# The Civil War

**Other Books of Interest from St. Augustine's Press**

Jeremy Black, *Defoe's Britain*

Jeremy Black, *Smollett's Britain*

Jeremy Black, *The Importance of Being Poirot*

Jeremy Black, *The Age of Nightmare*

Jeremy Black, *In Fielding's Wake*

Michael Davis, *Electras: Aeschylus, Sophocles, and Euripides*

David Ramsay Steele, *The Conquistador with His Pants Down: David Ramsay Steele's Legendary Lost Lectures*

Kenneth Weisbrode, *Real Influencers: Fourteen Disappearing Acts that Left Fingerprints on History*

Marvin R. O'Connell, *Telling Stories that Matter: Memoirs and Essays*

Thomas F. Powers, *American Multiculturalism and the Anti-Discrimination Regime: The Challenge to Liberal Pluralism*

John von Heyking, *Comprehensive Judgment and Absolute Selflessness: Winston Churchill on Politics as Friendship*

Peter Fraser, *Twelve Films about Love and Heaven*

Gene Fendt, *Camus' Plague: Myth for Our World*

Ralph McInerny, *The Defamation of Pius XII*

Will Morrisey, *Herman Melville's Ship of State*

Roger Scruton, *The Politics of Culture and Other Essays*

Roger Scruton, *The Meaning of Conservatism: Revised 3rd Edition*

Roger Scruton, *On Hunting*

Stanley Rosen, *The Language of Love: An Interpretation of Plato's Phaedrus*

Winston Churchill, *My Early Life*

Winston Churchill, *Savrola*

Winston Churchill, *The River War*

# The Civil War

JEREMY BLACK

ST. AUGUSTINE'S PRESS
South Bend, Indiana

Manufactured in the United States of America.

1 2 3 4 5 6 30 29 28 27 26 25

**Library of Congress Control Number: 2025932171**

Paperback ISBN: 978-1-58731-117-8
Ebook ISBN: 978-1-58731-118-5

∞ The paper used in this publication meets the minimum requirements of the American National Standard for Information Sciences – Permanence of Paper for Printed Materials, ANSI Z39.48-1984.

St. Augustine's Press
www.staugustine.net

For
Jason, Mark, Paul, and David

## Table of Contents

# PREFACE

In the two World Wars, as well as the conflicts of the Cold War and struggles since, America has been centrally involved. However, what little fighting has occurred on American soil was largely at the extremes of Japanese military capability—though this is not to say that the attack on Pearl Harbor in 1941, eighty years after the outbreak of the Civil War, was inconsequential. The Civil War (1861–5) is more striking precisely because all fighting on land was on American soil, while at sea American waters were crucial. States that are central to American history—notably Virginia—were contested, and cities such as Columbia, South Carolina, occupied and devastated. The disruption in combat zones was intense, both deliberate and unintentional, causing a range of unsettling trends from the seizure of livestock to population movements. The latter encompassed civilians fleeing or forcibly moved and prisoners of war, and all were multi-directional. This was generally accompanied by the spread of disease.

The Civil War was the most traumatic conflict, indeed event, in American history, and more so than the War of Independence in part because the divisions of the latter were not lasting: many of the Loyalists fled, notably to Canada; there was no *revanchist* movement; and the conflict could be presented as a war of independence (which it was) and not a civil war (which it also was). Indeed, the Civil War helped define American politics and human geography for a century, and its echo remains strong today—and in some respects very strong. To a lesser extent, however, the War for Independence (1775–83) also continues to define American politics, notably in the shape ultimately given to the Constitution.

The decision to hold the Second World Fair in New York in 1853 reflected America's confidence in its economic development, status, and future. Already in 1851, the major American role in the Great Exhibition held in London had underlined its status in cutting-edge technology.

Moreover, territorially, America was already very far removed from the thirteen colonies of 1775 that had won independence in 1783, and it was further transformed in 1846–8 with the solution of the Oregon Dispute with Britain and, more successfully and dramatically, the victory over Mexico. This meant that America achieved transcontinental status with a Pacific coastline, and this the trans-Pacific potential was quickly seen with the transformative entry of a squadron into Tokyo Bay in 1853.

There were differences concerning domestic politics, notably over the status of slavery in the newly-acquired territories, but a compromise in 1850 suggested that these were not insoluble. There was no comparison to the Year of Revolutions in 1848 when most of Europe was in turmoil, and Charles Sumner, then a prominent Massachusetts opponent of slavery and later a senator, observed from Boston: "America now seems to be *terra firma* compared to the volcanic earth of Europe."[1] Yet by 1861 America was in a civil war that was to be more sustained, and played out on a greater scale, than any in Europe in the period.

This was not the first American Civil War. Indeed, from the perspective of both Patriots and Loyalists, the War of Independence of 1775–83 was a civil war, both within the British empire and in the thirteen colonies that were to be the kernel of the United States. Unlike the Civil War of 1861–5, the earlier struggle had both been waged across the thirteen colonies and broadened out from 1778 to become an international struggle. A comparison of the two conflicts, both separatist efforts rather than attempts to overthrow existing governments, is instructive in that it can serve on many levels to contextualize the Civil War of 1861–5. Contextualization is indeed a principal intention of this work, and one intended to help make it distinctive.

Contemporaries certainly made comparisons, with Abraham Lincoln beginning the Gettysburg Address in 1863 with a direct, scene-setting reference: "Four score and seven years ago our fathers brought forth on this continent, a new nation, conceived in Liberty, and dedicated to the proposition that all men are created equal." In 1864, Emanuel Leutze's dramatic painting *Washington Crossing the Delaware* (1851), which indeed occurred on Washington's way to victory at Trenton in 1776, was hung in the place of honor at the New York Metropolitan Fair, a fundraising event for relief efforts for Union troops.[2] German-born but brought to America as a child, Leutze had painted the work to encourage European liberals. Also in that year, there was on display in Philadelphia before a very large crowd Peter Rothermel's *State House on the Day of Germantown* (1862) that depicted an episode in Philadelphia as battle raged nearby. This was an instance of the use of history painting during the Civil War to cultivate in citizens the memory of a past heritage of liberty (in these cases the effort made in the War of Independence in 1777). The *Chicago Tribune* of 17 April 1865 published the proclamation of William Bross, the Lieutenant-Governor of Illinois, declaring Lincoln the "second Washington" and "the Washington of this generation."

Contextualization, however, must come from a variety of perspectives. For Blacks, the War of Independence brought freedom in the northern states for those who had served in the Patriot armies or for the British who helped the latter resettle elsewhere at the end of the conflict. But the war accentuated racism in the south where there was great hostility toward British interest in recruiting slaves; although this interest was very different than the commitment shown by the Union, eventually.[3]

The quest for emancipation was to become a shared element in liberal opinion between American/Republican and British Liberals, and the result of the Civil War has been advanced as just one aspect of the "birth of the modern world."[4] This is one perspective through which the conflict might be understood. Yet, it is also worth noting that the possibility of a new Conservative world was suggested by developments in America, Britain, and Mexico, including the establishment of Emperor Maximilian in Mexico, the prospect of a Conservative return to power in Britain in 1864, and pro-Confederate policies emerging as a consequence.[5] Moreover, although emancipation might seem modern, the Jim Crow laws simply replaced slavery. They were a product of reconstruction rather than the war, but the two are nonetheless inseparable.

A very different international context possibly arose from the eruption of Mount Dubbi in Eritrea during May–October 1861 when ash was thrown over 250 kilometers (160 miles) from the volcano. This, the largest known historical eruption in Africa, which produced a sulphate aerosol veil that may well have been the cause of the unusually wet winter and spring of 1862 and cold summer of 1862 in the Northern Hemisphere.[6]

The consequences for the Civil War—at the levels of resource, operation, and tactics—require consideration.

It is necessary at every stage to remember the horrors of the conflict, for example in the Battle of the Wilderness in 1864 in which the wounded were burnt alive as some of the undergrowth caught fire. In addition, the corpses of those killed a year earlier at Chancellorsville were still there in the fields. Lieutenant Robert Hubard of the 3rd Virginia Cavalry recorded the fighting near Spotsylvania Courthouse on 8 May 1864, where his unit was fighting dismounted against Union attackers: "[W]e were firing as fast as we could load.... It was one incessant, deafening rattle while the smoke arose so thick we could scarcely see."[7] Such smoke made situational intelligence and command decisions more problematic. At Perryville in Kentucky, on 8 October 1862, the battle was made far more difficult through the shortage of water (fresh or not), the heat, the dust, and the blazing sun. Sunstroke and heat exhaustion proved major problems in that battle. Yet battle, whatever its scale, could be more specifically brutal, and this remained the case until the close of the war, as seen particularly in the hand-to-hand fighting—for example, the clubbing to death with muskets at Selma on 2 April 1865.[8] Such brutal violence and base clubbing was common throughout the war not least because the successful use of bayonets required high levels of training, and proper instruction in the use of these weapons was largely absent.

Even for those who did not die or suffer wounds, there remained the sight, sound, and smell of the many who were dead or maimed. Bloated bodies and the primitive nature of medical care left a very disturbing legacy. Ulysses S. Grant's twelve-year-old son, Fred, who accompanied him on the Vicksburg campaign, was greatly shocked by the wounded, notably the amputations he saw after the Battle of Port Gibson on 1 May 1863. There was also the impact of the uncertainty of conflict.

War assaulted the senses and tore through the bodies of the troops.[9] The war caused the deaths, within a large possible range, of about 750,000 in the military (possibly about 36,000 of them Blacks), and affected many more, including the death and injury of many civilians. These were unprecedented numbers for America, and recent scholarship has raised the accepted number of deaths by assessing male survival rates in successive censuses.[10] This method has led to a figure that not only replaces the previous one of about 620,000, but also increases disproportionally the number of Confederate dead, as Confederate record-keeping was less complete, notably during the period of years 1864–5. Alongside casualties, all were affected by the possibility of and proximity to death.

There was also the devastation of the natural and built environment. This was readily apparent, as with woodlands that were cut down or trees riddled by bullets. But it could also be insidious, not least in the impact on the soil of millions of lead musket and cannon balls. This was but one instance of the polluting impact of the war, one greater than for other wars on other soils hitherto thanks to the possibilities now offered by industrial technology and production at a scale greater than in previous wars.

Civil war is a traumatic experience, one that tears the body politic and brings conflict to society as nothing else does. This trauma abounded in Baltimore where troops shot down Confederate rioters on 19 April 1861, killing at least twelve (five soldiers were killed). Among the Confederate civilians imprisoned in nearby Fort McHenry, the lodestar of national resolve against the British in 1814, was the grandson of the composer of "The Star-Spangled Banner." Although the Crimean War was fairly extensively photographed by the British, French, and even Russians, the Civil War was the first in which photography was used on a major scale, and as a result battlefields, combatants, and destruction were readily seen by others everywhere.

Every advance, however limited and whatever the extent, led to a wave of disruption, for the extent of the likely advance was always unclear, as was the likely forward projection of cavalry raiders. There was also the uncertainty bound up with the military response to the advance, the inroads of foraging, and the devastation of conflict.

Separately, it is necessary to appreciate the nature of the sources—not least the difficulty of establishing what was going on,[11] but also the extent of rival accounts. Written subsequently in the mid-1880s, in part as a comment on other versions, Ulysses S. Grant in his *Memoirs* (1885–6) reflects on the account of the bitter Battle of Shiloh (where he had commanded Union forces) written by the son of the Confederate commander:

> The description of the battle of Shiloh given by Colonel William Preston Johnston is very graphic and well told. The reader will imagine that he can see each blow struck, a demoralized and broken mob of Union soldiers, each blow sending the enemy more demoralized than ever towards the Tennessee River, which was a little more than two miles away at the beginning of the onset. If the reader does not stop to inquire why, with such Confederate success from more than twelve hours of hard fighting, the National troops were not all killed, captured, or driven into the river, he will regard the pen picture as perfect.... I see but little in the description that I can recognize.[12]

Yet Shiloh, a battle that lasted two days, itself shows how popular accounts require correction by scholarship, not least due to the common intention to shape, for narrative purposes, a battle that was more complex and multi-faceted. In particular, as is true with campaigns, the simultaneity of battles defies such coherently rendered narratives.[13] For both contemporaries and those after, this then invites the question of emphasis, and—linked to this—the question of what is the impact of "missing the spotlight."[14] Why then had this war occurred and how had it broken out? We turn in the next chapter to consider these crucial questions.

In writing a deliberately short book on a subject that has attracted towering intellects and many millions of pages, I am trying to cut to the quick on some key issues. At the same time, I would urge readers to pursue the subject by consulting the stimulating literature available. My thanks are obviously due to those who have written on the subject, to those across 37 states who have invited me to lecture, to those who have taken me to see battlefields, and to the very many Americans I am pleased to call friends. For me, particularly instructive invitations included those to compare the American and English Civil War for a University of Virginia summer school, and to give the Gettysburg lecture at the Union League Club in Philadelphia. I am most grateful to Ian Beckett, John Broom, Kevin Farrell, Jason Gehrke, Bill Gibson, Crawford Gribben, Caleb Karges, Al Nofi, Ethan Rafuse, Brian Holden Reid, David Stewart, Adrian Brettle, and Ken Weisbode for their very helpful comments on earlier chapters. They are not responsible for any errors that remain.

This book is dedicated to Jason Gehrke, Mark Moyar, Paul Rahe, and David Stewart, and their colleagues at Hillsdale with thanks for their welcome hospitality on an enjoyable visit to speak at their impressive institution, one where teaching is married with scholarship.

# 1. TO THE FIRING PLACE

*Westward the Course of Empire Takes Its Way* is the name of the mural that Emanuel Leutze painted in 1861 in response to a Congressional commission to decorate a stairway in the Capitol building in Washington. A war over the New West explains much about the Civil War, but like all one-phrase descriptions it leaves out more. Nevertheless, the future and influence of the new territories that had been gained for America from 1845 (when Texas became a state) to 1848 (when the Mexican American War ended) were issues made more important by the pace and prospect of western expansion. Combined with the California Gold Rush of 1848–55, the expansion of railways, the defeat of Native Americans, and confidence in "Manifest Destiny," the West appeared integral not only to America's potential in the future but to the developing present as well. California rapidly acquired a large enough population to transfer early, in 1850, from territory to state, thereby tilting the balance in the Senate toward the 'Free States.'

Texas becoming a state had led to the war with Mexico (1846–8), which resulted in America gaining vast territories between Texas and the Pacific, including what were to become the states of California, Nevada, Utah, New Mexico, and Arizona, as well as most of Colorado and parts of Oklahoma, Kansas, and Wyoming. This was not least because the subsequent Gadsden Purchase of border territory from Mexico in 1853 would not have been possible but for the gains of 1848. The Gadsden Purchase sought to strengthen the southern interest in the New West by easing a rail route from New Orleans to California. The status of slavery in the newly acquired territories soon became a key topic of controversy. This is an example of how conquest can create internal instability.

Meanwhile, the profitability of the cotton economy in the south ensured that slavery in America was not going to be stopped by economic factors as Thomas Jefferson, among others, had anticipated; although there were in fact geographical limits to this economy, as moderates on the slavery issue frequently pointed out. This profitability owed much to Eli Whitney's invention in 1793 of the cotton gin, a hand-operated machine that made it possible to separate the cotton seeds from the fiber. This possibility encouraged the cultivation of "upland" cotton. It was hardy, and therefore widely cultivable across the south, but was very difficult to deseed by hand, unlike the Sea Island cotton hitherto grown, which had been largely restricted to the southern Atlantic coastlands. Annual cotton output in America, as a result, rose from 3,000 bales in 1793 to over 3 million in the 1850s. American cotton became the key source for British cotton manufacturers, which were a major force in the British economy and at that time the largest in the world.

Rather than slavery proving unprofitable or inconsistent with industrialization, or, indeed, challenged by slave revolts, political developments relating to this issue were crucial. Slavery indeed played a more prominent role in divisions within America from the 1820s, helping both to cement a sense of separate and particular southern identity, and also give it an expansionist dynamic. Racial exclusion was presented as both form and focus of southern cultural identity, and was defended on the grounds of providentialism, rights, necessity, and prudence.[1] There was scant ebbing of support for slavery on the earlier pattern of the situation in Britain, where slavery had been prominent in its Atlantic empire. The moralization of the abolition argument in the late 1810s and 1820s, lessening the earlier focus on arguments about economic development, both strengthened northern abolitionism and led southern slaveowners to stake out a moral defense based in the supposed 'savagery of the African race' and how they needed to be paternalistically brought into the 'modern' world. At the same time, there were significant differences in the world of slavery within America, differences that greatly affected the pattern of behavior during the Civil War on the part of white southerners.

"Like well-boiled rice, they remain united, but each grain separate." The British diplomat Henry Addington was ably observant in 1823 about the United States. However, in 1832 South Carolina attempted to nullify a new tariff on the grounds that it was unconstitutional as well as unfair, and that individual states could protect themselves from such acts by interposing their respective authority, and thus nullify the federal law. The state raised an enthusiastic army of more than 25,000 men, purchased arms, and threatened secession if the federal government sought to enforce the tariff. This was far more active, developed, and overt than the Hartford Convention of 1814–15 in which New England Federalists opposed to the War of 1812 discussed how best to change the Constitution. Yet in this case these men took no action.

In 1832, the federal government did not give way and Charleston's garrison was reinforced by General Winfield Scott who was to be commanding general of the United States Army from 1841 to 1861, and therefore in command when the Civil War broke out. Unsupported by the other southern states and likewise facing opposition to nullification from within, South Carolina was compelled to back down in 1832, abandon the threat of nullification, and accept a settlement of the tariff issue that did not meet its goals. The dispute indicated the fragility of political and constitutional conventions, the clash between southern notions of the Union as a voluntary compact among independent states, and northern views of the indivisibility of the one American nation, and the possibility of conflict. In 1832–3, talking about disunion proved an alternative to conflict, but the situation was to be very different in 1861.

Texas' independence from Mexico in 1836 was followed by the reversing of earlier Mexican attempts to limit the scope of slavery, and the spread instead of the norms of the American south. In 1840 the immigration of free Blacks to Texas was restricted. The spread of cotton cultivation led to a major increase in the number of slaves in Texas from 443 in 1825 and about 5,000 in 1836, to 58,161 in the 1850 census and 182,566 in the 1860 census. The annexation of Texas to America in 1845 was opposed by the American Whigs, who were suspicious about the likely consequences of increasing the number of slave states.[2] From that perspective, Texas' entry as a single state, rather than (as had been feared given its size) as multiple states (each of them with slaves) was very important.

Southern politicians sounded off on the argument that slavery should be illegal in the lands conquered from Mexico and, instead, a compromise in 1850 left the new state of California free. It became very difficult to be a southern Whig. However, slavery was to be legal in the New Mexico and Utah territories, subject to popular sovereignty in the shape of the settlers, as well as in the as-yet-unorganized territory that in 1907 became Oklahoma. Furthermore, far from simply championing states' rights, the south was also the champion of federal authority over both northern states' rights and, in the territories, of a federal code protecting slavery.

Yet, in the 1850s, the situation became more complex. The admission of California as a free state gave the free states a majority in the Senate. Indeed, the minority status of the south in the Union, which had been recognized since the debate in the House of Representatives in 1819 over the Tallmadge Amendment on limitations on slavery in Missouri, was an immediate feature of the sectional controversy of the 1850s. Minnesota and Oregon followed as free states in 1858 and 1859, respectively. This minority status for the south interacted with the growing economic links between the west and the east, with the key relationships being between the midwest and the northeast, and from the midwest, westward. There was a symbiotic relationship between a rapidly industrializing northeast and a rapidly mechanizing agricultural midwest and west. The McCormick Mechanical Reaper, built in Chicago in1847 for grain crops, was a success that far-surpassed cotton-picking machines. Differential economic expansion helped lead southerners to migrate northward for opportunities. The southern view of American development was increasingly becoming redundant, whatever the strength of the cotton economy.

Being under challenge, and more especially the very sense of being under challenge, ensured that southern secession was more frequently threatened in the 1850s than ever before; although this also underlines that this course of action was not taken during this time. South Carolina's interest in secession in 1851 as protest against the Compromise of 1850 was not backed by other states.

There were apparent alternatives to secession, involving the attempt to make America acceptable for the south and slavery. Constitutional and political means appeared possible, not least acquiring more slave states, a key issue earlier in westward expansion. Some Democrats had wished to annex more of Mexico in 1848. There were subsequent hopes of gaining Cuba, and again more of Mexico, and this drive helped further embitter relations within America from the mid-1850s onward.

Volatility was enhanced by the attempts of American filibusters (those pursuing unauthorized warfare against a foreign state) trying to seize and hold territories by force in order to establish new slave societies, although there were also northerners who sought to expand into Canada. William Walker (1824–60) was the filibuster who made the biggest splash. A Tennessee-born doctor, Walker became a newspaper editor in San Francisco, a city of apparently boundless prospects. There he conceived the idea of a central American state that was to fulfill his views of Manifest Destiny for White men like himself. Demonstrating how pro-slavery elements existed in free states, Walker sought to create a state ruled by Whites and resting on a slave-based agriculture—basically a transposed south. Walker's first step was an invasion of Baja California, then part of Mexico, in 1853. Capturing the capital, La Paz, Walker declared that it was independent, as was the neighboring Mexican province of Sonora. He put the new "Republic of Lower California" under the laws of Louisiana, which provided a legal basis for slavery. The Mexican army swiftly drove Walker's band out. In 1855, Walker tried again, this time seeking to exploit the civil war in Nicaragua. Having conquered it, he declared himself President in 1856. The Emancipation Edict of 1824 forbidding slavery was annulled, and Walker encouraged the idea that Nicaragua would be a key partner of the south. The following year, however, Walker was defeated and left. He was to be executed in 1860 when he sought to intervene in Honduras.

The actions of Walker and others stirred in many a sense that there was nothing to be fixed and that conflict was manly—an approach also encouraged by the presentation both of the Mexican War and of conflict with Native Americans. This masculine culture was an aspect of the commitment to mission, duty, and salvation that was so important to the prevailing trends of Providentialism: it was considered manly to fight sin,[3] and this approach was to encourage determination, in the face of great odds, among soldiers as well as civilians. Despair was unacceptable to the larger masses.

Southern advocates, such as Jefferson Davis, a Democratic Mississippi politician and the future president of the Confederacy, saw the expansion of slavery as a way to guarantee a labor force in the west that would bring prosperity. They argued that slavery would make irrigated agriculture feasible, and thereby overcome the constraints of geography and provide the security of continuous settlement, thereby eroding the power of the Native Americans. These were themes in Davis's speech to the Senate on 14 February 1850 and his annual report as Secretary of War in 1853.[4] A graduate of West Point, Davis had served on the Wisconsin frontier, served as a colonel of volunteers and was a war hero in the Mexican War, and was Secretary of War during 1853–7.

Visionary capitalism, geopolitics, interest in Asian markets in China and Japan, speculation, and anxiety all looked in the same direction. With slavery seen as a panacea or a 'fix-all,' slave labor was to provide support for railroad construction and mining. Slavery was seen as an aspect of a developing economic system and part of a future in which unfree labor was the basis for free trade and civilizational improvement. This idea was supported by many in the southwest, much of whose White population had come from the south, and saw it as model, partner, and protector. The army was used to provide help including in the surveying of transport routes. The subjugation of Native Americans was intended to provide opportunities for the spread of slaving interests.

This was not a would-be south pivoting around states' rights, but an expanded south that was to benefit from the federal government. Moreover, northern restrictions were circumvented, as with legislation in California in 1852 that allowed the retention of slavery for slaves there prior to 1850. In California, immigrant Chinese laborers were not legally slaves but in practice indentured servants due to the restrictions placed upon them. More generally, Native American labor was also coerced. The Mormons in Utah offered possible support for the states' rights cause.

In Kansas territory, disagreements over extending slavery escaped government control and became bloody. In the context of the idea of popular sovereignty (that is, settlers and not Congress determining slavery in the territories), protagonists for the two sides sought to terrorize their opponents in order to ensure a majority for their views, which was the consequence of the Kansas–Nebraska Act of 1854, the basis for the establishment of Kansas as a territory in 1854. This act allowed the people in the territory to decide on slavery, rather than settling the question at the federal level. In the event, rival governments were established in

Kansas in 1855 and, in 1856 conflict broke out that could only be constrained by the arrival of the army.

George, 4th Earl of Clarendon, the able British Foreign Secretary, was in no doubt that these issues would push slavery to the fore, although he got the eventual outcome wrong: "The Yankees seem to have got a good large internal bone to pick. The Nebraska and Kansas affair will I suppose bring the whole slavery question under discussion again, and in a manner the least likely to lead to an amicable solution. It may *threaten* the union, but I have no idea that anything in our time will dissolve it … much bluster and insult and menace will stimulate the sense of danger, and then some compromise will be patched up."[5]

The army was a growing presence in the west not only to contain Native Americans but also to deal with differences between the White population. Indeed, in 1857–8 troops were dispatched to the Utah Territory (which was far more extensive than the subsequent state) in order to ensure that the Mormons (who were in favor of legalizing slavery as ordained by God) did not take it out of the Union, creating a theocratic state named Deseret. This expedition and occupation encountered problems, including logistics, weather, and resistance; but it also demonstrated a willingness to employ force for political reasons,[6] albeit against far less violent opposition than was to be the case in the south in 1861.

Meanwhile, the Dred Scott decision of the Supreme Court in 1857 that affirmed slave-owners could take their slaves into any territory was unwelcome to anti-slavery advocates such as Lincoln, who sought the restriction of slavery (but in so doing did not necessarily identify with abolitionists) and owed much to the southern majority on the Court:

> It becomes necessary to determine who were citizens of the several States when the Constitution was adopted…. [T]he legislation and histories of the times, and the language used in the Declaration of Independence, show, that neither the class of persons who had been imported as slaves, nor their descendants, whether they had become free or not, were then acknowledged as a part of the people, nor intended to be included in the general words used in that memorable instrument.

This decision, which affirmed that slavery was national and freedom sectional, and not the other way around, contributed to the sense that the situation was inherently unstable. A harsher practice on hounding fugitives slaves much offended northerners.

The conflict in Kansas, for which competing constitutions were proposed and thus bitterly dividing the Democratic Party in 1858, greatly helped radicalize attitudes and provided longstanding fears on each side both of a territorial focus and a trigger to violence.[7] The threat of southern secession in 1858 was directed at ensuring the admission of Kansas as a slave state. In contrast, a Kansan constitution in 1859 gave Blacks the right to vote in school elections.

That year the federal arsenal at Harpers Ferry was seized by the abolitionist John Brown, who had led anti-slavery forces in conflict in Kansas in 1856. He saw the seizure as the first stage of a war on slavery, to be achieved in large part by armed slaves. But his rising was rapidly suppressed by Colonel Robert E. Lee and Lieutenant J.E.B. Stuart of the American Army.[8] However, this episode helped raise tension in the south where many were convinced that this effort revealed the true intention of abolitionists. Indeed, talk of a conspiracy to that end was an important background to the southern debate. The able British envoy, Richard, Lord Lyons,[9] who had taken up the post in December 1858, commented:

> [A]fter making due allowance for the tendency to consider the "present" crisis as always the most serious that has ever occurred, I am inclined to think that the North and South have never seen so near a breach.[10]

He was correct, and there was a strong sense of foreboding, one that itself helped encourage the move toward crisis. Lyons had noted the alarm triggered in 1859:

> The extraordinary excitement and alarm which exist in Virginia since the Harper's Ferry affair are not very confirmatory of the confidence which the planters profess to feel in the "happy and attached peasantry," by which euphonious appellation they love to designate their slaves. There have been

alarms and movements of militia and volunteers almost daily.[11]

The 1860 presidential election gave victory to Abraham Lincoln of the Republicans, who wished to prevent the extension of slavery into the federal territories, a prevention that was understood by Lincoln and others as a step that threatened southern interests and identity. The election of Lincoln, who, on the pattern of Andrew Jackson (president from 1829 to 1837), was described by one contemporary as "a rough Western, of the lowest origin and little education," reflected the refashioning of politics by the slavery issue, even though Jackson was a war hero and a national figure.

The slavery issue had played a major role in the "intolerable psychic tensions" that affected antebellum South Carolina from the 1820s,[12] and led thereafter, first, to pressure on the Whigs, as with the rise of the anti-slavery Liberty Party founded in 1839–40 and its essential successor the anti-slavery Free Soil Party of 1848–54, and subsequently to the disintegration of the Whigs in the aftermath of the Kansas-Nebraska Act of 1854 and the related rise of the Republicans as a northern sectional party focused on the restriction of slavery. There had also been the division of the Democratic Party, the only remaining bond between north and south, or between northern and southern Whigs.

The Whigs, the Free-Soil Party, and the Know Nothings (officially known first as the Native American Party) were absorbed into the Republicans who made their first run for the presidency in 1856, a course determined by opposition to the potential for new slaveholding that was opened up by the 1854 Kansas-Nebraska Act. Free control of the land was a key issue, as the party also sought 'free soil'—that is, free land for farmers in the west. Freedom was a moral position, which was embraced in the Republican party by pietist Protestants seeking public morality, whether it was against slavery, Mormon polygamy, or drink.

In 1856, James Buchanan, the Democratic candidate, won the south but also Pennsylvania, Illinois, and Indiana, revealing a winning national appeal. In 1860, in contrast, Stephen Douglas, the northern Democrat, competed with John Breckinridge, the southern Democrat. This competition allowed Lincoln, the Republican, who carried the northern states but none of the southern ones (the Republicans were not allowed to organize in the slave states that formed the Confederacy), to win on fewer than 40 per cent of the votes cast. Douglas and Lincoln were moderate candidates, but national politics were no longer being contested by effective national parties. Partly as a result, American mass democracy was unable to generate a consensus, which produced (and reflected) an instability that challenged the undoubted constitutional nature of Lincoln's election.

So also with religious groups, notably the Episcopal Church, with southern clerics such as Leonidas Polk, Bishop of Louisiana, supporting secession, and northern clerics taking a different view. A graduate of West Point, Polk was to become a general, albeit not a good one, and was killed in 1864.[13] The war also deeply divided the Baptists and the Methodists.

Compromise was on offer, but in a context of uncertainty as well as contingency this no longer seemed sufficiently acceptable, in either the north or south, and it failed to gather impetus. Lincoln rejected the proposal in December 1860 advanced by the highly-experienced Senator John Crittenden of Kentucky (a border state that had slavery) that called for the 36º 30¢ line of the 1820 Missouri Compromise accepting slavery for the Arkansas Territory to be run toward the Pacific. Such a line would include the New Mexico Territory acquired in 1848 in the world of slavery. Crittenden's system was an aspect of the more general attempt by the border states to prevent any move to civil war. Yet they lacked the heft to do so at the federal level. Possibly Lincoln, who opposed the extension of slavery into the territories, failed to provide them with sufficient backing, a situation parallel to George III's mishandling of American politics in 1774, but that would be to simplify the situation in these states. The north had already conceded much.

Ultimately, the border states were unable to prevent themselves from being dragged into the coming war. Indeed, with the exception of Maryland, which in part due to a seizure of power in 1861 was largely held under firm Union control throughout the conflict, the border states saw the most bitter conflict, with the exception of Virginia, a state in the upper south but on the border with Union-held territory. Virginia indeed was to be divided by the Union, which led to the creation of West

Virginia. The shouting of grievances after the war, and especially after 1900 and the various neo-Confederate revivals that have occurred since, was to be won by the deep south, notably as a consequence of Sherman's destructiveness in 1864–5. Yet, the social cost of civil war in the border states extended to a level of community division and guerrilla warfare not seen farther south. Many of those who supported the Union within the south were in the western frontier area of the Appalachians where there were fewer slaves.

Lincoln's election led to the secession of the south, beginning on 20 December 1860 with South Carolina, long a center of southern consciousness, and to the formation of the Confederate States of America. Yet, as a reminder of the significance of geographical factors and also of their uncertainty—and thus of the volatility of geopolitics—the Confederacy did not simply equate itself to the slave states. Only the lower south seceded at first—namely, Alabama, Florida, Georgia, and Mississippi—doing so after the rejection of Crittenden's plan in Congress, and Montgomery, Alabama, was the initial capital of the Confederacy. Moreover, much of the upper south, including Virginia, Tennessee, and Kentucky (all slave states) had voted for John Bell of Tennessee, the candidate of the new Constitutional Union Party pledged to back "the Union, the Constitution, and the Laws,"[14] rather than for Breckinridge. Crittenden had played a key role in the formation of that party in 1860, while its vice-presidential candidate, Edward Everett, spoke at Gettysburg in 1863 immediately before Lincoln.

As with the English Civil War in 1642, the apparently coherent blocs of support were shot through with many tensions and divisions, and there was no simple, single explanation of support. Thus, each seceding state still possessed many Unionists, and their support extended to the issue of bearing arms. Belief and self-interest both played significant roles in the alignments of the English and American civil wars. There were, however, particular differences. There was no equivalent in England to the states' rights issue, and the nearest similarity was the degree of earlier Scottish rejection of Charles I. Secondly, localism and loyalty in the American Civil War often reflected citizens points of origin, and many were recent settlers (relocated from locations of birth). This for example helped explain differences between counties in northern Georgia.[15]

Although Lincoln was willing to back a constitutional amendment prohibiting the federal government from interfering with slavery, secession was unacceptable to him and the Republicans; and Lincoln was very concerned about the consequences of his actions for his party.[16] Lincoln and the Republicans argued both that the maintenance of the Union was essential to the purpose of America as well as to its strength; and yet it was also necessary to understand how the superiority of the federal government over the states was important to America's international position and critical to the idea of the American nation. However, this presentation says nothing about images of honor, masculinity, and rights, and yet it indicates assumptions about necessity that affected both sides, the Union as well as the Confederacy.[17] The Republicans had the obligation to govern on the principles they had presented to the people in the 1860 election, but they failed to address the large number (60.2% of the electors) who had not voted for them.

In theory and practice, there were uncertain Constitutional issues and perceptions of the American Revolution that offered arguments to both sides. The right to secession was inherent to a federal system and indeed underlay the move to independence in 1775–6. Yet this left unclear the extent to which there was also a right to oppose secession. British commentators might see a parallel with the Declaration of Independence in 1776 from British rule, but Union advocates argued that America in 1861 was not an empire as Britain had been in 1775–6. Lincoln, moreover, cited the legal obligation to enforce the laws throughout the land.

In both cases, the reason for independence, real or alleged, was not the same as the justification of it either Constitutionally or indeed politically. The period of 1775–6 might as much be typecast as an anti-tax rebellion and 1861 as a pro-slavery year. Each element was very much present but scarcely exhausted the reasons for rebellion. Many of those who fought for the Confederacy were not slaveowners and, even if some were certainly racists, this was also true of many of those who fought for the Union, including slaveowners in the border states. Moreover, the attitude of Democrats in the north suggests that a different president in 1861 would have handled matters in a contrasting fashion. It is no justification of the hotheads in Charleston to argue that they might have been handled with more adroitness, and so also and far more might this be said of the upper south and the border states. Inevitably affected by his own worldview, Lincoln failed to grasp the varied views of southern conservatives and the possibility of working with them (although it could be argued that he conceded as much as he could without legitimizing blackmail). Lincoln was willing to grant five of the six Crittenden Compromise points, but did not let slavery expand into the territories, a point also taken in the peace conference of February 1861 held in Washington with former President John Tyler as presiding officer. Lincoln argued that Republican victory meant that the electorate did not want this expansion and therefore that conceding this point would mean denying the people what they voted for.

James Buchanan, the president until 4 March 1861, a Democrat from Pennsylvania who backed states' rights and aligned with southern Democrats, had supported the vice-president John Breckinridge in his unsuccessful bid for president. After the election, Buchanan largely kicked the can down the road on southern secession and did nothing to help Lincoln in the transition of power.[18] Looked at differently, his attempts at compromise based on the right to slavery in the southern states and territories were at least worth trying, if only to avoid isolating the deep south. Similarly, the Virginian Tyler emphasized the need to protect the rights of slaveowners in the territories and backed secession.

It is appropriate to note from the Irish example that there were several possible outcomes to growing tension. Under the Acts of Union of 1800, Ireland from 1801 was part of the United Kingdom of Great Britain and Ireland, with representation in Westminster until 1922. That much of Ireland thereafter would become independent was far from inevitable, and prior to 1916 there was only limited violence in Ireland. Instead, there were a series of proposals for Home Rule for Ireland from the 1870s, and one which came close to success in 1914. In turn, after the violence of 1919–21, the Irish Free State established in 1922 was itself far from stable and its government was to be replaced by a new Constitution in 1937.

Whether in 1861 Fort Sumter in Charleston harbor merited the turn to arms can at least be debated. The small size of the army meant that Lincoln had to respond to the growing separation of the south by turning to the militia, which offered numbers rather than expertise and was politically damaging given that it forced state governments and their populations to make decisions about showing up to fight. This small size of the army ensured he was in a weak position, and notably so for offensive operations, although the Massachusetts militia provided a valuable defense for Washington. For both sides, it was necessary to deploy force in unpredictable and fast-changing situations. The discrepancy in military force between government and rebels was far less than in the case of Europe, partly because prior to the war the government did not control a conscript army. Moreover, John Floyd, a Virginian who was secretary of war from 1857 until December 1860, failed to fulfill Buchanan's instructions to strengthen the southern forts and was later accused by Grant of deliberately weakening the army by deploying its troops and guns so as to facilitate southern action. That might in part be an instance of hindsight, although there was criticism in the press at the time. Floyd later became a Confederate general, but proved a failure.

The role of contingency was demonstrated on 18 February when Major-General David Twiggs, the Georgian-born commander of the army's Department of Texas, surrendered his command to Texas officials, a situation very different to that which was to occur at Fort Sumter. A supporter of states' rights, Twiggs had to be relieved of command and sought to avoid conflict. The situation in San Antonio moved to crisis when the War Department appointed a strong Unionist as his replacement—the Texans then moved to act and, under threat of attack, Twiggs surrendered. He was treated as a traitor in the north. Twiggs became a Confederate general and was appointed to command the Military District of Louisiana. A combination of the decentralization of a weak federal system, with the vitality of the idea of southern identity, gave rebels a greater chance in America than in Europe. This interacted with a political system that could not cope with the strains of the big issues that had gradually become more acute—notably expansion and slavery. Limited government in this sense had both a military and a political dimension.

The Union's superiority over southern identity and state views was demonstrated when Lincoln refused to yield to demands for the surrender of the federal position of Fort Sumter: This was the reality of national power in the face of a forge of southern consciousness and separatism.

Shots were fired on Fort Sumter at 4:30 a.m. on 12 April but it did not surrender until 14 April, after over 3,000 shell and shots had been fired, setting fire to the wooden buildings in the fort and exposing the malnourished troops to smoke, heat, sound, and shock.[19] The vulnerability of masonry fortifications was fully demonstrated. Fort Pulaski outside Savannah still shows visible damage to a masonry foot from bombardment. In iconic terms, the context and consequences of the attack on Fort Sumter were very different from the unsuccessful British naval bombardment of Fort McHenry outside Baltimore in 1814 (the origins of the song "The Star-Spangled Banner").

The aftermath was to be very different to the recent war in another western federal state abroad—namely, Switzerland. In 1845, seven Catholic cantons established the *Sonderbund* (separate alliance) to defend their interests against the majority Free Democratic Party that wanted a more centralized Constitution and was also hostile to the Catholic Church. The immediate crisis was delayed until 21 October 1847 when the Federal Diet proclaimed the *Sonderbund* unconstitutional, as it indeed was under the 1815 Constitution and ordered the federal army to dissolve it. Two cantons officially declared themselves neutral. Fighting began on 4 November, and under threat of attack the *Sonderbund* canton of Fribourg surrendered on 14 November, followed by Zug on 21 November. At Gisikon on 23 November—which saw the most significant fighting—the federal forces won in a battle in which 37 men were killed. Another victory at Meierskappel that day led to the fall of the city of Lucerne, and on 26 November to the dissolution of the *Sonderbund*. The last member canton surrendered on 29 November, after a war in which there were about 100 fatalities. A new federal Constitution in 1848 lessened the independence of the cantons and expelled the Jesuits.[20] The conflict in America was to be far longer, bloodier, and more consequential, and its background was quite different.

In 1865, in his second inauguration speech, Lincoln looked back and provided his retrospective account, one worthy of considerable attention though understandably weak on the short-term causes of conflict:

> These slaves constituted a peculiar and powerful interest. All knew that the interest was somehow the cause of the war. To

strengthen, perpetuate, and extend this interest was the object for which the insurgents would rend the Union even by war, while the Government claimed no right to do more than to restrict the territorial enlargement of it. Neither party expected for the war the magnitude or the duration which it had already attained. Each looked for an easier triumph, and a result less fundamental and astounding. Both read the same Bible and pray to the same God.

## 2. 1861: NO QUICK SOLUTION

The bombardment of Fort Sumter did not make the trajectory of conflict obvious. Indeed, the "sides" were still inchoate. But now, the drive to respond to action replaced the pressure to act. Far from the bombardment intimidating him into yielding, just as southern leaders had hoped, this clash led Lincoln to determine to act against what he termed "combinations" in the south. He went to war to maintain the Union and not for the emancipation of the slaves. More particularly, Lincoln acted to enforce the law against combinations too powerful to be suppressed through the normal judicial proceedings. There was responsibility on the part of the executive to see that the laws were faithfully executed.

Lincoln's call for 75,000 state militia, a formidable number given the size of the White population. His clear intention to resist secession with force and invading the lower south, however, played the major role in leading Arkansas, North Carolina, Tennessee, and Virginia to join the Confederacy: They had no intention to provide troops to put down what Lincoln termed an insurrection.[1] Missouri also objected.

In doing so, Lincoln offered an echo of 1773–5 when George III's government had initially thought opposition focused on Massachusetts and likely to be overcome by firmness and a show of force there, only to discover that the government had precipitated a more widespread and serious crisis. The militia that were called up on 15 April 1861 were only to be enlisted for ninety days, and that was seen as enough in a strategy of control via coastal forts, naval deployment, and force demonstration—overall a totally unrealistic timetable. Southerners were reassured by Lincoln's government that it had no intention of ending slavery. The declaration included:

> the first service assigned to the forces hereby called forth will probably be to repossess the forts, places, and property which

> have been seized from the Union; and in every event, the utmost care will be observed, consistently with the objects aforesaid, to avoid any devastation, any destruction of, or interference with, property, or any disturbance of peaceful citizens in any part of the country.

This subsequent secession of the upper south greatly altered the demographic and military context of the war—thta is, political events reshaped the geography and thus geopolitics of the war. Though protecting Texas, Arkansas was not otherwise able to contribute much to the Confederacy, but Virginia, Tennessee, and North Carolina were each more important in economic and demographic terms than any state in the lower south. In this order, they were the leading states in White population in the Confederacy, while together they were to field close to 40 percent of the Confederacy's forces. Additionally, they provided half of its crops and more than half of its manufacturing capacity, although by 1863, Georgia, and specifically Atlanta, Augusta, and Macon, was one of the major manufacturing centers. By then, probably only Selma in Alabama and the Tredegar Works at Richmond were as important.

South Carolina's ability to win over Virginia was important to the geopolitical definition of the south and contrasted with the earlier hesitation in Virginia. In military terms, the location of productive capacity in frontier areas was a problem for the Confederacy, as they were vulnerable and thus rewarded Union attackers while compromising the idea of a Confederate defense-in-depth. However, while the gain of these four states ensured that there was more territory to defend, it transformed the military potential of the Confederacy. The Union no longer had a common frontier with every seceding state (bar Florida) and thus the lower south became less vulnerable. It also became easier to think of the Confederacy as a bloc of territory that could be defended in a coherent fashion; and this therefore required a coherent and very wide-ranging Union strategy, of the type offered by Scott, in order to bring it down.

In particular, the secession of Virginia and North Carolina greatly altered the location of the likely field of operations in the east as, militarily, the front line of the secession was no longer on the northern border of South Carolina. Had that been the case, Columbia and Charleston would have been readily vulnerable to Union attack, just as Atlanta in Georgia would have been from Chattanooga in Tennessee (prefiguring Sherman's campaign in 1864). In this event, the war would probably have been at first primarily a coastal conflict, with Union warships enforcing the collection of customs of ports. In this case, 75,000 men probably would have been sufficient to begin the process, followed by an expanded regular army to sustain it.

Conversely, the Union was able to gain control of an important bloc of slave states: Delaware, Maryland, Kentucky, Missouri, and those parts of Virginia that in 1863 became the state of West Virginia. There were also slaves in southern New Jersey. Had these states joined the Confederacy, the situation would also have been very different. Instead, by gaining these states, the Union consolidated its superiority in resources, blocked invasion routes into the north, and exposed the south to attack. Missouri and Kentucky sympathizers were seated in the Confederate Congress, but this did not match the situation on the ground.

The use of force in St. Louis was crucial in keeping it and therefore all of Missouri in the Union, which was particularly important as Missouri controlled access to the Missouri River and the Great Plains. In addition, Benjamin Butler's clever amphibious movement in the Chesapeake in April, bypassing a sabotaged section of railway track and secessionist-inclined Baltimore, had important strategic and political consequences. His troops were virtually the first to reach Washington. As Maryland, whose governor was a Unionist, stayed in the Union, the central battleground of the war lay between Washington (which remained the capital of the Union) and Richmond, Virginia, which became the capital of the Confederacy in May 1861 (replacing Montgomery, Alabama). But for Maryland staying in the Union, there would have been the need for a Union capital that was farther north. Had that been Philadelphia, there would have been more of an echo of the War of Independence.

Their proximity helped give a geographical focus to the conflict, one that reflected the political importance of the two capitals, and also cut across the potential expansiveness of the conflict arising from the extent of the area in rebellion. Indeed, this proximity offered the prospect of the rapid end to the war that northerners sought, an outcome that was seen as Napoleonic in style. Moreover, these states in Union hands affected the offensive capability of the Confederacy. Given Lee's willingness to march north across the Potomac River in 1862 and 1863 into Maryland, it is instructive to consider what the military impact of having the frontier on the northern border of Maryland would have been. Maryland in Confederate hands would have proved a threat to Ohio, influenced developments in Kentucky, and provided greater potential depth to northward moves by the army of northern Virginia, the main Confederate force. There was also a key demographic dimension in state loyalty terms—namely, that of the manpower available to both sides.

The Civil War, furthermore, was a civil conflict within the states that seceded. In the latter, the prevalence of slavery varied greatly, with for example few slaves in Appalachia. Conversely, fears of an Abolitionist plot in Texas in late 1860 (a major instance of the sequence of panics following John Brown's attempt on Harper's Ferry in October 1859) helped stir up vigilante action and encouraged backing for secession.[2] The variation in the prevalence of slavery was linked to the degree of support for the war, though it was not the sole factor involved. A sizeable 104,000 White Southerners fought with the Union forces,[3] a major addition to the latter and a cause of Confederate weakness. For example, eight regiments of North Carolinians fought for the Union army, four Black and four White, and Arkansas sent fourteen, seven Black and seven White. Both states had large mountainous regions. To a degree, opposition to secession underlined the degree to which chance factors played a considerable role in ensuring that it would in fact occur.[4] Moreover, this opposition increased the military challenge to the Confederacy.[5]

So too was it for the Union in the case of those who backed the Confederacy. This was notably a feature in the border states; although, if not only there, it did not extend across the north as Unionist support did in every state of the Confederacy. There were many northern "dough faces" willing to accept slavery, including Franklin Pierce, Democratic President from 1853 to 1857, who was to be a bitter critic of Lincoln, and "Copperheads" keen on peace, but they did not provide a military support for the south equivalent to that of southerners who fought against separation.

For both sides, this situation provided an element in the politics of the war but also in the manner of campaigning. Support for sympathizers extended to the determination to give them political representation, as with the Union in the Red River Campaign in Louisiana and Texas in 1864. This support, as well as belief in its capacity, affected Confederate campaigning in Maryland, Kentucky, and Missouri, as there was the conviction that to move northward would be to be greeted with help. In any event, any peace would have had to consider the terms available to sympathizers.

Every extant secession proclamation advanced slavery as a cause. Alongside a commitment to slavery, which was extensive for example in the army of northern Virginia with, among its members, many informal links to the slave system, many who fought for the south did not own slaves. They were more motivated by a cultural commitment to the apparent need to defend communities, culture, and the states' rights that were believed to protect both. These states' rights, however, were defined in the south in part in terms of the defense of slavery, and certainly could be presented in these terms. Slavery was the litmus test for states' rights and the latter in themselves only became of prime significance after 1865–6, with Robert E. Lee, the commander of the army of northern Virginia, taking a prominent role in advancing the argument.

The extent of different beliefs in the south serves as a reminder of the complexity of the issues at stake, and thus qualifies any account of the geopolitics and strategy of the war in terms of homogenous blocs. Initially unprepared for the difficulty of the struggle, both militarily and politically, Union forces had to try to shift the political balance within the south in order to lead to its surrender. That did indeed occur in 1865, but not before. The military alternative of the conquest of the entire south was not viable given the size of the Confederacy. Nor had such an alternative been viable for the British in the War of Independence, whereas in 1782–3 as peace began to materialize Britain still controlled New York and Charleston, and the Patriot plan in 1782 to capture New York led nowhere.

The political option appeared clearer for the Confederacy. There was the hope that success in the conflict would lead the Union to change policy by abandoning the war and, secondly, that success might bring the

British and French into the war, thereby, again, ensuring that the Union would be compelled to change policy. There was considerable weight in both ideas, and, if electoral results, diplomacy, and the playing out of the war revealed that neither was viable, this was not readily apparent to contemporaries in America and abroad until well into the conflict (see chapter 3).

The impact of politics on strategy was shown at the outset when political pressure in the north for a rapid advance on Richmond (to destroy the Confederacy by seizing the capital) led to a departure from the plan drawn up by Winfield Scott, the experienced General-in-Chief and the victor over Mexico in 1847–8. He, instead, had called on 3 May 1861 for an advance by 80,000 troops down the Mississippi to bisect the Confederacy, combined with a blockade of the Atlantic and Gulf coasts. Superiority in resources was to be used and reaffirmed, with the strategic aspects of the Mississippi relied upon in both. Termed the "Anaconda Plan" by the press (referring to the snake), this was intended to save lives and, by imposing economic problems and increasing support for a return to the Union, to encourage the Confederacy toward peace or, failing that, to position the Union in the best state for further operations. Scott's plan foreshadowed the career of Ulysses S. Grant in the war and the anticipated war of exhaustion wherein the north had the advantage.

However, Scott's emphasis on planning, as well as on the indirect approach, training, and a delay in the offensive until the autumn of 1861, fell afoul of the pressure for decisive action. He unsuccessfully opposed the proposal of Brigadier-General Irvin McDowell, a West Point veteran with staff experience and the field commander in the Washington area, to attack the smaller Confederate army on the Potomac at Manassas Junction, Virginia, that July, fixing it while part of the army outmaneuvered the Confederates such that they had to fall back on the Rappahannock River. Scott sought strategy, "a war of large bodies," but, instead, what he termed "a little war by piece-meal" prevailed.

In the event, the hopes that the war might be rapidly brought to a close were shattered in failure on 21 July in what became the First Battle of Bull Run, or First Manassas, in which neither commander behaved adroitly. Each planned to mount flank attacks and thus collapse their opponents. However, the Union advance was too slow and disorganized, the force had little combat experience, and McDowell's flaws exacerbated the faults of his army (the army of northeastern Virginia, and half of which was not engaged). In the event, the fate of the battle hinged not on planning, but on the arrival of fresh troops. In that, the Confederates, who possibly had an initial advantage in the caliber of their officers, benefited from operating on interior lines. Their reinforcements from the army of the Shenandoah in the Shenandoah Valley under General Joseph E. Johnston, arriving by rail, decided the battle with an attack on the Union right flank that caused the inexperienced troops to flee. The south benefited from fighting on the tactical defensive at the critical part of the battle, setting up its ability to shift to the offensive when the northern troops were exhausted. Responding to such an attack was not in their repertoire. An army composed largely of state volunteers clearly needed training.[6]

In a major contrast with the anticipated success, the battle ended with the humiliating flight of the Union forces, who suffered heavier losses: 2,708 to 1,982, and losing much more equipment in what was known in the South as "The Great Skedaddle." Hawthorne's criticism of partisanship was seen as pro-southern, but he was rather critical of the war.[7] Herman Melville's poem "The March into Virginia Ending in the First Manassas" commented on the failure to anticipate the destructive "vollied glare" of the battle. However, the Confederates failed to exploit their victory, in large part because they had been exhausted and disorganized by the fighting, but also due to command disagreements. They remained in control of Manassas Junction until the following spring, although it did not serve as the basis for a subsequent advance on Washington, which was being fortified. Meanwhile, the Union forces were trained, both soldiers and officers.

The battle did not end hostilities for that year. Indeed, while it was the key event, there was a continuation of the conflict in the eastern theatre of the war. Already, there had been significant success in western Virginia, by Union forces under George McClellan, who had advanced from Clarksburg on 27 June and, at Rich Mountain on 11 July, his far larger force defeated Confederate defenders, its size helping it cope with the flow of success. Confederate forces then withdrew, giving the Union the opportunity to reopen the Baltimore and Ohio railroads. McClellan, his success winning promotion, was summoned to Washington on 22 July and he gained command first of the division of the Potomac and then, with the Department of the Shenandoah absorbed on 26 July, of the army of the Potomac. Meanwhile, the fighting that had begun west of the Appalachians continued. On 3 September, the Confederates occupied Columbus, Kentucky, a position dominating the Mississippi. In response, on 6 November, Brigadier-General Ulysses S. Grant, the Commander of the District of Southeastern Missouri, attacked the Confederate post on the opposite bank Belmont, only to be driven back the next day in a Confederate counterattack and then fall back.

So too were matters with the Union's use of its maritime power both for blockade and for amphibious action. Port Royal, South Carolina, was captured on 7 November 1861 by a force under Rear-Admiral Samuel DuPont, a veteran of the Mexican American War, and St. Augustine fell in March 1862. However, in each case, this was without successful exploitation, in large part because of the difficulty of moving from coastal positions to hinterland dominance. Looked at differently, it was the very pressure that could be brought to bear by Union joint operations that added a significant level of uncertainty to Confederate strategy. Moreover, the seizure of coastal positions by amphibious attacks gave added force to the Union blockade, which was one of the major campaigns of the war, cutting off the ability of Confederate blockade-runners to make port and bring in vital goods or export cash-earning commodities.[8] Given the absence, despite the Mexican-American War of 1846–8, of any experience of issues and operations at this scale, and the extent of friction and rivalry between army and navy, the Union proved able to improvise a joint military strategy, yet there was no real joint doctrine. The naval authorities were very jealous of their autonomy and distrusted the army. Gideon Welles, the Secretary of the Navy from 1861 to 1869, who had no prior experience, and Edwin Stanton, the Secretary of War from 1862 to 1868, who had no military experience, had an especially prickly relationship. Nevertheless, the blockade proved more significant as a framer of the context within which the Confederacy had to operate than as a basis for amphibious assaults. The recent argument that "the most effective naval action by either side was not the Union blockade but the handful of cruisers sent out by the Confederacy to attack Union merchant shipping"[9] totally fails to understand the strategic dimension of naval power in this war.

On the other hand, the lack of decisiveness in 1861 was itself crucial. This was not only in terms of the need for a longer war or negotiation, but also because a degree of stability provided both sides with the ability to consolidate their areas of control, which in turn made success harder for their opponent. This consolidation involved what in effect was a front line, but one that in many areas was rather a matter of very extensive gaps between fortified positions. That put a premium on combat in any effort to define the front line, and this meant small-unit clashes. These were particularly important in northwestern Virginia and eastern Kentucky in 1861 as that helped determine zones of control that were of wider significance for buffer zones and secure communication routes.[10] These operations fitted pre-war stereotypes—that is, they were quick, short, and with low casualties.

So too was it across the southwest, where the withdrawal of much of the federal army, as well as secession by Texas and uncertainty about the views of many other potential "players," led to considerable volatility. This was exacerbated by the absence, other than in California, of state institutions that offered coherence even if these views could be contested. It was as if the entire southwest was similar in fate to the border states, and notably their Appalachian portions. A key early move occurred in March 1861 when the Arizona territory was defined as Confederate by conventions held at Mesilla on 16 March and Tucson on 28 March. In turn, Major-General Earl Van Dorn (who boasted extensive military experience in the Mexican American War and in fighting Native Americans), the commander of the Confederate Department of Texas, seeking both to consolidate and enhance these possibilities, and also to protect west Texas from any Union action, sent the 2nd Texas Mounted Rifles (under Lieutenant-Colonel John Baylor) into the region. Having failed to take the Union position at Fort Fillmore, Baylor reached Mesilla and, on 25 July, drove off an attack from the Fillmore garrison after which they abandoned it. Baylor, on 1 August, declared himself the governor of Arizona territory and proclaimed martial law in a move that was very much like that of a filibuster.

Consolidation was also a matter of seeking to clarify policy. Thus,

Lincoln's attempt to preserve the loyalty of the slaveholding border states had been compromised on 30 August when Major-General John Frémont, a radical Republican (and buccaneer of power in 1846–7 in the Mexican-American War) who was commander of the Department of the West, confiscated the property and emancipated the slaves of Confederate activists in Missouri, as part of his policy of securing the divided state, which would challenge Union political and military authorities throughout the war. Control over Missouri was seen as important for securing Illinois, but this was challenged by the Confederate victory at Wilson's Creek near Springfield, Missouri, on 10 August. Fearful that Frémont's policy would lead to the loss of Kentucky, and thereafter of Missouri and Maryland, Lincoln on 11 September revoked the confiscation and emancipation provisions.[11] Partly for this reason, the headstrong Frémont, an authoritarian surrounded by corruption, was altogether dismissed on 2 November. He was given command of the Mountain Department in the Appalachians in March 1862 but held no command from that June onward. In 1864, he ran for president as the candidate of the Radical Democracy Party but pulled out before the vote.

There were separate front lines with coastal fortifications. If held by the Union on a Confederate coast, these could have a sphere of influence around them. There was also the question of offshore positions such as Fort Pickens, built in 1829–34 on Santa Rosa Island off Pensacola Bay and not in use during the 1850s. In January 1861, the fort was seen by the local Union commander as the most readily-defended local position. Other positions were therefore abandoned and the fort was tightly held by the Union throughout the war, although exposed to fire from Fort Barancas on the mainland. However, backed by Union warships, Fort Pickens played a key role in blockading Pensacola Bay. Somewhat differently, secession by the Confederacy led to the scuttling of federal warships off the naval yard at Norfolk.

As a parallel, in 1854 Sir James Graham, the First Lord of the British Admiralty, wrote to Fitzroy, Lord Raglan (at the time the Master-General of the Ordnance) about plans to defend the port of Hull and Humberside from amphibious attacks: "I quite concur in the opinion that the permanent presence of a large military force at Hull is not requisite: that inland concentration, with rapid means of distribution by railroad, is the right system."[12] At that point, Russia was the principal threat to Britain.

In contrast to America, many civil wars ended rapidly, in part because the opening campaign delivered an immediate verdict, or provided, in the result of the initial trial of strength, an opportunity to test the willingness to continue the struggle as opposed to beginning negotiations. Thus, a verdict had been delivered in 1860 in the Ecuadorian civil war between the rivals Guillermo Franco, president from 1859, and the conservative Gabriel Garcia Moreno, based in the rival centers of Guayaquil and Quito, when Juan José Flores, a former president and commander of the conservative army, won a decisive victory at Bodegas. Flores then advanced on Guayaquil, Franco went into exile, and Moreno was president until 1865.

The failure to settle the American Civil War in the opening campaign threw attention onto the international context (see chapter 3), and thus emphasized both the uncertainty and the danger that the war was slipping away from the north. Scott resigned on 1 November 1861 in response to Lincoln's favor for McClellan. This—and the abandonment both of Scott's design and of the effective integration of expeditionary operations within the larger context of Union grand strategy—committed the north to the timetable of success in what became an uncertain as well as slow war in the east.[13] However, in contrast, it has been argued that the Union generals were slow and victory possible much earlier.[14] This is an approach that puts an emphasis on the skill brought by Grant in 1864, although it was necessary for McClellan to have time to build his army, while a war of exhaustion, or, at least of more than a knock-out blow, is always going to take time.

American military doctrine—that of power projection to assert strength and fixed positions to secure control over large regions—was necessarily employed in a totally new political context. This doctrine was the same as in any other Western society although it was not formally articulated. The relationship with operational goals and means was not tight, but the latter were very much in line with Jominian principles, those in which Napoleon's generalship were presented (see chapter 5). Bases of operations, lines of operations, offensive operations to project power, defensive operations to secure territory, logistics, and fortifications were all aspects of how Americans thought about military operations. This was largely established practice, if not common sense.

However, it was the administrative apparatus to support this practice on the scale of the Civil War that was naturally in 1860 underdeveloped. That was because there was no need for more. Nevertheless, when more of an apparatus was required, it was largely a matter of expanding the pre-war systems. This was accomplished, although this expansion or up-scaling posed a major bureaucratic and managerial challenge, as well as great pressure on resources. Simon Cameron, the Secretary of War from March 1861 to January 1862, was held responsible for poor administration and was criticized for corruption. (Lincoln had been bullied by Pennsylvania to appoint Cameron to the Cabinet.)

The combination of the consolidation of the two sides and the duration of the conflict threw more emphasis on resources. Although the Confederacy contained about 30 percent of the country's wealth, the Union's advantages were formidable, not only in this wealth but also in the ease with which it could be employed—that is, Union resources were fungible. The Union had a 4:1 advantage in manpower, which was significant in tactical, operational, and strategic terms, although this manpower required equipment and training and there was no available experience in commanding such numbers. The Confederacy, in contrast, where conscription began in April 1862, was unusual among contemporary slave societies in that it did not conscript slave soldiers: it was more like classical Sparta than the Islamic tradition with respect to troops.

Although still fundamentally rural, the Union also had a formidable advantage in a manufacturing plant, railway track and bullion resources, and the gold and silver of the west (notably the silver-rich Comstock Lode discovered in 1859 in Utah Territory, and other deposits especially of gold in what became in 1861 the Nevada Territory) being particularly important. The importance of bullion encouraged southern interest in the southwest, and in both its silver and the gold. The Union was able as well as willing to stage costly campaigns. The Union had six times as many factories as the Confederacy and ten times its productive capacity, producing 97 percent of America's firearms, 94 percent of its pig iron, and 90 percent of its boots and shoes.

The disparity was accentuated by the economic and financial dislocation of the Confederacy stemming from the Union blockade of Southern ports, a blockade that became more effective as the war continued. This blockade ensured that immigrants from Europe persisted, as they had for decades, in going to the North, which provided their manpower as a resource for Union armies (although not all were so willing to fight).

The blockade, however, absorbed massive resources in both *matériel* and manpower.[15] Not all these resources would have been transferable to the war on land, but some of it would have been. That the Union could mount such a formidable effort on land and at sea was highly significant. Even Britain could not have done so other than in or near India where they had a formidable native army.

The north also had a marked advantage in agricultural production, even though the south was more agricultural in character. The south was oriented toward cash-crops—cotton, tobacco, indigo, and sugar—whereas the northern agricultural combination was more balanced toward food crops and livestock, and thus the north was better off nutritionally. The north had 800,000 draught animals to the south's 300,000, and the north's agricultural strength also rested on an ability to respond to new possibilities, specifically with respect to upgraded agricultural machinery. As a consequence, northern wheat crops rose in 1862 and 1863, and wheat, corn, beef, and pork exports rose, despite a full third of the agricultural workforce serving in the army and indeed requiring to be fed there. Much of the additional burden was met by northern farm women, a key instance of the wider societal and strategic significance of women (one also to be seen in World War II).

Helped by a wartime prosperity that impressed foreign observers, the north also had a far greater capacity to maintain liquidity and raise both tax revenues and loans, and thus to finance what was, for America, a conflict of unprecedented expense. War bonds provided about two thirds of the cost of the conflict, and the financial strength and stability of the north permitted the issue of close to 457 million dollars of Treasury notes, which held their value well. Income tax and paper currency were introduced. Nevertheless, the latter had to be supported by government action in the shape of the Legal Tender Act of 25 February 1862, which on the grounds of necessity authorized the creation of paper money called greenbacks that were not redeemable in gold or silver. Other acts of 11 July 1862 and 3 March 1863 authorized further issues of notes, once again in 150 million dollars for each.

Union resources made it easier to equip the large numbers of troops that were raised. For example, nearly 1.5 million Springfield rifles were manufactured (a total that reflected the capacity of contemporary industry) and one that could not be matched in the Confederacy. In April 1865, in his farewell address to his soldiers (an important part of what was to become a southern mythology) Lee argued that they had been "compelled to yield to overwhelming power," which was a way to excuse his own failures, especially at Gettysburg in 1863.

Lee still had a point in pointing to superior northern resources, but, although the war could not have been won by the north without them, this power alone did not ensure victory. It had to be used effectually. Furthermore, aside from the conceptual, methodological, historiographical, and empirical reasons that warn military history as a whole against any reading simply from resource advantages to victory, there was the degree to which the very implementation of resource availability could be countered to ensure Confederate operational superiority. This was notably so for example in the case of the use by the Army of Northern Virginia of the deployment of large corps, a measure helped by the Confederate Conscription Act of April 1862.[16] Furthermore, pre-war experience in controlling slavery, notably slave patrols and active militia service, helped ensure a degree of militarism in the south. Yet, what can be advantageous in a single fight is rarely so in a larger war and the portrayal of a militant south fails to capture this distinction, one that can be related to a contrast between traditional and modern definitions of masculinity. Moreover, for both sides, pre-war militias aided mobilization and provided both institutional rationale and practical experience.

Southern militarism extended to Jefferson Davis who took an active military role. This was due to Davis's combination of military experience and personality, but it would not serve the Confederacy well. He had no relevant political or military experience for the challenges it faced, although had he been successful (or less unsuccessful) the verdict might have been different.

No more did geography ensure victory. The Cumberland, Mississippi, and Tennessee Rivers provided the Union forces with raiding possibilities and invasion routes into the south, but this did not guarantee success even though pressure could readily be brought to bear. Grant recorded: "After the fall of Fort Henry, Captain Walke commanding the iron-clad *Carondelet*, at my request ascended the Tennessee River and thoroughly destroyed the bridge of the Memphis and Ohio Railroad' at Danville."[17]

The proximity of Richmond to Union territories left it vulnerable, but in 1861 this had not brought triumph. Although the violent emergence of two rival blocs that were each homogenous was better for either rail system than a civil war of two sides across the entire networked country, neither system had coherencey that matched these blocs. The existing rail mileage in the Confederacy was far shorter than in the Union and was mostly designed to link ports to hinterlands—as with Jacksonville and the Florida, Atlantic and Gulf Central Railroad from Jacksonville to Chattahoochee—rather than to provide an overarching network, which had also not been possible due to insufficient capital. Moreover, major problems were caused by different gauges. The weakness of the south's rail infrastructure was clear, notably in comparison with the far greater density of railways in more industrialized Ohio and Pennsylvania.

An aspect of this was the density and significance of junctions and major bridging points. There were fewer junctions in the south than in the north, which made it easier to interdict the rail system. There were rail-steamer junctions across the Mississippi in the south (where the river was larger), rather than bridges: the first bridge across the Mississippi was not finished until 1856 and it was found in the north, between Rock Island, Illinois (where a prison and a military manufactory were to be established), and Davenport, Iowa. It had taken three years to build during peacetime, which revealed the issues posed by adding to rail infrastructure during the Civil War.

Just as the confluence of rivers had traditionally explained operational planning and economic activity, with a common focus on logistics, so too was this true of the significance of rail junctions. Thus, Macon in central Georgia had train tracks thence to Atlanta, Columbus, and

Savannah, which explained Union attacks, in this case the two (unsuccessful) Union cavalry attacks in 1864. In turn, serious Confederate raids on the Baltimore and Ohio (B&O) line in 1861, with Harpers Ferry seized on 18 April (and the bridge blown up on 14 June) and Martinsburg on 20 June, led to an end to services, obliging the Union to use west-east lines further north (the North Central and Pennsylvania Railroads) to the benefit of the corrupt Simon Cameron, the Secretary of War, a Pennsylvania businessman and politician. Harpers Ferry and Martinsburg were not recaptured until February 1862. Yet, the reality that the Union had these lines was a factor in its railway capacity. Such strategic depth was an important aspect of the military significance of rail because it reduced the vulnerabilities arising had there only been a single railroad line and also from the proximity to the frontline, with the resulting exposure to opposing forces.

Similarly, the importance of particular river-rail crossings emerged from the lack of other crossings, although rivers above the Appalachian fall-line often had many crossing points. This was the case for example on the Rappahannock River below Fredericksburg, or for many miles farther upstream. This situation enhanced the significance of Fredericksburg as a target, and a major battle was to be fought there in 1862, and another (Chancellorsville) in 1863.

In late 1861, however, it was Washington itself that needed protection. On 4 December, the front page of *The New York Times* carried the story, "The National Lines before Washington. A Map exhibiting the defenses of the national capital, and positions of the several divisions of the Grand Union army." The accompanying text began:

> The interest which attaches to the military operations of the National army on the line of the Potomac, has induced us to present the readers of the Times with the above very complete and accurate map of the impregnable lines on the Virginia side of the National Capital.... The principal permanent fortifications, which the rebels, if they attempt them, will find to be an impassable barrier to their ambitious designs upon the Capital, have been enumerated by title and position in the General Orders of General McClellan, but are, for the first

> time, located and named upon the present map.... Another novel and useful trait our present map is its geographical definition of the territory occupied by each of the eight divisions constituting the grand defensive army.[18]

The army's commander, McClellan, furiously demanded that the paper be punished for aiding the Confederates. The Secretary of War, Cameron, restricted himself to urging the editor to avoid such action in the future. The following spring, however, the War Department established a voluntary system to prevent journalists with the Army of the Potomac from publishing compromising maps.

In response to Union failures, the Joint Committee on the Conduct of the War was created by Congress on 10 December. Comprised of three senators and four representatives, it held 272 meetings until May 1865. It proved to be a source of pressure on the generals and a means for political influence by radical Republicans. However, the committee's assumptions about strategy and emphasis on willpower were flawed. Particular steps, such as in favor of Major-General John Frémont in March 1862, were poorly judged.[19] On 3 December 1861, in his first annual message to Congress, Lincoln warned about the need to not to allow the war to "degenerate into a violent and remorseless revolutionary struggle." That, however, was indeed the direction in which it was going.

Comparisons with the War of Independence are instructive, with timing being one of the most significant elements in this. The opening years, 1775 and 1861, were very similar in many respects, with the rebels gaining the advantage and their opponents unable to use a demonstration of force to achieve a speedy and successful response. A law enforcement problem had likewise escalated in part due to ambitious leaders who, depending on the circumstances, were recklessly irresponsible.

Indeed, there was great similarity between Bunker Hill and First Bull Run in that the display of force by the British and Union forces, respectively, failed to produce the intended outcome. The obvious differences on the ground in part resulted in the ability of the British finally to gain control of the battleground, whereas the Union army failed to do so. Professionalism played a key role in the eventual, but costly, British success at Bunker Hill by troops and officers (many of whom had had service in the Seven Years' War during 1756–63). Yet, there was an inability to prevent the consolidation of rebellion over a widespread area. This was also to be the case in 1861, although the area in question here was only a portion of the country and, indeed, among the slaveholding states.

At the end of 1775, the Patriots had bottled the British forces in Boston and had also invaded Canada, where the British, having lost Montreal, were besieged in Quebec. There was no comparison with the situation for the Confederates, the rebels in the later war, at the end of 1861. Indeed, the Union was in control of much of America and boasted dominance at sea. It looked as though the following year would bring Union success, which also seemed to be the prospect for the Patriots in 1776. At the same time, British preparations meant that this was likewise a prospect for Britain in 1776, and not least because it was not then at war with France. The international context was also very important in 1861–2, but for very different reasons. We turn to these in the next chapter.

## 3. INTERNATIONAL CONTEXT

Mexican revanche was scarcely an element in the American Civil War. Nor was there a united Native American uprising. As so often happens, it is the elements that did not occur that are highly significant and yet also tend to be slighted. Mexican resilience was to be demonstrated in these years, and successfully so; but it was at the expense of the French-backed imperial effort of Maximilian to usher in a counter-revolution in Mexico and not in an effort to reverse all or part of the Mexican losses in the War of 1846–8. As a result, the potential role that Mexico might have taken in a neighboring country was greatly lessened.

Similarly, many Native Americans fought for the Union or Confederate causes. Others fought White settlers. Yet, and unsurprisingly so as there was no united Native American bloc, there was no united Native American revival or even effort, and certainly no equivalent to the Native American element in the War of 1812. As a result, the international context that is considered becomes almost exclusively that of the European powers, and this alone offers a different agenda of might-have-beens.

The literature on the international dimension of the war is good, but far less copious than that on the military dimension. Moreover, the linkage between the two is not always what it should be. This is especially the case as far as the strategies of both sides are concerned. Yet in the war's context, course, and consequences (not least the economic aspect mentioned in the last chapter) the international dimension was crucial, just as it was in the War of Independence of 1775–83. Indeed, as a result, that dimension provides the vital counterfactual that helps explain the different fate of the 1861 rebellion or, at the very least, provides a crucial contextualization. This chapter shows that for a number of reasons the Anglo-French intervention did not occur, and it was never as simple as being one Confederate victory or stalemated battle—notably Antietam—away from happening.

In throwing light on the potential impact of international intervention, the result of the War of Independence (in which France formally intervened onward from 1778) leads to a stress on that factor in the Civil War. At that time there was no such military intervention nor recognition for the Confederacy. This was the case not only at the outset, but throughout the war. Indeed, this factor must be considered for the successive stages of the conflict rather than as a one-off factor of cause and consequence. Doing so helps ensure that the international/diplomatic element is not simply seen as a structural or contextual factor—rather, as one that developed and sometimes more significantly so than its military counterpart.

Furthermore, the sequential nature of French and Spanish entry into the War of Independence—in 1778 and 1779, respectively—once again throws suggestive light on the Civil War when suspicions and differences dividing Britain and France arguably limited the chances of either intervening. Yet, the War of Independence showed that it was not necessary to have both powers in line. That was also the case in Mexico where France had moved into military intervention, whereas Britain and Spain had not.

The nineteenth century saw the rise of America that prefigured a change to the world order, one readily apparent with the crucial nature of American intervention in the two World Wars and the Cold War. Had there been any inherent desire to stop this, the opportunity would have been strongest at the time of the Civil War. It offered the possibility of ensuring a permanent division of America and advancing the British and French hopes—at the time of Texan independence—of finding an ally in North America, an outcome that the pro-slave promoters of Texas annexation had greatly feared.

British North America had been partitioned in 1783, with Spain gaining Florida, Britain retaining Canada, and America becoming an independent state with, in addition, hegemony over the Native Americans beyond the Appalachians. Now, there was the prospect of sustaining the division of the independent section acknowledged in this partitioning. Consequently, North America might follow a trajectory more similar to the very divided Spanish New World (at least by 1861), rather than its still-united Portuguese counterpart, Brazil. Regional risings in Brazil in the 1820s–40s had not enjoyed external support, which stood in contrast to the situation of the American Patriots against Britain in 1775–83.

Nevertheless, there was no such planning on the part of Britain, the leading naval power. Prior to the start of the Civil War, the British government was determined not to intervene, just as they had not done so in the 1840s during the Mexican American War. And this was not because the British followed the logic of the American Monroe Doctrine of 1823, with its stipulation of European non-intervention in the New World. Instead, as earlier with the War of 1812, America was not the principal priority for British policymakers in this period, which helps explain Britain's accommodating position toward America on a number of occasions, including during the Civil War.

In addition, America was an important investment and commercial sphere of activity, but this did not render conflict impossible. Instead, from the outset of the Civil War, there were projections of the possibilities of international intervention, not least because of the war's consequences for international trade, the freedom of which was a matter of ideological commitment for British politicians and significant for other important economic interests.

There was also the relationship between the war and broader intellectual-political divisions—notably between liberalism and conservatism. The ability of northern and pro-northern commentators to argue that the war was a liberal struggle against a conservative south cut across the stress of the latter on self-determination. Indeed, the nationalist trope, so strong in liberal European opinion, did not help the would-be nation of the south.[1] Many European liberals, indeed, fought for the north. But not Giuseppe Garibaldi, who was offered a major-general's commission in 1861, but then unsuccessfully demanded the command of the forces and the abolition of slavery. More particularly, the contrast promoted by the north was between democracy and oligarchy, and between freedom and bondage. Ironically, the liberals in the economic sense were the low-tariff cotton producers of the south.

While permeable by small, fast steamships until late in the conflict—which enabled British merchants to supply munitions, including rifles, saltpeter (necessary for gunpowder), and lead—the blockade of the Confederate states, organized by the Union's Blockade Board established in

1861, indicated the potency of economic warfare by limiting Southern exports. The blockade, however, led to a host of disputes with commercial states, and most prominent among them was Britain, the leading trader in the world. In the diplomatic archives, one is struck by the amount of time spent on quarrels over the fate of individual ships.

The blockade, which drew from American experience against Mexico in 1846–8, also helped to limit the Confederates' efforts to build up their own fleet. Even before the blockade became effective, the Confederacy had made insufficient efforts to import rolled iron and machinery,[2] which was a serious issue because they were so short of iron that they had to pull up railway tracks and could not adequately maintain their rail system, even when attempting to relay track.[3] Had Britain fought the Union, then such factors would have limited the ability of the Confederates to provide support.

In May 1861, Richard, 2nd Lord Lyons, the able British envoy, noted, in his confidential correspondence with Rear-Admiral Alexander Milne, the commander of the North America and West Indies station, that non-intervention was the order of the day for Britain: "The present policy of the government at home is to keep entirely aloof from the quarrel which is raging in this country, to show neither favour nor disfavour to one side or the other." Although obliged to protect British subjects and property, Milne was not to interfere with the Union blockade, a key advantage for the north, but nor with southern privateers.[4] America's legal position vis-à-vis Britain was affected by the unilateral American refusal in 1856 to sign the Declaration of Paris, an international agreement codifying practice over blockade and privateering.

Simply announcing a blockade did not make it so. Since the Union refused to recognize that the Confederates were belligerents, there was a lack of clarity about the legal position. This was notably so as America blockading its own ports implied at least a *de facto* recognition of the Confederacy. Lincoln saw the Confederacy as engaged in defying legal authorities and not as a belligerent. International law, however, accepted searching foreign vessels for contraband as part of a blockade only in a public war between sovereign states. Britain declared neutrality and recognized both sides as belligerents, thereby permitting trade to continue. British subjects were instructed to observe British law and "the law of nations in relation thereto." The Union position was that stopping at a neutral port in mid-voyage did not eliminate the illegality of the entire voyage if contraband was being carried, this being its case when it seized the *Bermuda* 400 miles off the American coast in April 1862 when it was flying a British flag.

Britain did not use the crisis in America as an opportunity to "meddle," let alone to press its claims over the San Juan issue in Puget Sound (the basis of the very minor Pig War of 1859), despite tension over the issue in the winter of 1860–1,[5] and issued a neutrality proclamation on 13 May 1861.[6] However, even-handedness was unacceptable to the Union because, by treating both sides as belligerents, the British and French (whom the British government was keeping informed[7]) did not present the Confederates as rebels.

The Union proved reluctant to accept the constraints posed by this stance, and, later in May, Lyons noted: "I am seriously alarmed at the recklessness and imprudence of this government in their treatment of foreign powers,"[8] a point more generally true of American attitudes and European responses. He added in June: "I do not regard a sudden declaration of war against us by the United States as an event altogether impossible at any moment," an anxiety to which he was to recur on other occasions.[9] If Lyons believed the danger imminent and could not telegraph in cypher, he would send the message: "Could you forward a letter for me to Antigua."[10]

Lyons did not think that Bull Run would affect the British line of conduct, yet by ensuring that the war would continue it rendered his hope that the Union would not try to close the southern ports to international trade less plausible. For him to point out that Britain had faced a comparable issue in Colombia was unhelpful, as the Union would not let itself be treated in a similar fashion,[11] although throughout the Civil War and thereafter comparisons were to be drawn as all sides struggled to gain advantage in debate. Lord John Russell, the Foreign Secretary, observed in September 1861: "The great question of all is the American, and that grows darker and darker every day. I do not expect that Lyons will be sent away, but it is possible. Seward [the Secretary of State] and Co. may attempt to revive their waning popularity by a quarrel with Great Britain; but if we avoid all offence, I do not see how they can do it."[12] The danger of war for popularity on the part of the Union, as already seen earlier on a number of occasions, was to be revisited repeatedly by Lyons, but there was no real basis for his fear.[13]

The suggestion in June by Henry, 3rd Viscount Palmerston, the Prime Minister throughout the Civil War, that naval reinforcements be sent to American waters was not followed up, in part because of concern about tensions with France, and Anglo-American relations did not deteriorate in late 1861 until 8 November. Then a Union frigate, the *San Jacinto* (named after Sam Houston's dramatic victory over the Mexicans in 1836) fired across the bows and stopped the British packet (mail) steamer RMS *Trent*, in the Old Bahama Channel *en route* from Spanish-ruled Havana to the British possession of Nassau with an onward voyage to Southampton. Acting without orders, the *San Jacinto* removed from the *Trent* two prominent Confederate politicians, James Mason and John Slidell, who were being sent to Europe to try and win formal recognition of independence, along with their two secretaries, and they were confined in Fort Warren, Boston. The blockade thus compounded the weaknesses of Confederate diplomacy.[14] Congress voted Charles Wilkes, the Captain of the *San Jacinto*, the thanks of the nation.

"It is not lawful to take passengers out of a neutral vessel going from a neutral port to a neutral port," commented Russell.[15] This clear breach of British maritime rights, was exacerbated by the assurance from Charles Adams, the American envoy in London, that the ship would not be stopped, an assurance given in good faith as the difficult Wilkes had acted without orders. Informed of the incident on 27 November, the British government (after a Cabinet meeting on the 28th) demanded the return of the men and an apology.

Concerned that the American government that wished to win support through conflict with Britain would not agree, a longstanding fear on the British part, the British prepared for war. Edward, 12th Duke of Somerset, the First Lord of the Admiralty throughout the Civil War, ordered Milne to concentrate naval forces such that no ship be left isolated and vulnerable to attack. Benefiting from the naval build-up stemming from concern about French plans in 1859 and subsequently,[16] Somerset planned the dispatch of "our most effective ships and also smaller vessels to operate in shallow waters" and, in the meanwhile, dispatched warships from both the Home and Mediterranean Fleets (the two most important ones) in part to protect the steamships hired to transport troops.[17] Russell was confident on the naval side, but fearful of an American attack on an unprepared Canada, rather as Palmerston had been when fearful of war earlier in the year.[18]

From 29 November, reinforcements were sent to Canada and Bermuda, both troops and *materiel*, while the export of munitions to the Union—notably crucial the saltpeter from India for gunpowder—was suspended on the 28th. The British imperial system came into play with its multiple interconnections. Coal was sent to the West Indies to support a larger naval presence,[19] while Canadian Volunteer units gained recruits. In response to the prospect of war, the New York stock market fell.

British ministers speculated about the likely international consequences, and about the possibility that the Union's options might be constrained by domestic circumstances aside from their leaders seeking war with Britain (both points made by Palmerston)[20] whose extensive experience as a Foreign Secretary (1830–4, 1835–41, and 1846–51) included periods of Anglo-American antagonism while he had been Secretary at War in 1809–28 when the two powers fought each other in the War of 1812. Presenting Britain as having no other options, Russell observed on 6 December 1861: "I cannot imagine their giving a plain yes or no to our demands. I think they will try to hook in France, and if that is, as I hope, impossible, to get Russia to support them in some plausible philo-neutral proposition. Their government has all the genius of a country attorney," a remark (and frequently made) that reflected a social disdain and also a sense of the Americans as preferring narrow interests to statecraft. Russia was seen as hostile to Britain: the two had recently fought during the Crimean War (1854–6), with France at that time allied to Britain. On 16 December 1861, Russell added, "The President's message is prudent.... But the Congress will, I fear, intercept any rational solution." And yet, expressing optimism, Lyons wrote on 28 December: "[T]he only present danger seems to lie in the surrender causing so violent an outburst of public wrath, as to drive the government to some highhanded proceeding in order to satisfy the American populace."[21]

On 17 December 1861, Adams communicated to Russell Seward's letter of 30 November stating that Wilkes had not been authorized to act.

Four days later, the French envoy made it clear to Seward that France would not help America and, instead, urged compliance with British demands. Subsequently, the Union government, after a Cabinet meeting on 25 December, apologized, disavowed Wilkes, and released the envoys—this was a settlement and great relief to Russell, of which news reached London on 8 January 1862.[22] His letter of 10 January, announcing that the government was satisfied by these steps, was communicated to Seward on 30 January by Lyons, who worked hard to solve the crisis.[23] Russell had pointed out that the Union's best chance in the Civil War was to keep Britain and France neutral. But he also linked policy to American politics, expressing the hope that George B. McClellan, the commander of the main Union field army, whom he had been told found the seizures unjustifiable, "could be made Dictator."[24]

Counterfactuals come into immediate play, as both sides could have taken a different line. Indeed, the draft for the initial British protesting dispatch that was to be sent to the Union government was softened according to the advice of the dying Prince Albert as he felt it would endanger relations. Submitted to the Queen for consideration on the night of 30 November, the draft was countered the following day by a memorandum from Albert urging modifications that were approved by Palmerston and adopted by Russell.[25] Albert himself died from typhoid on 14 December, an event seen in the north as a loss to America. His views had influenced those of Victoria. Separately, while in America, the Prince of Wales's unofficial visit to America in 1860 (a visit in which he only went for a day trip to the future Confederacy and only to pay his respects at Washington's tomb) had revealed a degree of Anglophilia royal[26] alongside the recent hostile willingness to cheer on the Russians against Britain in the Crimean War. Yet, the strength of the British naval challenge was a more important source of continued peace than Albert's intervention as it acted as a potent restraint on American policy,[27] just as had been the case earlier in the century.

The *Trent* crisis and its resolution might seem to have drawn the sting on both sides of the Atlantic by showing the danger of conflict, but it also revealed the highly dangerous nature of relations. The outcome of the crisis, public support in Britain for the Prime Minister, Palmerston (a politician who had long cultivated public opinion as a means to advance and protect policy and his own position[28]), and a rapid close to the crisis on British terms, encouraged Palmerston. Palmerston had consistently been ready to use sea power as an integral aspect of his foreign policy of supporting British interests. Personally, he disliked America as an unpredictable force in international relations. However, his conduct in the *Trent* crisis was less belligerent and risky than that of Seward who kept talking up the threat to Canada.

Rather than criticizing Palmerston for risky belligerence, it is worth noting the views of the opposition (Conservative) leader, Edward, 14th Earl of Derby, who had been Secretary of State for War and the Colonies in 1833–4 and 1841–45, and Prime Minister in 1852 and 1858–9. The British party leaders had far more experience of international affairs than their American counterparts. Like Lyons, Derby always felt that the most effective way of dealing with America was with forthright directness as, otherwise, popular enthusiasm and democratic agitation would run unchecked. Over the *Trent* crisis, Derby advised both Henry, 5th Duke of Newcastle, the Colonial Secretary who had met Seward earlier in the year while visiting America, and George, 2nd Earl Granville, the Lord President of the Council, accordingly. Derby shared in the patriotic anger but did not want war, and supported Palmerston's policy of recognizing the south as a belligerent but not as independent. Palmerston, indeed, was a cautious realist as far as policy was concerned,[29] with his caution encouraged by the perception that Seward was somewhat unhinged.

Palmerston had no great desire to confront America because he focused on Europe. He read disputes with America partly in European terms, in the sense of wanting to use assertiveness in North America to underpin policy closer to home, or at least in giving that impression. If the material limitations of British power influenced the shape of policy in terms of the extent to which that policy would ever be pushed in practice, Britain, nevertheless, had intervened in China alongside France in difficult circumstances in 1856–60.

Successfully pressing the Union to back down in the *Trent* case of 1861 did not satisfactorily address the problems created by a blockade that Britain would have to accept as legal in order to maintain good relations with the north. Separately, the argument that military preparations, especially the maintenance of a considerable force in Canada, were the best way to get America to be reasonable[30] was not without risk as they could have encouraged Britain to pursue a policy that might have led to an unwanted war, although, in the event, British policy tended to be cautious. Seward likewise did not want the British involved. The challenge was in finding a way for both sides to get what they wanted without losing too much face. Lincoln and Seward decided in the *Trent* crisis that losing face a little was worth it for both sides.

However, Lyons pointed out the risks created by the willingness of Union subordinate officers to commit acts of violence on their own accounts,[31] risks that were enhanced as Britain clarified its position on trade with the south. Indeed, Lyons greeted the news of the safe arrival of Mason and Slidell at Bermuda by fearing that another dispute might soon arise.[32] Wilkes himself caused further controversy by his presence off Nassau, the capital of the Bahamas, St. George's Bermuda, and the French colony of Martinique—for example entering St George's and refusing to leave for six days when a belligerent warship could stay only for 24 hours. Wilkes was recalled in June 1863.

Meanwhile, European observers followed the war with attention, but it was difficult to understand developments from such a distance, and still less to get a grip on the relationship between the different fronts. There were also the problems of the accuracy of the information available. The European envoys were in Washington, and communications with Richmond, while possible (under a flag of truce via Norfolk) were such that it was even more difficult to understand the situation there.

Mason, who met Russell on 10 February 1862, found the latter unwilling to commit the government, and his reports offered scant grounds for optimism. Slidell encountered a similar response in Paris. The following month, parliamentary speeches on behalf of the Confederacy, in a debate claiming that the Union blockade was ineffective (and therefore invalid) were refuted by the Solicitor-General, Roundell Palmer. Yet Russell wished the Democrats success[33] and reports of their victories in the elections in late 1862 were keenly noted.[34]

Meanwhile, recognition of the Confederacy was pushed hard by Napoleon III, which reflected his hostility to the Union and his interest in Mexico. There was a more general trend in French policy toward keeping other states small, notably seen in efforts to keep Italy and

Germany divided into a number of kingdoms. This policy was regarded as a means to maintain French power and, in December 1861, Palmerston was concerned about the possibility of a forthcoming French attack on Austria and Prussia. Aside from backing southern secessionism, there was also the rumor that French diplomats supported the separation of Texas from the Confederacy "in order to further the supposed ambitious designs of the Emperor Napoleon upon this continent."[35]

A similar view was to be taken later by Robert, 3$^{rd}$ Marquess of Salisbury, Conservative Prime Minister of Britain in 1885–6, 1886–92, and 1895–1902, and Foreign Secretary in 1878–80, 1887–92, and 1895–1900. He was to argue during the Venezuela Crisis in 1895 that Britain should have supported the Confederacy as doing so would make American power more manageable. Understandably furious with American aggression, Salisbury, less plausibly, wished Britain had taken this earlier opportunity to break up America. Then as Lord Robert Cecil, he had pointed out that Britain recognized both Brazil and Spain, each of which accepted slavery (Spain in Cuba). In a less considered tone, Cecil was a critic of American democracy, and saw Lincoln as a despot, and also fancifully compared Sherman to Genghis Khan and argued that there was much Native American blood among the northern population.[36] Some of the press, for example the *Oldham Standard* of 30 May 1863, a paper from the cotton manufacturing county of Lancashire, was even more scathing.

The British government's emphasis, however, was not on divisiveness for America. Lyons, for example, wrote in November 1862: "The immediate and obvious interest of Great Britain as well as of the rest of Europe, is that peace and prosperity should be restored to this country as soon as possible. The point chiefly worthy of consideration appears to be whether separation or reunion be the more likely to effect this object."[37] Recognition of the south enjoyed influential support in Britain, not least because a war fought to preserve or overthrow the Union did not seem too different to other struggles—notably that for Italian unification, in which Britain had supported the cause of self- determination.[38] Indeed, in 1864, by the Treaty of London, Britain ceded the Protectorate of the Ionian Islands (which it had conquered from France in 1809–14 during the Napoleonic Wars and gained in the Vienna peace settlement of 1814–15) to Greece, which was a concession to Greek nationalism. British commentators compared the Confederate cause to the Italian and Polish struggles for independence, but that did not mean that they necessarily favored intervention by Britain. Indeed, Grant remarked:

> The hostility of England to the United States during our rebellion was not so much real as it was apparent. It was the hostility of the leaders of one political party. I am told that there was no time during the civil war when they were able to get up in England a demonstration in favor of secession, while these were constantly being got up in favor of the Union.[39]

Yet, after news of Confederate success at Second Manassas/Bull Run on 30 August 1862 reached London, Palmerston suggested that Britain and France should recommend a peace agreement on the basis of separation if the Confederacy won more battles. The Confederacy appeared not only to enjoy the firm backing of the majority of its (White) citizens, but also to be able to persist in the struggle with reasonable success.[40] The linked issues of recognition of the Confederacy and Anglo-French mediation of the war came to the fore. Indeed, on 2 October, Palmerston wrote to the Foreign Secretary, "The condition of things which would be favourable to an offer of mediation would be great success of the South against the North. That state of things seemed ten days ago to be approaching."[41] Russell and W.E. Gladstone, the Chancellor of the Exchequer throughout the war, both supported mediation.

A longer struggle directed attention to the role of the great powers because it made the blockade more important to Union success as the best means to hit the Confederate economy. Only the great powers were well positioned to end the blockade, but foreign intervention almost certainly would have meant a more damaging war for all. Not only did the blockade prevent exports that could finance foreign purchases including munitions, it also stopped southern coastal transport, which was an important means of internal trade,[42] as had been the case during the War of Independence. This stoppage helped push up prices in the south, and this was just an aspect of a more general difficulty in obtaining goods; the shortages and inflation hit civilian morale hard.[43] There was a general economic dislocation, one not seen in the north.

It is worth asking how far foreign intervention in the Civil War would have been more likely had France been stronger than Britain, as it had come close to being earlier in the century. This question raises the dependence of American developments on wider international events, or at least the close relationship between the two. The obvious conclusion is that, just as American independence owed much to the configurations of politics, in North America and more widely, in 1775–83, so too the Union's success in 1861–5 rested in part on the earlier failure of Napoleon I to defeat Britain and/or to leave a European system in which France was the leading power, and therefore able to limit Britain's naval and colonial position. Such a system might have left his successors more influential in the New World and better able to support power projection.

The extent to which America, far from being exceptional, was part of a wider international situation, made foreign intervention in the Civil War less likely, as did the likely costs of such intervention. France was already involved in Mexico from 1861, and, with its leading military commitment being longstanding in Algeria, was also active elsewhere. In 1862, for example, the port of Obok in what became French Somaliland was acquired. France also conquered part of Indochina during 1858–63 in a hard-fought conflict. Action against missionaries led to a Franco-Spanish expedition that seized Danang in 1858 and Saigon in 1859. Cochin China and Cambodia became French protectorates in 1863. Indeed, the range of French commitments, as well as the difficulties posed by supporting substantial forces in Mexico and at that distance, contributed to the situation in which too few troops were deployed in Mexico.

Spain under General Leopoldo O'Donnell, who had served in Cuba as Captain General from 1843 to 1848 (brutally repressing slaves and Free Blacks in 1844), had seized power in 1856 and held it until 1863, returning in 1865–6, and was already involved, from 1859, in a series of imperial episodes which were intended to ensure public support, but which left few resources available for additional commitments. O'Donnell was an interventionist with a strong penchant for dramatic gestures on the international stage, and Spain had the fourth largest navy in the world, although nothing in the Caribbean that could match the Union's ironclads. Aside from intervention in Mexico alongside Britain and France, in 1861, there was participation in French operations in Indochina. On her own, Spain was involved (with French[44] encouragement) in a campaign in Morocco in 1859–60, a conflict that concerned Britain,[45] as well as the resumption of control of Santo Domingo (now the Dominican Republic) in 1861 in order to help the president there resist domestic opposition, and naval action in the Pacific against Bolivia, Chile, and Peru. The success in Morocco, which led to the capture of Tetuán and Ifni in 1860, brought patriotic support for the government in Spain, but the cumulative pressure of these commitments was too great, and O'Donnell was affected by a rise in opposition from both radical and progressive directions. Support for the Confederacy, in any event, was too great a task for Spain,[46] which in 1862 did not pursue its commitment in Mexico. Such support was also too great a task for other powers unless undertaken as part of a European coalition.

Britain was not committed in Mexico, but the French pressed Britain to repeat over America the diplomatic and military co-operation already seen over the previous decade against Russia and China. However, although Anglo-French relations were based on an understanding of the value of co- operation,[47] the volatile Napoleon III with his opportunism and machinations repeatedly posed a problem for the British. Palmerston was particularly suspicious of France, and his correspondence from this period is full of his conviction of French enmity[48] as well as of suspicion of particular French steps—for example in Syria[49]—and rumored moves—such as reports of attempts to take over Iceland, Sardinia,[50] and an island in the Cape Verde Islands, the last as a naval coaling station.[51] As recently as 1859, an invasion scare in Britain concerning France resulted in the rifle volunteer movement, just as that which in 1851–2 resulted in the revival and reform of the militia.

Leaving aside Palmerston's concerns, there was the danger that Napoleon III, who wished to direct British policy in the New World as well as Europe, would fight America to the very last Briton. Seward, indeed, told the Russian envoy that he had no fear of intervention because he was convinced that Britain and France would not agree on the subject.[52] An Anglo-French *entente*, however, also offered the prospect of a measure of security from Union anger, and that also led to suggestions that a bigger coalition be assembled. In considering Union anger, Palmerston put military and diplomatic factors together, beginning with the seasonal geopolitics of North America:

> [W]e should have less to care about than resentment in the spring when communication with Canada opens, and when our naval force could more easily operate upon the American coast than in winter, when we are cut off from Canada and the American coast is not so safe.
>
> But if the acknowledgement were made at one and the same time by England, France and Some other powers, the Yankee would probably not seek a quarrel with us alone, and would not like one against a European Confederation. Such a quarrel would render certain and permanent that southern independence, the acknowledgement of which would have caused it.

Palmerston thought it best not to offer mediation but, rather, to suggest direct talks between the north and south; although he noted that, if there was an armistice, it would have to be accompanied by the end of the blockade or it would help the North: "[T]he whole matter is full of difficulty, and can only be cleared up by some more decided events between the contending armies."[53]

The correspondence of the British ministers was perceptive of these difficulties, not least the incompatible preconditions of the two sides. Antietam (see chapter four) definitely had an impact in leading to emphasis on the problems involved in any negotiations, Palmerston cautiously observing on 22 October 1862 that he was "inclined to change the opinion on which I wrote to you when the Confederates seemed to be carrying all before them, and I am very much come back to our original view of the matter, that we must continue merely to be lookers-on till the war shall have taken a more decided turn."[54] At the same time, British suspicion of France challenged the prevalent northern view that the British were likely to intervene up to Antietam and that only the diplomacy of Charles Francis Adams, combined with

Seward's frequent threats to take the war to Canada, kept that from happening.

Napoleon III proposed to Britain and Russia that they recommend an armistice, a step that lent urgency to the ministerial discussions in Britain. Different scenarios were sketched out, including the north rejecting the Allies' good offices, which would entitle the latter to recognize the south,[55] a course that Lyons saw as pointless unless the blockade was ended.[56] Conversely, there was the fear that Britain might be exposed to trouble, uncertainty, and defense costs if the north won,[57] an argument that the Americans were to use toward foreign powers.[58]

On 11 November 1862, the Cabinet met and rejected the French proposal of joint intervention, a measure also urged by Belgium. Pope Pius IX's support for the Confederate cause was scarcely going to recommend it to Britain—the pope also backed Maximilian in Mexico. Gladstone, who had argued at a public dinner in Newcastle on 7 October that the south "had so made a nation," had produced a paper advocating joint intervention, but he noted that Russell had "given up *the* point."[59] Somerset thought that raising the issue of an armistice might lead the American navy to become troublesome, and plans for naval reinforcements were therefore in hand. The four available ironclads were sent out to Lisbon, from which they could be readily deployed to Bermuda, the key point from which to threaten the Chesapeake.[60] Had Gladstone been prime minister, then the situation might have been more serious. Be that as it may, he had infringed convention by speaking about another minister's brief, and Adams was told by Russell that Gladstone's speech was not government policy, although Palmerston was more sympathetic.[61]

Subsequently, Gladstone disavowed the position he had taken and spoke in favor of strict neutrality. Yet, his sympathies were clear. He responded on 27 December to the news of southern victory at Fredericksburg, a fortnight earlier, by writing "surely this will end the madness," by showing the north that it could not win.[62] Other ministers who, in early November, supported mediation nevertheless felt that the moment was not yet opportune, in part because of the state of the campaigning, but also due to hopes that the mid-term elections would see Democrat successes, and that then would be the time to suggest peace.[63]

European intervention would certainly have altered both the

resource issue and pushed the question of naval power to the fore. This was not less true as the blockade of the south was regarded as the key point.[64] Such intervention would also have led to a spread of the war, certainly into Canada and probably also into Mexico and the West Indies.

The wider international context, however, was scarcely defined by the American crisis. Sir Frederick Grey, the First Naval Lord of the Admiralty through the Civil War, noted that "we have an insurrection in Greece or rather a revolution and little quarrels of our own both with Brazil and Chile so our hands are full."[65] In Greece, King Otho was deposed in 1862, and the crisis, which involved a British naval deployment,[66] ended in 1863 when George I was elected by the Greek National Assembly. In 1863, the Polish crisis was to focus European attention, dividing Russia from France (they anyway had different views on the Civil War) and leading Palmerston to fear Napoleon III's ambitions. This division between France and Russia, and more generally among the European powers, was taken forward into the Schleswig-Holstein crisis of 1863–4. Important developments in America then were to attract less attention than they might otherwise, and this separateness of America from the European system provided the Union with a vital margin of opportunity. So also, more generally, from the development of America during the European wars of the French Revolutionary and Napoleonic period.

Nevertheless, the possibility that external intervention would affect this situation was raised in America and abroad. On 9 February 1863, the House of Representatives was warned "unless some success in a short time crowns our arms, does not every man in this House feel that the nations of Europe will essay to intervene in our affairs," and, indeed, in early 1863, the French government pressed the Union to negotiate directly with the Confederacy without suspending hostilities, only to have the approach rejected by the Union, which insisted on unconditional surrender.[67] Aside from opposition to such negotiations, France's position was compromised by Union anger about Napoleon III's interventionist policy in Mexico, and indeed, on 3 February, critical resolutions about the latter were introduced in the Senate.

Convinced that independence for the Confederacy was best, Edouard Henri Mercier, the French envoy from July 1860 to December

1863, saw foreign action as a necessary precondition. He complained to Lyons in a fashion that showed scant sympathy for democracy: "American politicians are timid. They sought to sail with the current—they followed public opinion, they did not attempt to lead it. Now separation was an idea too repugnant to the pride of the people to be willingly admitted, and those Americans who themselves entertained it were afraid to announce it boldly. 'Impulsion' from abroad might be eminently useful in such a case." Mercier argued that the war might end if Britain and France recognized the Confederacy, and that it was worth seeking Russian support; but Lyons retorted that the failure of the French proposals had compromised the idea of European mediation and Britain was against interfering by force.[68]

Moreover, that July, meetings of the Conservative leadership in Britain confirmed that the opposition was opposed to recognition of the South.[69] This reduced pressure on the government. Thus, there was no comparison with the divisions between Democrats and Republicans.

The French attitude helped draw suspicion and unpopularity in the Union away from Britain,[70] and Lyons became more confident that he could finesse disputes. The most dangerous occurrence seemed to be that the Union would, as threatened, issue letters of marque for privateers, enabling them to detain neutral ships on charges of breaches of blockade, and that the activities of the privateers would lead to clashes with Britain.[71] As a consequence, Lyons was glad that Milne abandoned the idea of a cruise in Caribbean waters, a deployment that would make it harder to bring the threat to bear of the prompt use of force against the Union.[72]

Relations, however, were put at risk by the *Alabama*,[73] a commerce raider built at Birkenhead on the Mersey for the Confederacy. The British government's role in permitting the construction of this large (990 tons) and fast ship became a matter of great controversy, as it seemed to present a serious linkage between itself and the Confederate cause. Sailing from the Mersey on 29 July 1862, the *Alabama* collected its armament outside Britain in the Azores in August, but there was little doubt of its intention, and the ship captured (numbers vary) between 65 and 71 merchantmen, causing an insurance crisis in America before being eventually sunk off Cherbourg on 19 June 1864 by the Union warship *Kearsage* (an event seen from shore and thus recorded on canvas by Edouard Manet). The *Florida*, which had been built in Liverpool, launched in December 1861 and sailed from England in March 1862, was another successful raider, capturing 37 prizes before being illegally seized by a Union warship in Brazilian waters in October 1864. The *Sea King*, a British merchant ship, was purchased by Confederate agents in October 1864, renamed the *Shenandoah* and made successful raids, notably against Union whalers in the Pacific in 1865.

While the *Alabama* was at Birkenhead, the Union made representations to the British, whom the government referred to its law officers for advice, but the ship was not detained pending their report, and it was able to sail. On 27 March 1863, Lyons wrote: "There is so violent an exasperation now against England, on account of the proceedings of the *Alabama*, and of the rumours that other such ships are fitting out in our ports for the Confederates—that it is more than usually necessary to be careful not to give our susceptible friends any just cause of offence."[74] Subsequently, he noted an increase in anger, and the danger that letters of marque would be issued if Britain did not adopt a satisfactory policy.[75] Lyons was also concerned about the actions of American warships, and feared that because many naval officers wanted war with Britain they ignored all conciliatory instructions.

The British ministry pursued a policy of careful, but conciliatory, vigilance. Russell noted in March 1863: "I do not apprehend anything unless our naval forces on the American station and our troops in Canada are diminished."[76] The following month, Somerset instructed Milne accordingly: "The irritation on the part of the Federals on account of the *Alabama* and probably also of the numerous deceits which have been practised upon them by the assumption of the British flags renders Lord Russell [the Foreign Secretary] anxious that you should still continue in a central portion from which you may be able to watch and to advise on the innumerable questions which arise and which cannot be foreseen."[77]

At the same time, the British government took the necessary steps to prevent the construction of further warships for the Confederacy, being careful to block the risks posed by the use of intermediaries. A key instance arose later that year, again at Birkenhead, and Russell, anxious to avoid a repetition of the *Alabama* case, acted more swiftly and with a willingness to test the law (albeit cautiously) that was a pale shadow of the policies of the Lincoln government, driven as they were by the exigencies of war:

> The conduct of the gentlemen who have contracted for the ironclads at Birkenhead is so very suspicious that I have thought it necessary to direct that they should be detained. The Solicitor-General has been consulted and concurs in the measure as one of policy though not of strict law. We shall thus test the law, and if we have to pay damages we have satisfied the opinion which prevails here, as well as in America, that this kind of neutral hostility should not be allowed to go on without some attempt to stop it.[78]

Charles Adams, the American envoy, sent a note to Russell on 5 September that threatened war if the ships were allowed to leave harbor. The pragmatic Palmerston recommended that Britain buy the two ships, "Laird rams" equipped with "rams" intended to smash in the wooden hulls of Union warships.[79] That was done for £220,000 each, but only after they had been detained, blockaded, and boarded, a clear demonstration of the primacy of policy of state over legal complexities. Seward was secretly informed in advance.

Moreover, with the Conservatives divided, the faction hostile to the Union in a minority, and others unenthusiastic about alliance with France (and furthermore, skeptical about the chances of Maximilian in Mexico), pro-Confederate lobbying was again defeated in Parliament. A call for recognition of the Confederacy failed in the Commons on 30 June 1863, and on 10 August Russell rejected Mason's request to alter Britain's stance on the blockade. The government's position was supported by the Conservative opposition.

The purchase of the "rams" was scarcely the language of ministers seeking war, and there was also restraint on the American side, albeit with a significant clash between Seward and Gideon Welles, the Secretary of the Navy. The Union needed to stop Britain from providing a navy for the Confederacy, but in searching for a way to avoid war Lincoln focused on expedients that would preserve the peace. These were more important to him than either legal interpretations or public anger. Lyons noted, "There is a want of firmness in checking individual officers who transgress international law, but certainly a strong desire on the part of those highest in authority here that no transgressions should take place."[80]

Charles Sumner, the Chairman of the Senate Committee on Foreign Affairs, was convinced that any war with Britain would be wide-ranging and not restricted to North America. He warned John Bright, a radical Liberal politician, that the Irish would take the opportunity to rebel against British rule, and suggested that Russia would fight France, creating an alignment to counter an Anglo-French–Confederate–Mexican alignment. To Sumner, American Anglophilia was at risk and "Western civilization" at stake.[81] In practice, Sumner was a notorious Anglophobe who, relying on Cobden and Bright's alarmist correspondence, misunderstood Britain's position. Cobden passed along Sumner's warnings to Russell.[82]

Although, in a dispatch of April 1864 printed alongside the detailed accompanying naval report for the benefit of the Cabinet, Lyons warned of bitter Anglophobia and American willingness to consider an attack on Britain.[83] The possibility of war, nevertheless, eased after the *Alabama* crisis. In part, this reflected the gradual working out of a form of *modus vivendi* between the two powers, such that, for example, Lyons advised that if a British warship be sent to Charleston (which was blockaded by the Union) he hoped that the captain would be "conciliatory and cool headed."[84] In January 1864, the American government took care to reassure the British that no warships would be supplied to Japan until its differences with Britain were over.[85]

Yet other factors also played a role, not least among which were the Union successes at Gettysburg and Vicksburg, as well as the mutual significance of Britain and the north as markets. Moreover, the Union's commitment to emancipation was affecting British opinion—notably, but not only, its public opinion. The international audience was in Lincoln's mind, especially in framing slavery as the main cause of the war, when he issued the Emancipation Proclamation but also earlier. By presenting slavery, beginning in his Inauguration Address, as the root cause of the conflict, Lincoln helped ensure that the Anglo-French political dialogue associated slavery with the Confederacy. Even Napoleon III's ramshackle regime could not ride roughshod over French public opinion. When, in 1862, the American government agreed to a search treaty that would hit the slave trade, a measure for which the British had long been pressing,[86] this pleased British opinion, including that of the ministry. The trans-Atlantic Abolitionist cause rose to a height during the Civil War, with Abolitionists seeing their calling as a universal one. The *Daily Dispatch* [Richmond] commented on 12 March 1862:

> the Abolition of feeling, prejudice and influence in the present ruling party combination in England is very powerful, and the Government hesitates to take part with slaveholders, however just their cause.

Thus, the prominent British Abolitionist George Thomas, who was very well received when he lectured in Massachusetts in September 1864 on behalf of the cause, wrote: "On the side of the North the battle must be fought upon the very highest moral grounds and with the most uncompromising fidelity to the principles of equal absolute impartial, universal liberty."[87] Such a universal quality was central to Christian ideas of political action because they were moralized as issues of the human condition.

The diplomatic position of the free-Black states was also transformed. President Jefferson had refused to extend diplomatic recognition to Haiti when it won independence in 1804, in part due to his wish for friendly relations with France, but largely as a product of racism. A Black state proved too much for the influential slaveholding interests, for Black republicanism was perceived as a serious threat to the racial order in America. It was not until the Civil War, when most of the slave states had disenfranchised themselves by secession, that the independence of Haiti and Liberia were recognized: Only in April 1862 did Congress authorized the dispatch of American envoys. Opposition to recognition then was led by Garrett Davis, a Union Democrat Senator for Kentucky from 1861 to 1872 opposed to southern secession, who claimed to be able to imagine no sight so dreadful as that of "a full-blooded negro" in Washington society. Diplomatic relations with the Dominican Republic followed in 1866.[88]

Moreover, France's interests in the Americas were primarily focused in Mexico, not the United States. Napoleon III was also concerned about Russian-ruled Poland, where the suppression of a large-scale, but poorly-organized, Polish rebellion[89] maintained the territorial order created in the late eighteenth century and reinforced in 1814–15, an outcome unwelcome to Napoleon. France, supported in part by the British ministry, was interested in the idea of an independent Poland; but this idea was unwelcome to Russia, whose government took the view that the insurrection was simply an internal affair, and this view was directly pertinent to the Civil War. The Polish crisis was important to European international developments, both then and subsequently, and as a result also greatly affected the situation in America. The crisis led to the end of the Franco-Russian alliance but also weakened relations between France and Britain, whose Cabinet rejected, on 24 June 1863, the French proposal for a joint declaration on Poland by Britain, France, and Austria. The failure to agree on this made any joint declaration on America unlikely.

Separately, again lessening any chance of pressure on America, relations between Britain and Russia were tense because of British concerns about Russian expansionism in Central Asia, while Alexander II was also seeking an opportunity to recover prestige from the blow to Russia's international position suffered in the wake of the Crimean War of 1854–6. Already in 1859, Russia had offered to sell Alaska to America, a step seen as challenging Britain's position in the Pacific, while in 1860–1 the Russian navy had played a role in the Middle East. In 1863, six Russian warships were sent to New York and others to San Francisco, in part to benefit from any tension between Britain and the Union. Aside from uneasy relations with Britain, Alexander II's emancipation of Russia's serfs in 1861 led to a degree of sympathy from Union Abolitionists. Congressional interest in early 1862 in surveying a telegraph route across the North Pacific from San Francisco to the Amur estuary (as a key link between American and Russian communication systems) testified not only to American interest in East Asia, including the Philippines and Australia, but also a belief in the value of good relations with Russia.[90]

The Polish crisis looked toward eventual international tensions. Prussia gained more freedom for maneuvering in European power politics as a result of the new tensions between Britain, France, and Russia, whereas by the end of the crisis Austria had alienated both sides, which helped Prussia further.[91] The Polish crisis spilled into conflict over Schleswig-Holstein, duchies with large German populations that were joined to the Crown of Denmark by a personal union. Frederick VII of Denmark sought to strengthen this link by incorporating Schleswig into Denmark, a step that led the German Confederation to threaten military action. Palmerston recommended that Frederick withdraw this constitution, but on 23 July 1863, he told Parliament that if any power tampered with Danish independence "it would not be Denmark alone with which they would have to contend." The recent marriage of Edward, Prince of Wales (later Edward VII) to Alexandra (the daughter of Frederick's heir, Christian of Glücksberg), a marriage that had attracted enormous attention in Britain,[92] was a significant complication, but at that time it was unclear how Britain should respond. (In September, Russell withdrew from his draft the pro-Danish remark that Britain would regard foreign intervention in Holstein as an act of international hostility.)

That November, the Danish Parliament ratified the incorporation of Schleswig, but this step was unacceptable to the German Confederation that invaded to give effect to its demand for the abrogation of this constitution. Danish refusal led to the outbreak of fighting on 1 February 1864, and to an Austro-Prussian invasion of Schleswig. In response to the Danish request for assistance, Russell, without Cabinet approval, proposed a joint naval demonstration in the Baltic to France and Russia, but Gladstone complained and on 24 February the Cabinet refused to send a British squadron to Copenhagen. Palmerston was against joint action, as he did not trust Napoleon III's intentions.

This was not the background for unilateral or joint action in America, and thus the international situation greatly improved for the Union side. This improvement was increased by serious French problems in Mexico. This, again, was not the basis for speculation and contingency planning about foreign intervention in America, although Britain remained anxious with respect to Canada's defenses, while Mexico continued to be a central issue in relations between France and the Union. In 1863, Lincoln became concerned about the build-up of French forces in Mexico, their capture of Mexico City, the stage-managed offer of the crown to Archduke Ferdinand-Joseph Maximilian of Austria (he was crowned Emperor of Mexico in 1864),[93] the subsequent move of French units toward the American border (in order to suppress opposition in northern Mexico where Juárez's support was concentrated), and the nature of French intentions.

The major failure of the Union's Red River Expedition, an attempt to invade Texas in the spring of 1864 (see chapter 7), revealed Union weaknesses in the Trans-Mississippi. It was reported that France saw its presence in Mexico as a bar to American dominance of the region, and Napoleon III was certainly opposed to the Monroe Doctrine.[94] There were also reports in 1865 that France was seeking a territorial position in Mexico, and these were linked to French interest in colonization by Confederate supporters, in part in order to ensure that mines were worked successfully and revenues raised to reimburse French loans.[95] Lincoln had long been anxious about French moves there, and during the Civil War Benito Juárez, the Mexican republican leader, received covert support from Union forces.

Lincoln's concern led him to clash in 1863 with Halleck, the General-in-Chief of the Army. Lincoln wanted Union forces built up on the Texas coast to address the threat he saw posed by the French army in Mexico. But Halleck circumvented these instructions because he did not share this concern and, in contrast, saw deployment to Texas as part of the strategy for action against the Confederacy.[96] Strategic goals were therefore set in part by international priorities. In practice, French forces based in Veracruz and struggling to establish themselves in central Mexico were in no position to make a significant intervention in Texas.

Affected by Congressional pressure, Seward (although cautious about appearing to dictate the nature of Mexico's government[97]) protested against French policy, while in 1864 Lincoln pressed successfully for the dispatch of a Union force to the Texas coast. That April, the House of Representatives unanimously passed a resolution that it would not acknowledge "any monarchical government erected on the ruins of any republican government in America under the auspices of any European power." This position very much contrasted with Palmerston's view that Mexico needed a monarch, although Britain, unlike Austria, provided no troops to help the French.

By 1864, despite the clear goal of one war at a time, the Union was taking a more active international stance in which they sought to elicit cooperation as well as to display strength. In May, Seward, pressing Lyons about Spanish conduct toward Peru and Santo Domingo, suggested that the two states cooperate in a settlement to the dispute. However, the possibility of Spanish action against Haiti was a matter of concern the following month.[98] That September, the American corvette *Jamestown* cooperated with British, French, and Dutch warships in Japanese waters, in acting against batteries erected by the Prince of Nagato that threatened the international use of the Straits of Shimonoseki by foreign shipping. Issues continued to emerge, but as the international situation (with the exception of Mexico) became more benign toward the Union, so counterfactuals, instead, came to focus largely on operations within America. The international dimension was of continuing interest, but it was at this point in time no longer of central governmental concern.[99]

## 4. 1862: CONFEDERACY REVIVED

"Chiefly About War Matters," a pseudonymous essay published by the famed novelist Nathaniel Hawthorne in the July issue of the *Atlantic Monthly*, begins:

> There is no remoteness of life and thought, no hermetically sealed seclusion, except, possibly, that of the grave, into which the disturbing influences of this war do not penetrate … the universal fear and sorrow.

As in 1776, the second year of the war saw a reversal, but the differences between the two are instructive. The year 1776 began with the British in a dire position, and this worsened in March under the threat of American artillery dispositions at the British anchorage when they evacuated Boston, their last remaining significant position in the thirteen colonies. Yet in the summer the situation greatly improved. There was a parallel in this to the situation in 1862 for the Confederacy—a parallel that helps raise questions about who was respectively stronger in the two cases, and how both strength and goals are assessed. In 1776, the British struck back, using their amphibious power to great effect in the New York campaign, while also driving the Americans out of Canada.

The comparison for the Confederates is less than exact, and there was also no equivalent to a success in both major theatres of war, as was the case for Britain in 1776. Nevertheless, the ability of the British in 1776 and of Lee in 1862 in the eastern theatre radically to alter their respective circumstances indicates the potential for change, and the danger of reading from structural factors to more specific outcomes. In 1862 at Antietam—as in 1776 at Trenton—the riposte, Confederate and British respectively, ultimately ran out of steam, but, again, this indicated the contingent nature of battle.

One contrast is that 1862 did not see the equivalent of the British peace propositions of 1776 nor of the Staten Island Peace Conference of 11 September 1776 in which the British was unable to meet the American demand for independence.[1] The closest comparison was in fact to events on the Union side—namely, the Harrison's Landing Memorandum that McClellan, the Commander of the Army of the Potomac, gave Lincoln on 8 July 1862. This urged keeping the war goals moderate, which would have served to make peace easier to negotiate. Had McClellan been victorious—capturing Richmond as planned and anticipated—then that might have been possible. However, peace would also have required that both sides agree on the military achievements for it to be a verdict.

On 27 February 1862, Lyons reported that the Union government expected the fall of New Orleans and Savannah within days; in fact, the first occurred on 1 May 1862, but the second only on 22 December 1864. Thinking William Seward, the Secretary of State, "always excessively sanguine,"[2] Lyons nevertheless explained the difficulty of assessing the situation, a point that could have been made more generally, and this remains valid. Lyons also speculated on the contrast between output and outcome:

> The United States have recently had a series of successes—not perhaps any one taken simply of very great military importance—but taken all together they constitute a great advantage morally and materially. The impression produced by the surrenders at Roanoke Island and Fort Donelson certainly is that the Southern Men do not manifest in action the desperate valour to which they lay claim in speech.... If this is a specimen of the spirit which prevails generally among them, they will hardly make any effective resistance to the Northern armies, which are greatly superior in numbers, and still more so in arms and equipment.... The fall of Fort Donelson and Fort Henry has given the Federals the command of the Cumberland and Tennessee Rivers— They expect to be thus enabled to occupy the Western part of Tennessee, to obtain possession of Nashville and the railroads

which united at that point, and in this way to interrupt the communication between Virginia and the South through Tennessee….

The month of May is to see the Federal armies in undisputed possession of Missouri, Kentucky, Virginia and Tennessee, and of the seaboard of the other states. This is going very fast indeed, as all that has been done yet is to take two small river forts…. Nevertheless, if the Southerners do not recover their military superiority by gaining a battle on a large scale, or some other great success, the state of affairs may not be unlike what the ardent Northern partisans expect. But will this end the war? If the South acts with the determination and possesses the endurance to what it lays claim, the contest may be maintained for years in the interior of the Gulf states…. At this moment the North is full of confidence and spirit.

Lyons also wrote that the Army of Northern Virginia at Manassas was to have its communications cut by a Union advance and "being thus isolated, is to be compelled either to retreat or to accept a battle under unfavourable circumstances."[3]

Lyons' emphasis on railway support as a means of enabling forces to remain in position is instructive. In tactical and operational terms, the combination of the "brown-water" navy with army units was often effective, as was true along the Cumberland and Tennessee Rivers.

The battlespace was defined during 1861 into 1862. This was not simply a matter of the success or failure of Union operations. Instead, Confederate plans were bold and far from restricted to simply defending the south. Indeed, in marching north in 1862 and 1863, Lee leaned into a wider determination to take the war to the Union. This was designed to seize resources, gain political capital, and still protect the south, not least by drawing the Union forces northward and putting them on the defensive. In accordance with both military and political need the states that had joined the Confederacy late were to be protected, secessionists in the other slaveholding states encouraged, and a forward buffer established.

Thus, in January 1862, Major-General Earl Van Dorn, newly appointed to command the Trans-Mississippi Department, wished to capture St Louis, advance into Illinois, and thereby lead Union units to withdraw from Tennessee. This entailed using a position in Missouri west of the Mississippi to affect operations to its east. Instead, however, the Confederate army was driven out of Missouri by the Army of the Southwest, and Fayetteville in Arkansas was occupied by Union forces on 21 February. A Confederate counterattack was checked at Pea Ridge on 7–8 March in confused fighting arising from the problems surrounding implementing plans both before and during contact with the enemy (not least when senior officers were killed). This battle secured Missouri, an important Union objective, protected it from Confederate attack (which weakened the Confederacy as a whole because many from Missouri were willing to fight for it), and left the state in bitter guerrilla and counterinsurgency conflict.

With the Confederate army of the west moved into Mississippi to attack Grant, Arkansas, in turn, was invaded by Union forces. Many slaves were freed, although that was not yet government policy, and farms were plundered in order to support the poorly-supplied Union soldiers. (That the Union was comparatively resource-rich did not necessarily mean that resources were readily available.) A Confederate force was assembled to protect Little Rock, much of it deriving from Texas, together with local men drafted under the martial law imposed by Major-General Thomas Hindman. His control saw a mobilization of resources that anticipated much that was subsequently to become normal. In addition, Hindman backed partisan activity behind Union lines, including in Missouri. Union forces did the same. Guerrilla activity led to reprisals and to the destruction of the food that might have fed the guerrillas. This part of America was sparsely populated and full of woodland, providing perfect terrain for guerrilla operations.

Hindman's autocratic tendencies led to disaffection in Arkansas among the Confederates, which was part of a more general crisis surrounding their cause of monetary and food shortages, inflation, and social tension, lawlessness, and desertion. The destruction caused by campaigning made further campaigning more difficult. On 7 December, at Prairie Grove, Hindman's attempt to cover western Arkansas and open the way into Missouri failed when two Union forces that he had sought to defeat separately (in Napoleonic fashion) were able to combine. Thereafter, there was a stabilization of the ruined frontier zone, with both sides moving troops east across the Mississippi to fight. With the fighting at that location difficult to supply and apparently less significant, Arkansas was largely left in Confederate hands.[4]

Meanwhile, in northern Virginia, due to the density of their forces in the area and the deficiencies of the Centerville Road, not least the amount of fodder eaten by the ox teams, the Confederacy turned to the railways to funnel supplies and constructed a spur off the Orange and Alexandria Railroad (O&A) at Manassas Junction toward Centerville: the Centerville Military Railroad, five and a half miles long, intended to support the Confederate defenses. The iron for the track came from storage and from raids on the Baltimore and Ohio lines, notably the Great Train Raid of May 1861, which included the seizure of 14 locomotives at Martinsburg. They were disassembled and then moved by horse-drawn teams to Virginia. As a classic instance of wartime improvisation, the speed of the railroad's construction ensured that no ballast was used, while the spacing of the ties was twice the usual. The withdrawal of the Confederate troops to the Rappahannock River in March 1862 led to the speedy abandonment of the line. The greater population density of Virginia, relative intensity of its agriculture, and extent of its rail lines made it easier to sustain operations in the region, unlike in the west.

By May, the war seemed won by the Union, which serves as a reminder of the multiple uncertainties of the conflict, but also the extent to which events contributed to a perception that itself was of great significance as a basis for morale. Nashville, the key position in western Tennessee, not least as a major rail junction, fell on 25 February and most of Tennessee had been captured. Then New Orleans, the most populous city in the Confederacy was taken on 29 April. The fall of New Orleans greatly affected the Confederacy's export of cotton and affected its shipbuilding capacity. Confederate attempts to regain New Orleans failed, while the very able Rear-Admiral David Farragut, commander of the West Gulf Blockading Squadron, and Major-General Benjamin Butler pressed on up the Mississippi to capture Baton Rouge on 12 May.

In addition, Natchez, a major river port and the largest city in Mississippi, surrendered after being bombarded by an ironclad. This both provided valuable defense in depth for the Union position in New Orleans and deepened the Union threat to the Confederate position in the Mississippi Valley. This position was also threatened by poor morale, which on 27–8 April had extended to the mutiny of the garrison at Fort Jackson (which was a key element in the fall of New Orleans). Capturing major cities posed major issues of security, control, and governance, but also served to demonstrate military success and brought with it economic, transport, and political value. All cities were foci of local transport networks and nodes in regional ones.

In February, Grant had taken Forts Henry and Heiman on the Tennessee River and Fort Donelson on the Cumberland River. Grant's insistence on unconditional surrender won him the nickname "Unconditional Surrender Grant." These successes provided a welcome victory for a Union short of success, although these remarks scarcely capture the difficulties, for both sides, of operating with scratch forces—on land and river—in harsh winter conditions. Confederate command limitations proved more serious.[5] Grant had then been instructed to advance into Tennessee, a process aided by a Confederate commander, General Albert Sidney Johnston (a friend to Davis), who did not rise to the challenge, although he had not been helped by a lack of sufficient manpower.[6] The Confederate commanders at Fort Donelson had likewise performed poorly.

Deployed at Pittsburg Landing on the Tennessee River, Grant was unexpectedly attacked by the Confederates on 6 April when Johnston tried to win back what he had lost in the campaign. The inexperience of commanders, officers, and soldiers caused problems as the Confederates sought to advance into position. This led General P.G.T. Beauregard to press for the abandonment of the project, only for Johnston to seek to win, in part by will and on the impetus of morale. He did in fact push forward but not by maneuver, rather through what he termed "the iron dice of battle" that were cast at the start of what became the bitter battle of Shiloh.

It initially seemed likely to end in southern victory, with the surprised Union units driven back toward the river. Union resistance, however, soon exposed the limitations of the attacking force, and the

Confederate advance lacked coherence in scale or timing. The death that day of Johnston (who had not adequately planned the battle), the resilience of the Union forces that had been pushed back, and the arrival of Union reinforcements overnight all helped lead to Union victory in the fighting on April 7th, albeit with the Union suffering heavier losses. The Confederate force was seriously outnumbered on the second day, but their troops put up good resistance and did not break. Even with winning the ground, the Union army was still unable to exploit its victory. The Confederates suffered 10,699 casualties and the Union a staggering 13,047.

This is a bald summary of a complex and bloody battle. At the same time, the summary captures the unpredictability of the conflict and the extent to which that was felt by those involved. Grant was to observe:

> The endeavor of the enemy on the first day was simply to hurl their men against ours—first at one point, then at another, sometimes at several points at once. This they did with daring and energy, until at night the rebel troops were worn out. Our effort during the same time was to be prepared to resist assaults whenever made. The object of the Confederates on the second day was to get away with as much of their army and material as possible.[7]

The losses demonstrated the need for reinforcements if dynamism was to be maintained, and thus put pressure on both operational coordination and on general recruitment. The losses as well as the fighting furthermore showed that both sides were determined to fight hard, which increased the stakes in the war as a whole. To that extent, the battle was very similar to that of Long Island in 1776. The great loss of life at Shiloh brought with it concern and anger, notably in the Union where there was an attempt to settle the controversy by removing one of the generals Grant criticized—namely, Lew Wallace.

More generally, the Union exploited its inland naval supremacy in the Mississippi basin, particularly to sustain logistics and to maintain the dynamic of campaigning; and the Confederacy was unable to counter this, a situation that owed much to the disproportionate allocation of

Confederate units to Virginia.[8] At the same time, alongside such general factors, the specifics of conflict remained important. Shiloh, the loss of Johnston, and other serious logistical problems challenged Confederate morale—inciting poor discipline—and forced responses that led to the abandonment of territory, notably with troops withdrawn from Arkansas. The weakness of the Confederates near New Orleans was also a product of concentration farther north. Repeatedly during the war, prioritization was a key element at the strategic, operational, and tactical levels.

In turn, Major-General Henry Halleck, who took command of the Union western field army after Shiloh, moved south on Corinth in a very slow fashion, one determined by a concern for another Confederate surprise attack, but also affected by a move away from river-based logistics. This concern also led Halleck to pull in troops from other commands, which lessened the prospects for simultaneous Union attacks. In light of the size of Halleck's army, the Confederates evacuated Corinth on the night of 29–30 May. Halleck occupied it on the 30th having moved just 22 miles in 29 days. This was unimpressive, but Union forces were now established in northern Mississippi. On 23 July, in response to the failure of the Peninsula Campaign in the eastern theatre, Halleck was made General-in-Chief.

Separately, the Confederate expedition under Brigadier General Henry Sibley sent to capture Santa Fé failed (as did their hope to overrun Arizona and open a way to the Pacific). This ended plans for a Confederate hegemony in the southwest. Such a hegemony would have ensured a very different post-war America to one simply focused on the Confederacy from Texas eastward; yet these plans encountered a formidable logistical challenge.[9] Any such operations also underlined the significance of control and furthermore the security in the Mississippi Valley.

Setting out from Fort Thorn on the Rio Grande in February, the Confederates were victorious at Valverde on 20–21 February and captured Albuquerque on 2 March, and then Santa Fé on 13 March. However, Union forces from Colorado strengthened the resistance and the two armies clashed at the Glorieta Pass on 28 March. The Confederates pushed the Union force back, but their supply train was badly damaged, which forced the Confederates to retreat. Under pressure, they first abandoned Santa Fé and then Albuquerque, the lack of supplies here proving a key factor. Separately, the California Column of Union volunteers advanced eastward through Arizona, capturing Tucson on 7 June and moved into west Texas where they captured Franklin (today called El Paso) and Fort Quitman.

Confederate logistics were not up to a major advance through the southwest, in part due to the difficulties of obtaining sufficient food and water locally. There was also, as for the British in the War of 1812, the problems of cooperating with Native Americans who, understandably, had their own agenda to pursue as well as their own problems. (The Comanche were hit hard by smallpox and by drought, the latter greatly affecting bison numbers.)

Most regular troops were withdrawn from the west during the American Civil War. They were replaced by local volunteers who reacted very violently to Native American actions, and continued their tradition of being far less able to keep the peace than regulars. The situation was particularly tense in Colorado. Pressure on Native lands had risen in 1858–9 as gold found west of Denver led to a surge in immigration. The gold itself was to be valuable to the Union in the Civil War.

Pressure on native lands led to the Treaty of Fort Wise in 1861 by which the Arapaho and the Cheyenne gave up much of their territory. However, many members of the tribe did not accept the treaty and violence between these and settlers led to an increasingly tense situation. In June 1864, the Governor of the Colorado Territory, John Evans, instructed "friendly Indians" to present themselves at military posts, but also prepared a military response. In August, Evans was given governmental permission to raise the Third Colorado Cavalry, a regiment of hundred-day volunteers that was to be commanded by Colonel John Chivington, the head of the army (Union) military district in Colorado. Native chiefs sought to negotiate a settlement and thought they had done so with Evans and Chivington at Camp Weld on 28 September. Consequently, Arapaho and Cheyenne moved to Fort Lyon in accordance with Evans' proclamation of June and what they believed to be the Camp Weld agreement. However, Evans was preparing to destroy the tribes. At dawn on 29 November, Chivington's men attacked the native encampment killing many both there and a mile farther on where the fleeing natives adopted a defensive position only to be bombarded by twelve-pounder mountain howitzer guns. In the Sand Creek Massacre, at least 150 and maybe about 200 natives—mainly women, children and the elderly—were slaughtered. Ten soldiers were killed. Chivington's men were applauded in Denver, but the episode was swiftly condemned in Washington. This massacre helped to touch off a major bout of fighting across the plains.[10]

There had already been serious fighting farther north. The Minnesota rising of 1862 also affected the Dakota Territory, and again was a response to the pace of settlement. Eastern Sioux attacked American settlements in Minnesota, although they failed to capture the forts, while other Sioux attacked Americans crossing their lands on the Bozeman Trail *en route* to gold stations in Montana. Just as in 1779 during the War of Independence, American troops were sent against the Iroquois instead of being focused solely against the British, so the American army responded by driving the eastern Sioux back from Minnesota, and then, during the summers of 1863, 1864 and 1865, launching columns under Brigadier Generals Henry Sibley and Alfred Sully against the Sioux in Dakota and Montana. Sully beat Sioux opponents at Whitestone Hill on 3 September 1863, and defeated Sitting Bull at Killdeer Mountain, North Dakota, on 28 July 1864.

Farther south, plans for a winter campaign against the Navajo in 1860–1 was abandoned due to the gathering political crisis. However, freed of concerns about any Confederate advance, federal columns forced the Navajo to agree to move to reservations in 1864. This is a bland description of the use of scorched earth policies and of the subsequent forced march of the Navajo and their confinement in the bleak reservation of Bosque Redondo. There was no systematic equivalent across the entire south in the case of the "hard hand" policies against Confederate civilians, although there was the Union clearing of nearly four counties in Missouri in 1863 in an attempt to suppress guerrilla activity.

In Texas, the Confederates were not able to protect their western settlements, and an outnumbered ranger force was routed by Kickapoo at Dove Creek in January 1865. In contrast, again proving a basis for Union activity, California troops defeated Shoshone in Idaho and Ute in Utah in 1863. That year, treaties were negotiated with Native American tribes in California and Oregon. It is possible that attacks on natives during the war were in part inspired by rumors of native support for the Confederacy. There was indeed such support, and a number of treaties were signed. The Cherokee leader Stand Watie served as a Brigadier-General in the Confederate Army, leading a full brigade drawn from Oklahoma's native population. At the same time loyalist natives also rallied to the Union and fought alongside them.[11]

Potential support for the Confederates was weakened not only by the tensions between settlers and Native Americans, as in Texas, but also by the geographical limitations to cooperation farther north (not least the substantial buffer to Union core areas posed by the Union presence in the Trans-Mississippi).

There was also no prospect of cooperation between the British and the Native Americans, despite Seward claiming that the Canadian authorities were feeding the Sioux who had taken refuge.[12] In fact, the British were unwilling to provide arms to the Native Americans, and there was no prospect of a British-Native-Confederate alignment (comparable to the other desired alliance between France, Mexico, and the Confederacy). The potential geopolitics of the 1775–1815 period had shriveled, and notably the British-Native American cooperation of the early 1810s.

Meanwhile, in early 1862, in the eastern theatre, Union pressure focused on the Confederates with considerable success. On 23 March, Thomas "Stonewall" Jackson was defeated at Kernstown in the Shenandoah Valley when outnumbered Confederate attackers were beaten back by defensive fire. Yet, as a classic instance of prioritization, concern about the Shenandoah affected Union plans, leading to Lincoln's reinforcement of the troops near Washington and bolstering their defensive potential by taking a corps originally assigned to McClellan. This measure infuriated the latter and exacerbated the urgency stemming from his exaggeration of Confederate numbers.

Separately, the Confederate coasts were threatened by Union naval superiority, a superiority that provided an opportunity for amphibious operations. These put pressure on Confederate force-deployment and led to local anxiety regarding moving troops to the main field armies. After the fall of Norfolk on 10 May, Lyons (wrongly) anticipated that Savannah and Charleston would likewise be lost.[13]

Alongside the wider range of operations, Union forces continued to be focused on Richmond and what was intended as the decisive blow was launched against it—such a blow being seen as both possible and necessary, bearing both military and political consequences. The capture of Richmond was regarded as likely to end the Confederacy by destroying its legitimacy and lessening its prospect of winning foreign support; although, ironically, this had not occurred when the British captured Philadelphia in 1777, and so too was their (very short term) seizure of Washington in 1814 was also without political consequence.

For the Confederacy, control of Virginia was economically and industrially (as well as politically) crucial. The Tredegar Iron Works in Richmond was the Confederacy's sole large-scale foundry. The significance of Virginia meant that the Confederacy would fight to protect it and adopt a policy of forward defense if not of outright attack. That was the stance adopted by Davis. Like George Washington in 1776—who recognized that it was difficult to defend Long Island and Manhattan but nevertheless fought for both—Davis was compelled to demonstrate his will and ability to defend Confederate territory.

Instead of attacking the Confederates at Manassas Junction and advancing overland from the north, as he had initially intended as General-in-Chief of all the Union Armies, by turning the Confederates below Washington and with a point of concentration at Urbanna on the Rappahannock River, George McClellan (from March 1862 only commander of the Army of the Potomac) advanced on Richmond westward along the James River. There is a strong similarity here with Sir William Howe's decision to abandon the idea of advancing on Philadelphia *via* New Jersey in 1777, which seemed too hazardous after the American victory at Trenton in December 1776, and instead to land his troops at Head of Elk sailing *via* the Chesapeake. This was akin to Scott's pivotal decision in the Mexican War.

McClellan advanced on Richmond after a landing to the east of the city and then lengthy siege of Yorktown, a position resonant of the War of Independence and one that would not have been possible had the British navy in 1862 been a factor. The time taken up by the siege significantly lessened the impetus of the Union operation, but, in one respect, the example of the capture of the port of Veracruz before Scott's advance on Mexico City provided a necessary template. This advance from the east rather than from Washington was an approach that worried Lincoln, whose anxiety to ensure the defense of Washington anticipated the problems caused by the subsequent northward advance of Confederate troops in September—the very advance that led to Antietam. By approaching from the east rather than from Washington, the Union divided its forces in the eastern theatre.

McClellan was no Moltke (the Elder), the Prussian Chief of the General Staff: McClellan organized the scene for battle but could not win it. In so far as he was the dubbed "Young Napoleon," the pertinent comparison was to be with Napoleon III, who was rapidly defeated by Moltke in 1870, and not with the famous and intended comparison, Napoleon I. McClellan lacked Moltke's fixity of purpose and ability to give rapid operational effect to strategic planning. On a pattern frequently seen with Union commanders, McClellan, whose caution spread to others, also greatly overestimated Confederate strength, which led him to accentuate his natural hesitancy and may have reflected political ambition. At the same time this is a comment rendered from hindsight. His army used gas-filled observer balloons, but they proved of little value in practice. They were inflexible, saw little, and it was difficult to act on the information received. This was a reprise of the French Revolutionaries' use of balloons in the 1790s, a course abandoned by Napoleon.

McClellan both drew on Scott's knock-out blow against Mexico City in 1847 (although he certainly lacked Scott's tempo and dexterity), and also sought to use coordinated pressure with supporting operations in Kentucky and eastern North Carolina as part of what he had presented in February as a "general plan."[14] There was certainly pressure, direct or indirect, throughout the Confederacy—including the occupation of parts of states, as with the seizure of Huntsville, northern Alabama, in April 1862, a process that expanded and accentuated the pressure on the Union.

McClellan's campaign initially seemed promising, with the Confederate forces retreating in the face of their numerous, but ponderous, Union opponents. McClellan, however, expended time and effort on the successful siege of Yorktown from 5 April to 4 May, an operation in which he could use Union naval power. This also played to the Union strength in position warfare—notably logistical support, artillery, siege crafts, and numbers, all of which offered the possibility of a systematic approach. McClellan, who expected his campaign to be like the Anglo-French capture of Sevastopol in the Crimean War in 1853, did not match this strength an embrace of the opportunities that could be thrown up by the chaos of war, and, more particularly, by seizing and applying manoeuverist ability. His failure to advance drew criticism from Lincoln and a demand for action.

However, McClellan was concerned about respective troop numbers and affected by a wet spring season that slowed movement, notably of artillery, and also by problems of cooperation with the navy. Himself nearly being killed by one of the early Confederate mines (pressure detonator-operated artillery shells) probably encouraged McClellan's caution, although it was not possible to manufacture sufficient quantities to make any appreciable difference.[15] McClellan also had malaria in late May. Lyons predicted that McClellan would reach Richmond before the end of June; yet with an instructive reference to the international context, he thought that the south would fight on, so as to make it unlikely that the Union could spare many forces to act against any other power[16]—in other words, Britain.

In any event, helped by the disruptive consequences for Union force-allocation of Stonewall Jackson's successful diversionary campaigning in the Shenandoah Valley (where he was victorious over McDowell at Sitlington's Hill, west of Staunton, on 8 May), Robert E. Lee reversed the pattern of Confederate retreat. This pattern had been set by his predecessor, Joseph Johnston. Lee, who had encouraged Jackson's aggressiveness that led to the diversion of Union reinforcements from McClellan, replaced Johnston in command after Johnston was wounded on 31 May at the battle of Seven Pines, an unsuccessful and costly counterattack on the converging Union forces. At the same time, Johnston's focus on defending Richmond was a matter of safeguarding troop numbers prior to a counterattack, and he understood the strategic need for an offensive and its value for morale. Johnston was able to retire without his forces being broken, and to retire on his chosen axis, one that permitted the replenishment of his forces.[17] Brigadier-General Jeb Stuart's cavalry circumnavigation of the Union army on 12–15 June compounded McClellan's uncertainty.

Succeeding the wounded Johnston, Lee successfully drove back McClellan's cautious advance in the Seven Days' battles (26 June–2 July 1862) and thwarted the approach toward Richmond. He went on to regain the initiative, in measures designed to undermine McClellan's emphasis on position warfare and, hopefully, to clear Virginia of Union forces. Lee was able not only to block McClellan but also to use Jackson's command to turn McClellan's forces by threatening their logistics.

Mobility was to be the main Confederate characteristic. This involved costly attacks that might be criticized, such as Lee's decisions at Malvern Hill (1 July), where frontal attacks led to 5,000 casualties without inflicting serious harm. Battles that ended with the opponent retreating after frontal attacks on their positions, as with the Confederate attacks at Mechanicsville (26 June) and Malvern Hill, should not necessarily be seen as vindications for those attacks, for the Union forces did not need to retreat in either case. Indeed, at Mechanicsville, the outnumbered Confederate attackers had to abandon their attack after suffering over 1,400 casualties. They had been outshot by defenders in good position further protected by earthworks and logs. The following day, at Gaines's Mill, the Confederates were present in greater numbers and the Union earthworks less impressive; but the Confederates again took considerable casualties and only broke through after several attacks. The Confederates' casualties were greater, again a product of their dangerous proclivity for the frontal offensive. Yet, the Confederates were still in a position to cut off the railroad sustaining McClellan's army after Mechanicsville, and the navy's unwillingness to support a forward position at Malvern Hill made Union retreat necessary.

McClellan lost his nerve, retreating and blaming the government for sending insufficient numbers. This was a key point for him as he was convinced that Lee's army was more than twice the size of its actual 92,000 troops. In response, and fearing that he might be cut off from his supply base at Harrison's Landing, McClellan determined to pull back or, as he put it, pursue a "change of base," from the White House on the Pamunkey River to the James River. On 28–30 June, he withdrew southward while being hit by Lee's pursuing troops in a number of clashes—namely, Savage's Station on the 29th and Glendale and White Oak Swamp on the 30th. On 1 July, at Malvern Hill, McClellan's army stood, and Lee launched a frontal attack that did not work. McClellan continued his fighting retreat to Harrison's Landing where there was a degree of naval protection and plentiful supplies.

At the same time, McClellan (an inveterate complainer and man who accumulated grudges) continued to press Lincoln for reinforcements. McClellan's backers in the press, for example in the *New York Herald*, blamed Lincoln accordingly, and suggested that the general had pursued a successful change of base. Republican newspapers, in turn, castigated the general for lying as well as for failure, and added that there was on his part a lack of will to win. Both sides, as is so often the case, had a point. There was division within the army and dismay across the north. Understandably so, and it would have been greater had more been known about McClellan's insubordination. He scarcely had the personality of a Douglas MacArthur and he hated politics, but many former generals had indeed become presidents.

McClellan at Harrison's Landing offered an echo of Charles, 2nd Earl Cornwallis surrendering at Yorktown in 1781, particularly emphasized on 4 July when McClellan's father-in-law told Edwin Stanton, the Secretary of War, that McClellan might have to capitulate. At no time, in fact, did he consider this. Nervous Lincoln advisors did fear he might be forced to capitulate, but not McClellan. In practice, in McClellan's situation there was no equivalent in place to the French navy blockading the British in Yorktown in 1781, and the situation was more similar to that of the British field army in 1778 after the battle of Monmouth Courthouse, when it retreated to the New Jersey shore where it relied on naval support from New York.

The Seven Days' battles started a series of Southern advances and victories in the east that affected the political as well as the military development of the struggle. Yet, one axis of advance was closed down when Jackson and his force, having defeated Union forces at Cross Keys and Port Republic on 8–9 June, was moved from the Shenandoah to assist the protection of Richmond, a consolidation of Confederate forces that helped Lee to turn the tide, not least by having the confidence and capability to do so. Without Jackson's command, Lee could not have turned McClellan's position the way he did.

The Seven Days' battles not only hit McClellan, who lost his nerve, but also disoriented his earlier and highly problematic attempt to put coordinated pressure on the Confederacy from a number of directions. In practice, the wars east and west of the Appalachians were largely distinct conflicts at that point with no military man charged with the overall direction of both. The responsibility for this belonged to Lincoln and Stanton. There is little evidence of any overarching strategy in which west and east were operating with an eye on each other after McClellan was deposed in March 1862 as General in Charge, a post left empty for some time. As things were going well, such coordination did not appear necessary. But after the Seven Days, Lincoln called Halleck to Washington to be General at large, but, from July until November, the north was stuck in a reactive mode to Confederate actions in both theatres. Not until December 1862 would Lincoln and Halleck again attempt to coordinate operations in the various major theatres.

Lee was a figure around whom the Confederates could rally, and this was important in helping to create a Confederate "nation" from people who still identified themselves with their states, a difficult task which matched that of George Washington in the war of American independence. If the army of northern Virginia was not quite the equivalent to Washington's continental army as a symbol of Confederate unity, it was nevertheless close, and notably so after the battle of Chancellorsville of 30 April–6 May 1863. Many of the army of northern Virginia's middle-ranking officers were strongly pro-slavery. Lee understood that Confederate public opinion had a preference for taking the initiative as opposed to responding to northern moves, that it sought offensive victories, and that control of Virginia was politically crucial. He gained valuable personal prestige from the Seven Days' battles, and as Jackson did not perform particularly well there, Lee's reputation was further enhanced. No Union general, not even Grant, achieved this singular status.

As another instance of a turn of the tide, the Union attempt to exploit the capture of Port Royal by advancing on land against the Savannah-Charleston Railroad, as well as to attack Secessionville, failed. The latter was an attempt on 16 June to take nearby Charleston by land, but it was defeated by defensive firepower notably from cannons. This failure led to a reliance on naval action in the (unsuccessful) attack on Charleston the following year.

In turn, naval firepower, notably the ironclad *Essex*, was significant in the Union success at Baton Rouge on 5 August 1862 in driving off a major attack by Confederate forces, but the Union garrison was pulled out soon after. The Confederate force had been greatly strengthened by the result of conscription, and this was given political attention and acceptability through opposition to the emancipation and arming of slaves by the Union.

Union naval strength had already been challenged on 8 March when the *Virginia* (the renamed *Merrimack*) attacked the wooden Union blockaders who employed blunt ramming to sink one and gunfire to destroy another. However, the Union was stronger in ironclads, and on 9 March the *Virginia* was countered by the *Monitor* (a more revolutionary ship design) in an indecisive clash. Moreover, the impact of Union amphibious capability and control of the littoral was seen that May in the Peninsula Campaign; as Union forces advanced, the Confederates scuttled the *Virginia* on the 11 March.

On the inland waterways, the Union added iron armor to many of its ships. Some were "tinclads," with only thin iron armor, but others, the "city class" built in St. Louis, were dressed in 2.5 inch thick armor. The Confederate loss of New Orleans and Memphis that year reduced its ability to build or convert warships for service on the Mississippi and other inland waterways, although the mobilization of the Confederate economy and the adaptability of the available manufacturing resources led to building ships at other river shipyards, such as Selma and Shreveport. This permitted the construction of ironclads at places away from the coast and major rivers, and thus not as vulnerable to capture by Union forces.[18] However, it was quite an ordeal for the Confederates to get their ironclad *Tennessee* down the Alabama River from Selma to Mobile Bay.

Most of the naval conflict in the war involved clashes between warships and shoreline defenses, or between individual ships, as in the War of Independence and the War of 1812. The dispersed nature of the Confederate fleet, and southern interest in blockade-running and privateering, ensured that larger actions were a matter of Union actions rather than Confederate responses (again as was true in the previous wars for Britain). To a certain extent, Confederate force, structure, and goals can be seen as prefiguring those advocated by the proponents of the *Jeune École* in France, particularly in the 1880s. Rather than focusing on conflict between battle fleets, they argued that France should respond to British naval power by emphasizing commerce raiding, the *guerre de course*, a strategy that required fast cruisers. The torpedo boat was seen as a way to undermine British battleships.

In contrast, although it did not create a deep-sea fleet because it did not need one to fight the south, Union goals looked toward the command of the sea later pressed, and in a different context, by Alfred Thayer Mahan, especially in his important *The Influence of Sea Power upon History, 1660–1783* (published in 1890). It is very unlikely that the Union could have done so well had the Confederacy been an equal, let alone superior, at sea, which was utterly impossible given the Union maritime strength. The scuttling of eleven warships at the Gosport Navy Yard at Norfolk, Virginia, on 20 April 1861 so that they would not be seized by the Confederacy (as well as many of the harbor buildings) was a contributing factor to this reality,[19] as was the Union blockade. Lee, understandably, did not place any of his focus on naval activity.

Appreciating the implications of large-scale conflict between democratic societies, Lee fostered a strategy designed to hit the northern popular will[20], and at a time when Union strategy was still unfocused. This indeed remained the case throughout 1862, though one's evaluation of it now is again a matter of hindsight. Union war-making in the east was in part affected by the political and personal tensions between John Pope's army of Virginia, which was dominated by Republicans and affected by "hard war" proponents, and McClellan's army of the Potomac, which from its commander downward was more Democratic and conciliatory; although the appeal of a limited war vanished for soldiers in McClellan's army too after the Seven Days. Indeed, even there, as McClellan himself observed in his Harrison's Landing letter, the logic of attacking slavery was seen by everyone. The army of Virginia attracted acute Confederate hostility due to its harsh treatment of civilians. Pope was heavily influenced by his experience in Missouri.

Jackson's wish to cut Pope off from Washington and then chew up his army led to the battle of Second Bull Run/Manassas on 28–30 August. Poor coordination and command flaws were problems for both sides, but the Confederates were able to inflict significantly more casualties and Pope retreated. Pope's failure left McClellan in a stronger position, and Lincoln merged the two armies under the latter. This provided the background to the Antietam campaign, ensuring that McClellan could bring more troops to bear against Lee.

Lee's advance across the Potomac River near Leesburg into Maryland on 4 September obliged the Union forces to follow and to seek to obstruct the advance,[21] and thus reduced the possibility of any renewed threat to Richmond. Lee kept the initiative. The Confederate advance also circumvented the vulnerabilities of the defense apparent in Lee's earlier command of South Carolina, Georgia, and Florida to which he had been appointed on 5 November 1861. There, Lee was criticized for his failure to prevent the bombardment of Fort Pulaski into surrender on 11 April 1862 that effectively closed the port of Savannah.

The advance was designed not only to shock Union opinion by carrying the war to the north and inflicting defeat there, as well as to convince foreign opinion of Confederate strength and potential, but also perhaps to encourage Maryland to secede or, at least for more in this state to offer support. This captured the extent to which Maryland, though part of the Union, was regarded as a potential member of the Confederacy—it was believed that this state might change allegiance if a military opportunity was provided. This again offered a parallel to British counterinsurgency strategy during the War of Independence, notably the "Southern Strategy" onward from late 1778 and, more particularly, in 1780–1. Lee was briefed on the limits of Confederate appeal in western Maryland, but he had to advance there if he was to pull the Union army northward from Virginia.

Lee turned the tide of the war, but to a political as much as a military end. That autumn, there was a possibility that Democrats might capture the House of Representatives and press for peace, and indeed they were to make gains in the elections: 28 seats in the House of Representatives, as well as the governorships of New Jersey and New York. However, the Republican defeat could have been worse.

The reading of the situation in Maryland was part of a more general Confederate perception of the border states, one, for example, that encouraged military moves into Kentucky. It was hoped that these areas would rebel against the Union and provide significant numbers of recruits for the Confederate forces. This was an example of the more general tendency to employ optimism, not only at the strategic level, but also in operational and tactical thinking. Above all, in both places, the need to seize the operational initiative in response to the situations that commanders faced was the major consideration. (So too in Mississippi where there were offensives against Iuka and Corinth.)

Had Lee's invasion of Maryland maintained its initial dynamic that September, the subsequent mid- term elections might not have gone well for the Republicans. A prospectus for Confederate success would have been emphasized if Braxton Bragg's simultaneous operations in Kentucky been successful. In particular, Lee's forces surrounded the garrison in Harpers Ferry on 13 September and it surrendered two days later, at the time an unprecedented surrender of American troops (12,500 men were involved). In this there was a parallel with the surrender to the British by the garrisons of Fort Washington and Charleston in 1776 and 1780, respectively.

Lee could have outmaneuvered a less cautious commander (like Pope), but McClellan was more difficult. Instead, in part due to the speed of Union preparations, Lee lost the initiative as well as divided his army in the face of the Union forces, a measure made more necessary by the need to advance along a number of roads. The Union on 13 September had discovered a copy of Lee's orders that indicated the divided nature of the Confederate units, and this encouraged McClellan to advance on 14 September and attack the valley gaps in South Mountain, later breaking through at Crampton's, Fox's and Turner's Gaps.

Lee was now in a vulnerable position and risked being cut off from northern Virginia. He decided to recross the Potomac before resolving to concentrate his units at Sharpsburg, taking advantage of Antietam Creek, part of a familiar pattern of commanders using water obstacles in order to hinder assailants.[22] It was there that McClellan determined to attack. In a battle that abundantly reflected the friction of war, both sides fought each other to a costly draw at Antietam on 17 September. The Confederate defenders took heavy casualties because, as in the fashion of western conflict in the period, they were not entrenched. But McClellan's command of the larger Union forces was woefully poor.

Having failed to attack on 16 September when he was clearly numerically superior, McClellan commanded on the 17th from far in the rear. This was where his command post should be for conducting a battle against an enemy who occupied interior lines, just as Lee's would be at Gettysburg the following summer. Yet McClellan, like Lee at Gettysburg, failed to master the flow of the battle.

He did not sufficiently coordinate the attacks on the Confederate left, right, and center. As a result, McClellan failed to implement his plan for hitting the Confederate flanks before breaking the center. Instead, a series of sequential attacks were unable to provide mutual support, and this failure exacerbated their costly character as frontal assaults. The attack on the Confederate left was mounted before that on the center, let alone the right.

More positively, the timing and sequence of McClellan's attacks resulted in Lee's right weakening to the point that it was rendered vulnerable. Lee's army was in serious trouble at 3 P.M., not despite the way McClellan conducted the battle but precisely because of the way he did so. McClellan, however, can be criticized for then failing to take full advantage of this. The eventual Union breakthrough, on the Confederate right on Antietam Creek, came too late to then determine the flow of the battle. The Confederates had defended what became known as Burnside's Bridge over the Creek against successive attacks for over three hours, when Burnside's corps pushed the Confederate right back, only for this corps, in turn, to be driven back by Confederate reinforcements. Moreover, McClellan failed to commit his reserve, which might have broken the Confederate center. The chaos of battle played a major role at Antietam, making coordination difficult.[23] Moreover, this contributed to the differences in evaluating the battle. This was very much unlike a Napoleonic battle of maneuver, but instead more similar to the attritional pounding seen in the Franco-Austrian battles of Solferino and Magenta in 1859, the former of which had played a role in the establishment of the Red Cross. Antietam was an unnecessary battle for Lee, with heavy losses and no corresponding benefit. By then, the campaign had lost its impetus and was no longer delivering results.

Lee held the ground during the battle and likewise on the next day before withdrawing. Having failed to win a convincing victory, McClellan also could not develop the potential for success.[24] Yet a retreat in the face of the enemy, as carried out by Lee, was inherently dangerous. All these factors reemerge with Gettysburg the following year, which raises the question of Lee's ability to learn from his mistakes. In 1862, Lee's generalship had brought a reversal in the flow of the war, but at Antietam he failed to sustain his earlier success. The pro-Democratic *New York Times* felt inclined on 20 September to offer the following misleading account:

> The Most Stupendous Struggle of Modern Times. The Battle won by Consummate Generalship. The Rebel Losses Estimated as High as Thirty Thousand [they were actually 10,337]....
>
> Wednesday, Sept. 17, 1862, will, we predict, hereafter be looked upon as an epoch in the history of the rebellion from which will date the inauguration of its downfall.

In practice, although not crushed, the heavy losses of the army of Northern Virginia forced Lee to a cautious exploitation of the battle. He withdrew from Antietam two days later and was relatively untroubled on his return to Virginia—both immediately after the battle and later when retreating across the Potomac. The Antietam campaign indeed ended with one final clash at Shepherdstown, West Virginia, where the vanguard of the pursuing Union forces advanced across the Potomac on 19 September. The Confederate counterattack on 20 September pushed these forces back to the other bank, showing that Lee's forces had not lost their fighting capability and determination. Lee then withdrew to the Shenandoah.

Both sides were suffering fatigue and from the impact of the logistical failure that had characterized the campaign, as well as the desertion caused by campaign issues and combat stress. A further consequence of the campaign was the earlier Confederate seizure at Harpers Ferry of escaped slaves and free Blacks, both moved to Richmond for re-enslavement. Separately, the campaign demonstrated the lack of Confederate support in western Maryland, as confirmed by the depredations of the campaign carried out by Confederate troops.

The retreat from Maryland had an impact in the south because it ended the extravagant hopes built up after the Seven Days that summer.

McClellan had not been forced to retreat anew, and it was difficult in the south to shape the battle into a triumphalist account, a process that had helped ensure that the heavy damage of the Seven Days might be minimized. Even if McClellan had not achieved all that he could have, and all Lincoln wanted, he had nonetheless denied Lee the victory he sought and the Confederacy needed.

Antietam both ruptured the run of Confederate success but also suggested that the war would be longer and more costly than had been anticipated. (This reality was brought home by the stark images of the Antietam dead photographed by Alexander Gardner and Matthew Brady.) It was clear, moreover, that success in an individual battle was not going to bring the destruction of the opponent's military strength. There would be no Waterloo, in part because of the number of independently operating forces on both sides and also due to the difficulties in exploiting success. Even Waterloo was less important than the overall situation for Napoleon's final abdication. Yet, the outcome of Antietam was extremely important for the timing of the Emancipation Proclamation, and for the international situation as it discouraged those who advocated recognition of the Confederacy.

From a different direction, a longer struggle directed attention to the role of the great powers because it made the naval blockade more important to Union success as the best means to hit the Confederate economy. Only the great powers were in a position to end the blockade (see chapter 3), although it might have been thwarted by blockade-runners. Not only did the blockade limit southern exports that could finance foreign purchases, including munitions, it also stopped southern coastal transport, which was an important means of trade.[25] This stoppage helped drive up prices in the south, as an aspect of a more general difficulty in obtaining goods, and the shortages and inflation hit civilian morale hard[26] and increased bitterness toward the Union.

Meanwhile in the west, the Confederates faced serious failures albeit not of the significance of Antietam. More than Halleck's lackluster generalship was involved in the inability to wield the success at Shiloh and the size of Union forces to make a fundamental change in the western theatre. The occupation of major towns (Memphis on 6 June) and large areas was important, but there were difficult issues in advancing south, not least among them being the need to control disaffected territory, to confront guerrillas, and to cope with significant logistical and manpower problems. Halleck had also entered the south's notorious "sickly" season, with massive illness sweeping through his command that produced in sick soldiers what was jokingly referred to as "the evacuation of Corinth," a reference to debilitating diarrhea. However, the Union would occupy the area until 1864, and thereby critique, debate, and develop assumptions and policies about how best to treat southern civilians.

Corinth was a center of operations and railroad junction. The Confederate army of the west was defeated at nearby Iuka, Mississippi, on 19 September, although Grant's attempt to coordinate his forces' arrival on the battlefield was thwarted. In turn, a Confederate attack on Corinth was driven back on 3–4 October, and having suffered heavier losses (in part because the Union forces fought behind breastworks) the Confederate army retreated. However, as happened at Iuka, Grant once again felt let down by William Rosecrans, the commander of the army of the Mississippi.

Success at Corinth encouraged Grant to propose an advance on Vicksburg, a stronghold that provided the surviving west-east route a connection between the Trans-Mississippi and the rest of the Confederacy and also blocked Union navigation of the Mississippi River. There had already been an attempt in May–July to attack Vicksburg from the south using ironclads and supporting troops, but that attempt was defeated by disease and the strength of the defenses, both natural and manmade. The new campaign against Vicksburg was launched in November; The first attack, in December, failed, and the campaign was not brought to fruition until July 1863 (see chapter 6), which serves as a reminder that not all of the war can be nicely divided into year-long sections.

Grant's logistical vulnerability was seen on 20 December 1862, when Confederate cavalry destroyed his supply depot at Holly Springs before inflicting further damage to the north along the Mississippi Central Railroad. Grant was forced to pull back. He was weakened by the independent moves of Major-General John McClernand who had spread intrigue in Washington against Grant in an attempt to gain a separate command, which he later obtained.

Meanwhile, in Kentucky, a Confederate invasion in September that thereby threatened Ohio was opposed by the army of Ohio under Major-General Don Carlos Buell, and blocked at Perryville on 8 October. This was a very bloody battle, after which the invaders were unable to sustain the advance and fell back into Tennessee. Buell had failed to use his much larger numbers to fight or pursue with energy, and he was replaced on 24 October by William Rosencrans. Buell did not serve again.

There was much still to fight for as 1862 came to its close. The elections (which were held on a number of dates set by the individual states) had revealed the strength of support for the Democrats, as they gained 27 more seats in the House and took New York, New Jersey, Pennsylvania, Ohio, Indiana, Illinois, and Wisconsin; all bar New Jersey that voted for Lincoln in 1860. Moreover, this was a more impressive list because the south was not part of the election as a result of secession. In New York, Horatio Seymour, an opponent of Lincoln and conscription, beat the Republican James Wadsworth for governor in a state where the previous governor had been Republican. The Democrats also had strength elsewhere, for example in Connecticut where there was only limited commitment to the Emancipation.[27]

Lincoln's dismissal of McClellan on 5 November arose in part because of dismay regarding his generalship, but it was correctly perceived as a defiance of the Democrats,[28] whose goals the general had shared.[29] On 22 September, Lincoln's preliminary Emancipation Proclamation proclaimed slaves free in the states in rebellion if they had not ceased rebellion by 31 December. McClellan was furious, while, in response to the Emancipation Proclamation issued on 1 January 1863 and the use of Black soldiers, Jefferson Davis, on 5 January 1863, issued an address presenting the war as a 'race war' and declared that from 22 February onward all free Blacks were to be slaves. The Emancipation Proclamation helped make the war about slavery, although Lincoln was opposed to the immediate emancipation pressed for by the radical Republicans.

Reflecting suspicion about Lincoln's intentions and concern for the war and its direction, the elections registered Democrat gains, but these were less than the Democrats had hoped. The Republicans maintained control of the Senate and the House. The Democrat tally in the House rose from 45 to 72, the Republican fell from 108 to 87, and the Unconditional Union, who were linked to the Radical Republicans, from 28 to

25. Moreover, the Democrats in the north were increasingly divided over the war. Indeed, in returning to Washington from London *via* New York, Lyons noted that the Democrat leaders he met in the latter felt their hope dashed that Lincoln would become more moderate and seek an end to the war.

After the Antietam campaign ended, McClellan focused on rebuilding his forces, which he did not think ready for a fresh campaign. This was probably correct, but it also enabled Lee to rebuild his army and compensate for its partial ruin in the recent campaign. McClellan also conducted a fairly impressive advance on Warrenton before being relieved. Nevertheless, McClellan's attitude helped ensure his dismissal on 5 November and replacement on 7 November by an unwilling Major-General Ambrose Burnside once the Congressional elections were largely over. Burnside, a good friend of McClellan, a graduate of West Point and a veteran of conflict with Apache, had earned Lincoln's favor from his operations on the North Carolina coastline earlier in the year, but had not done particularly well at Antietam. He only accepted the command to keep it away from the scheming Major-General Joseph Hooker.

Burnside's plan for a rapid advance on Richmond fell apart before Confederate resistance, helped by Virginia's geography in the shape of the rivers that flowed from the Appalachians to the Chesapeake. For political reasons, Burnside had been pressed by Lincoln to cross the Rappahannock River at Fredericksburg and march on Richmond, despite it being the winter season.[30] This was a repeat, in less promising circumstances, of the approach taken by the Union in 1861. Burnside moved the line of operations from the Orange and Alexandria Railroad to the Richmond, Fredericksburg, and Potomac Railroads. However, the government badly mishandled the management of pontoons Burnside needed to cross the Rappahannock before Lee seized the high ground outside Fredericksburg.

In a battle that began on 11 December 1862 and lasted until he withdrew on 15 December, Burnside was defeated at Fredericksburg. He sought to turn Lee's right, so as to cut off his direct route to Richmond, and thus compel him to fall back. In practice, however, far from turning them, the far larger Union forces (122,000 to 78,500) attacked positions on the Confederate right, who were inadequately supported and were repelled. In the battle, the Union army relied on frontal attacks on 13 December on the Confederate left, attacks which in turn fell victim, with heavy casualties, to well-positioned musket and cannon fire (although there was some hand-to-hand fighting).

Although aware of the "awful arithmetic of losses" that hit the smaller Confederacy hard, the heavy casualties of the battle, which greatly troubled Lincoln, were a somber underlining of the vicious toll of the continuing war. "If there is a place worse than Hell, I am in it," Lincoln's response to the heavy Union casualties at Fredericksburg (12,653 compared to 5,377 Confederates), casualties without any redeeming success, followed after Charlottesville by his "My God, my God, what will the people say?" captured the challenge weighing on him of both human and Providential responses. This was a challenge for many and one not necessarily lessened by significant military experience. Lee remarked "It is well that war is so terrible, or we should grow too fond of it." Yet, whatever their personal faith, generals had to be phlegmatic about casualties, both their own and those of opponents, a characteristic very much seen with Grant. Concern about losses was largely driven for generals by instrumentalist factors, notably the impact on morale as well as the number of troops still fit for service and the resulting vulnerability to opponents.

Meanwhile, both sides consolidated their positions. For the Union, this involved not only the states that supported it and the border states, but also areas in the Confederacy that had been conquered. This was not an easy process. Thus, the occupation of New Orleans was an unhappy one, compounded by corruption by the Union military governor, Benjamin Butler. While some there did not wish to hear about the war, and Butler's administration was admirable in dealing with the city's awful sanitation and health problems, many of the citizens disliked the Yankees and expressed this by public displays of Confederate support and by actions such as pouring chamber pots over Union officials and troops including, allegedly, Farragut. An attack on the Union flag above the mint led to a hanging.

The merchants adapted, however, to the occupation, notably because they were able to continue their trade to the Caribbean and were happy to ship sugar to New York. Moreover, Butler won over many by his reasonably effective administration and enjoyed the support of the recent German and Irish immigrants who prior were not integrated into the local society. Criticism of Butler must be balanced by other factors as well, and this is yet another reminder of the problems caused by selective citation.

As with the British after the capture of Charleston in 1780, there was an attempt to reintroduce established forms of constitutional government. Elections in Louisiana in December 1862 in two Congressional districts saw Republicans chosen by an appreciable number of White voters. The Military Governor felt inclined to wrote to Lincoln: "The election passed off quietly, the vote was quite respectable in point of numbers."[31] The British success in coastal South Carolina in 1780 was to be brought to an end with the peace in 1783, whereas the Republicans in Louisiana lasted until the failure of Reconstruction (see chapter 9), and it was this which proved politically crucial. Associated with the Union, free Blacks found themselves in a difficult situation due to local hostilities, but in 1863 thousands of slaves were freed in Louisiana. Ultimately, at New Orleans, as elsewhere, control over Confederate sympathizers rested on force, although "control" could have different meanings, and there was in particular control that did not preclude guerrilla activity. Attacks on railroads were frequent and increased the need for the Union to rely on shipping, which was much less vulnerable to guerrilla activity.[32]

There was significant Confederate support in Baltimore, but Lee's advances north in 1862 and 1863 were not sufficiently sustained to make to incite an uprising there or elsewhere and in 1862 there was Confederate disappointment surrounding the response in Maryland. The slaveholding parts of Maryland were out of reach for Confederate arms, while western Maryland was solidly Union and more aligned with Appalachia.

Nor was there any prospect of Confederate amphibious operations. The latter was far less possible than a Confederate advance west of the Appalachians, and it is worth asking whether the latter might have been more of a possibility had more of the troops from the region remained there instead of being transferred to Virginia—for example Hood's Texas Brigade, the fighting quality of which was highly praised by Lee, but praise that in part was earned by very heavy combat casualties. Any such questions invite the reflection that transport support and logistical resources should not necessarily be anticipated for such campaigning in the west. Yet, the area with its agrarian strength was more comfortable for operations than many others. Conversely, with the Union threat to Richmond, it is understandable that Confederate resources were focused there, for attack as well as defense. Indeed, that was a particular advantage in centering Confederate resources in northern Virginia because Union sensitivity to the region, due largely to the vulnerability of Washington, meant that a Union response could be coerced.

The year 1862 saw the need for both sides to switch from short-war planning and preparation to an uncertain longer war, a process that continued into 1863. This entailed both planning, understood subsequently as modernization and presented accordingly, but also coping. The latter was particularly significant and brought together traditional expedients and new responses. Medical care and the burying of bodies, for example, were each necessary at an unprecedented scale. The former saw the emergence of crude surgery and provisions of large amounts of opium and mercury derivatives. Diagnosis was limited and aftercare minimal, but Major Jonathan Letterman, Medical Director of the Army of the Potomac, improved the treatment of casualties through the use of forward first and stations, standing operating procedures, mobile field hospitals, and an efficient ambulance corps. As a result, the poor treatment of Union casualties in the Seven Days' Battles in 1862 was replaced by a much more effective response at Gettysburg in 1863.

As with other examples of innovation, prisoner-of-war camps had to be established and supplied. There was also necessary improvisation in the use of railroads, in entrenchment, and more generally in turning large numbers of recruits into soldiers and officers.[33] Due to its weak industrial base, it was especially important for the Confederacy to improvise, and it succeeded in doing so, in particular by developing arms, ammunition, and gunpowder manufacture.

At the same time as improvisation, there was planning for the future on the part of the Union that included a reconceptualization of the west as a key area of modernity. On 20 May 1862, the Homestead Act encouraged settlement there (and thus immigration), although not for those who had fought for the Confederacy. It promised that 160 acres per adult citizen was to be provided so long as the grantee cultivated the land, a measure designed to ensure independent freeholders (and not slaveholding estates), the earlier goal of Andrew Jackson, President from 1829 to 1837. This was legislation made possible by the Civil War, as the Democrats, in contrast, had wanted western land to be open to slaveowners. As a result, the Homestead Act of 1860, a Republican measure, had been vetoed by President James Buchanan, a Democrat.

In addition, a transcontinental railroad was authorized on 1 July 1862. This measure was seen as important in securing western support. The railroad scheme also helped in the planning of a new America and would be significant in shipping bullion from Nevada.

Confederate measures were more defensive, not least because, once the early advance into New Mexico had been checked, there was less of a prospect for a new geopolitics in which the Confederacy would stretch to the Pacific. This was despite the presence of Texas in the Confederacy and the lack of effective Union pressure on it, certainly on land. Texan troops were extensively used to the east, and this might well have ruined Davis's hopes for gains from the Trans-Mississippi.

There was also little real benefit for the Confederacy from Mexico, in large part because the French presence was unable to ensure success for the Royalist side. Yet this only became apparent after a while. Prior to that, there were possibilities for cooperation between the French and the Confederates. Indeed, in this and much else, there was still scant sense that the outcome of the war was foreordained.

As General-in-Chief from 23 July, Halleck sought to provide strategic coordination to the Union. He advised Lincoln and Stanton and served as coordinator of efforts across the theatres to the extent that circumstances allowed. In December, with the Confederates on the operational defensive in those theatres, the Union war effort went on the offensive in Mississippi, Tennessee, and Virginia. Due to particular circumstances on each front, the Union forces did not do so simultaneously the way it was intended to happen in May 1864, but the idea at any rate was to provide pressure on the Confederacy at different points at the same time. This helped explain the frustration of Halleck at Rosencrans's delays while Grant was operating against Vicksburg in 1863. The Union planned for major gains in the forthcoming campaign. In particular, the failure to carry through earlier success in the first half of 1862 was, it was hoped, to be remedied. How far Confederate forces would be able to make substitutions to their own agenda was still very unclear.

# 5. MILITARY CONTEXT

The speculative, counterfactual fiction *Gettysburg* (2003), *Grant Comes East* (2004), *Never Call Retreat: Lee and Grant,* and *The Final Victory* (2005) capture the enduring fascination with the Civil War and the extent to which this can be, and often is, manifested in speculation of different outcomes for the conflict. The authors are William Forstchen, an academic and novelist, and Newt Gingrich, who is famous not as a one-time history professor at the University of West Georgia, but as Republican Speaker of the House of Representatives from 1995 to 1999. The first book has Lee win Gettysburg. This is followed by an advance on Washington, which is unsuccessfully attacked before Baltimore is captured by the Confederates. In any event, Lee is defeated in the third volume, leading to the end of the Civil War in 1863.

The military possibilities offered are somewhat improbable, not least in the pace of operations, but also in the interest in counterfactuals[1] for this conflict that has been insistent. In *Intruder in the Dust* (1948), William Faulkner writes of the "Everlasting If" of Gettysburg: "For every Southern boy fourteen years old, not once but whenever he wants it, there is the instant when it's still not yet two o'clock on that July afternoon in 1863." As another instance of counterfactualism, Grant could have suffered from throat cancer earlier than he did. Anglo-French intervention was another "if," as discussed in chapter three.

This process can also throw renewed attention on why the war developed as it did if only to explain why the counterfactuals are wrong. For every pro-Confederate counterfactual, it is possible to suggest a pro-Union one, but the former are more prominent because the Confederates lost. Counterfactuals, nevertheless, are useful for advancing and analyzing alternate courses of action.

In practice, however, with counterfactuals there can be a failure to keep attention on both political and military goals, and to underrate the extent to which both can change as a result of events. Separately, a resource-based approach to the explanation of Union victory emphasizing the strength of the northern economy and the size of its armies, is apt to downplay the role of objectives and to treat conflict simply, or largely, as an elemental struggle for total and absolute victory. Instead, the goals of the north were up for debate, not only until the 1864 presidential election but also, differed beyond this point as the probable peace terms dictated debate and perspective.

An entirely separate counterfactual centers on the possibility of Lincoln not winning the previous presidential election, that of 1860, thus ensuring that the Civil War did not occur, or did not occur in the 1860s, which in turn yields instructive questions about the prior and subsequent course of American history, questions that endure to the present. The possibility of a triumph for the Democrats in the congressional elections of 1862,[2] and of a McClellan victory in 1864, provided the south with a viable military goal—namely, trying to mull among Union public opinion a sense that the war was going badly, and doing so at a time when the Republicans were seriously divided.

This strategy had operational consequences for the Confederates, which might seem foolish if the emphasis, instead, is only on a resource-centered interpretation with the stress for the Confederacy on preserving resources, and therefore resting on the defensive. Instead, the Confederate goal encouraged offensives into the Union in 1862 and 1863, which were designed to suggest to a war-weary northern public that the Union would never win and that the Confederacy retained the initiative.

In any event, in 1864, in large part because of Sherman's success near Atlanta, the Confederate strategy failed, whereas by then Lee was locked into the defense of the Confederate capital, Richmond, such that he could no longer advance northward in strength as he had done in 1862 and 1863. This failure of Confederate strategy does not, however, invalidate counterfactuals centering on the issue of whether it could have succeeded. Indeed, the Confederate strategy was not made inherently unviable by eventual failure, notably as a consequence of superior Union resources, as might be assumed if the emphasis is on the marked disparity in resources in favor of the Union. All things being equal, the Union had a higher probability of winning, and the south had serious disadvantages from the outset. Yet, to argue that this situation made the eventual outcome likely ignores the political dimension as well as the role of contingency.[3]

In one sense, the Civil War was a nationalist struggle, as were the contemporary wars of German and Italian unification. Although, very differently, it was an attempt to contest and, on the other side, preserve unity, rather than—as in Germany and Italy—to *create* a new united state. In the circumstances of America, this task proved more formidable, both militarily and politically, than what faced Prussia or Piedmont, where the initiating powers were the eventually successful German and Italian unifications.

In contrast, the Carlist wars in Spain provide an example of a European struggle over state identity in the face of massive political and regional cleavages. This provides an analogy to both the Union's challenges and, in some limited sense, the outcomes: The regionalists and arch-traditionalists lost the military struggle on both continents, but the causes and the rhetoric of those nineteenth-century struggles, in both America and Spain, have continued to be potent.

The Civil War was also a nationalist struggle on behalf of the would-be nation of the south or rather of White southerners. There is a kind of parallel in the unsuccessful Polish rebellion against Russian rule in 1863–4.[4] In America, alongside rival nationalisms at stake, on the basis of a separatist movement, there were, as in the War of Independence,[5] additional religious divisions and elements.[6] (The Blacks could exercise a degree of agency by various forms of resistance, but it was less effective and more readily countered than that of Native Americans in the West.[7] This is in parallel with the War of Independence of 1775–83.) This was likewise true with the creation of a new country of the envisioned Confederacy, a primitive vision of the future United States: There was no simple defiance on behalf of provincial or states' rights, but, instead, the attempt to create a new state altogether. This had several consequences, for a nation or state in the process of establishment is inherently weaker in its position than that which already exists.

Yet, in the case of the southern insurgency in 1861–5, there was also an asymmetry of grand strategic aims, something that helps explain why the Union did not have a decisive edge over the Confederacy. The Confederacy, ultimately, had only to fend off the Union, a goal which did not require total conquest. In contrast, the Union had to at the very least crush Confederate military power and probably occupy considerable swaths of the Confederacy in order to force it back into the Union. Thus, as is often the case, the weaker power was helped by having the more modest goal, although it had to persuade the stronger power to stop attacking. Although there was no political parallel, this was also the case with North Vietnam and America during the Vietnam War.

At the same time, the counterinsurgency goals changed. For the Union, the failure of initial efforts and limited goals (not to mention means) as a way to end the conflict was eventually linked to the definition of more radical war goals by Lincoln and of more arduous means by some key generals. This, in turn, rendered the political dimension even more significant because it ensured that a change in control in Washington would have greater consequences.

At the level of political direction, Lincoln exerted pressure in the formulation of the agenda, but encouraged and helped by the telegraph he also shared James Polk's propensity to micromanage during the Mexican American War of 1846–8. The ability of the military commanders while making the relevant military decisions to try to affect the politics of the war, however, posed major problems, which, to a degree, the Confederates were spared. In part, this was because despite his serious problems with state governors Jefferson Davis maintained more control, but also because Confederate politics were less divided (other than the disagreement between the demands of the central government and the views of particular states, notably Georgia).

The pace of operations, however much set by military considerations, had a political impact, especially when the tempo appeared deficient and the determination lacking, and this led to intervention by Lincoln. In this respect, he played a role similar to that of Winston Churchill with regard to British operations in North Africa during World War II. Both felt they had to sack generals who were showing insufficient drive, although critics will argue that Churchill truly micromanaged this campaign.

Reflecting the refusal for any prospect of compromise, more radical Union goals, however, put even greater priority on military victory, and, in turn, this priority rendered the warlike ardor and political determination in the north of utmost importance. Yet as so often happens, shifting goals became important to the viability of both the insurgency and the attempt to suppress it. Frustration on the home front with the intractability of the struggle affected the shifting sands that moved unstably beneath Union goals, both political and military. This frustration was linked to campaigning. McClellan, the commander of the army of the Potomac, who had advocated a conciliatory strategy to undermine southern support for the insurgency, was replaced by Lincoln in November 1862 after the former failed to deliver militarily.[8]

Strategic coordination on both sides was limited, but in part this was because the physical scale of operations was more akin to Napoleon's field of Europe as a whole in 1799–1815, rather than to Moltke's far more limited sphere of operations in an individual conflict during the successive Wars of German Unification (1864–71). Civil war meant the commitment to exert power, hold territory, and back supporters across the area in contention, which led to the grand scale of Scott's Anaconda Plan of 1861 and Sherman's wildly ambitious March to the Sea in 1864. Scott and Sherman both perceived the strategic and operational problems quite clearly and had great prescience.

Moreover, as in Napoleon's Europe, there were very major variations in the terrain and the cover. In America, the nature of both physical and human geography—often heavily wooded and with a limited presence of roads and tracks—affected tactical coordination and operational execution. In turn, this situation enhanced the significance—as goals, means or both—of the tracks that were indeed available; military positioning was much easier where such links were more common, not least for logistics. Failure of integration within armies in this regard accentuated the impact of terrain obstacles.

Furthermore, there were important institutional limitations, and for both sides. Creating new militaries was harder in practice than on paper, as was also shown by other conflicts that century. The U.S. Army (the Union army) expanded from 16,000 men in 1861 to perhaps two million by 1864, and its Confederate counterpart from zero to perhaps 800,000. This was robust expansion into something that none of the commanders could have imagined prior to the war. In Europe, in contrast, large armies were longstanding. During the War of Independence, American generals understood and copied their European counterparts, whereas decades later the relative isolation of America meant that European tactics and techniques were far more hypothetical since only the Mexican War had generated sizeable American armies, and even then it was only for a brief period. In turn, the French discovered in 1870–1 with the new republican armies (raised after the Third Republic was declared in September 1870) that raising large forces rapidly created serious problems of supply, training, and command. These new French armies, for example, had scant success against the Germans.

Despite Lincoln's efforts, civilian government did not provide the necessary direction or coordination for either Union or Confederacy, and, in addition, there was no effective general staff for either: even the War Board created by the Union in 1862 was short-lived. Henry Halleck, appointed General-in-Chief of the Armies of the United States in 1862 (a post in which his critic Grant was to succeed him in 1864) had administrative ability, yet despite all its efforts it failed to provide the necessary strategic coordination. As a result, on both sides, army-navy cooperation was generally (although not invariably), poor; generals often fought in certain regions with only episodic strategic oversight or strictly operational cooperation. Nevertheless, movement of units between regions was frequent, and this compelled armies and their leaders to coordinate, however unwelcome this enterprise.

These issues were compounded by the tensions involved in incorporating the ethos of amateur soldiers, an ethos made more problematic in the support it received from home state amateur officers and commanders, which extended to the regimental election of junior officers.[9] This situation clashed with the difficulties of shaping and sustaining military chains of command, a situation made more difficult by the small size of the regular military in 1861, and then its further division between Union and Confederacy. Finally, there was the need to elaborate the political aspects of these chains of command, and what professionalism meant in that context.

The pursuit of glory and a culture of honor complicated matters even more by stirring complaint. This included public complaint as well as complaint that ignored the chain of command. This encouraged responses, but in the context of the factionalism and jealousies that prevailed on each side in the command and often reared its head when deciding between complainants. Difficult generals, such as Lew Wallace, might be disciplined,[10] but problems proved incessant. Even for the Union, Benjamin Butler and John Fremont were more difficult generals than Wallace.

Furthermore, generals and admirals had no experience in directing the size of forces they were expected to command: corps-level organization was unprecedented in America. The navy only created the rank of Rear-Admiral in 1867 (precisely to address this problem). Prior to this, the highest rank in the U.S. Navy was Captain. Indeed, alongside the flaws of the Union generals, their Confederate colleagues were not nearly as brilliant as their post-war collective reputation presents. This was abundantly clear with Joseph Johnston, Pierre Beauregard (commonly referred to as P.G.T. Beauregard), Braxton Bragg, and John Pemberton, whereas the reputations of Stonewall Jackson (who had in fact only a mixed command record) and, to a lesser extent, Albert Sidney Johnston were enhanced and preserved by their early deaths. Moreover, their early careers had them fighting some of the Union's most lackluster commanders.

The Napoleonic legacy in the Civil War was ironically evidenced with the reference to the unsuccessful Union general Nathanael P. Banks ("Nothing Positive" Banks to some) as Napoleon, and, more positively, with McClellan (who was actually considerably older than Napoleon during his early triumphs) being nicknamed "Young Napoleon." This legacy was seen more in tactical and operational elements, rather than in the strategic. If any officers on either side had combat experience, they received it during the Mexican American War, when Scott's appreciation of those Napoleonic principles apparently led to decisive victory. An obsession with "decisiveness" in battle owed much to the Napoleonic "ghost," though it was prone to neglect the extent to which a battle might be "decisive" in its prolongation of war rather than ending it.[11]

To a degree, the ideas and ethos associated with Napoleon failed (as shown in Lee's generalship) to take adequate note of successive improvements in firepower technology, and the destructive capability this endowed on the defensive. Yet, as an example of the danger inherent in coming to a simple conclusion, it is also pertinent to suggest that, as later seen in World War I (1914–18), most generals were aware of this strength but could see no other way to achieve their goals. The action of attacking reflected more than cultural factors and attachment to outdated notions. It also appeared as a way to fix opponents, to force engagements, to win ground, and to obtain results (both tactical and operational), each of which was an important objective. This focus on the offensive, with the Confederates attacking in eight of the first twelve big battles (and taking heavier casualties[12]), was rendered disastrous by the increased use of rifled muskets by defending forces. But it has also been argued that the potential of the weaponry was not fully grasped during the Civil War, in part as a result of inexperience among soldiers and officers.[13] Indeed, bayonet charges remained quite important,[14] as did smoothbore muskets.

The Napoleonic legend set incredibly high standards for American generals to emulate, but Civil War battles were not that indecisive even in a culture that mistakenly tended to assume that warfare was easy to organize. The assumption that "natural genius" and courageous leadership would readily find a way to defeat the enemy completely ignored expertise and the importance of structure, planning, and organization; but the latter were developed to a degree in the heat and urgency of campaigning.

If attacking brought together strategic, operational, and tactical perspectives, an emphasis on the offensive for itself, however, posed serious problems in coordination. Training of staff officers gave the Prussian army a coherence its opponents lacked; and the Americans conformed more to the French system of 'muddling through,'[15] which was simply a method of responding to circumstances. Lacking peacetime conscription, the Americans relied heavily on untrained citizen-soldiers, even at senior levels. The peacetime army could not act as the kernel of a wartime equivalent, not least because it was divided by civil war, and the expansion in scale was far greater (thus far more unwieldy) than European forces. In terms of coherence and training, there was also no equivalent of an adequate reservist system. State militia was not set up and could not act in this fashion, not least due to a lack of preparation for conventional war.

The large number of wartime commanders and officers who had been through West Point, the military academy at Northfield, Vermont, and southern military training institutions, such as Virginia Military Institute, provided a cadre of valuable skills, and Lincoln and Davis both prioritized and valued soldiers with prewar experience. No less than 294 West Pointers became Union generals and another 151 of these graduates became Confederate generals. Lee had been Superintendent of West Point, where Henry Halleck had taught, who was much influenced by the work of Antoine-Henri Jomini. In addition, William Hardee, later a Confederate Lieutenant-General who was wounded at Shiloh and was a corps commander in the army of Tennessee, taught at West Point from 1853 to 1860 and his *Rifle and Light Infantry Tactics* (1855) was used by both sides during the war. Hardee's earlier service experience was in the Seminole Wars and the Mexican American War, and he had been sent to France to study tactics in 1840.[16]

The graduates of West Point and other pre-war military institutions lacked experience in the direction of large forces, and even West Pointers studied more engineering than military doctrine and practice. Nor had many American officers acquired experience by serving abroad in the various wars of the period, notably those in Latin America but also the frequent European conflicts of 1848–60. McClellan himself, as observer, only reached the Crimea in 1855 after hostilities had ceased.

The recovered experience of a civil war dimension during the War of Independence was not relevant as the key struggle in this conflict had been with British regular forces. Neither the War of 1812, which was often referred to as a second War of Independence, nor the Mexican American War had involved 'civil war dimensions.' The latter was not distant in terms of personal experience and memory, but it was still a war of choice fought at a distance, and not one of the proximity and scale of the Civil War. With Washington seized by the British in 1814 and public buildings burned (more damage was visited on Atlanta in 1864 and Charleston and Richmond in 1865), the War of 1812 had its own echoes. However, a major contrast was that 'the west' then was closer inward with respect to the area of Anglophone settlement and this meant that conflict involving Native Americans played a far larger role in that conflict. It was likewise true that the factors arising from the war made it distinctly Anglo-American, much of which revolved around the border between America and Canada and the problems of operating on it.

The Civil War is commonly studied at the level of the individual armies of the Confederate and Union forces, which, indeed, was the key for the implementation of strategy and for the ability to devise, adopt, and adapt operational plans. Yet, in the swing of campaigns, coordination within and between particular armies on both sides proved difficult. This was especially true on account of the sheer impact of any conflict with the enemy. As a consequence, a fundamental level of command was often that of the corps, and this was the case both on campaign (when corps in the same army were frequently separated at a distance) and in battle (when they were more commonly in close proximity), and furthermore of the commanding general.

Although there were undoubtedly failures on their part, Prussian staff officers very differently were given an assured place in a coordinated command system, and the system of joint responsibility between commanders and staff officers provided not only a necessary coherence but also a means to ensure the high level of forward planning that was valuable in maintaining the effectiveness of offensive operations. Prussian operational technique provided generally informed responsiveness under pressure, and therefore an ability to clinch victory despite all the fog and friction of war. It was also central to a self-conscious and intellectual professionalization of war.

In contrast, although the Confederate General James Longstreet, a West Pointer who served in the Mexican American War, organized (as a corps commander under Lee in 1862–3 and 1864–5) an effective staff and then wisely used it to take over particular tasks, the Union and Confederate forces were more dependent on individual ability and initiative.[17] This was the long-established practice of command, but one more suited to a battlefield that could be scanned by one pair of eyes than to more complex campaigning. Both sides in the Civil War took longer than the Prussians to appreciate the value of organizing artillery at the level of the corps such that it could be utilized in more than just an *ad hoc* fashion. Both sides also took time to develop effective systems for accumulating, assessing, and implementing intelligence, which was an important adjunct to staff work. Yet, progress was made. Joseph Hooker founded the Bureau of Military Information as an intelligence unit in February 1863 and in July 1864 Grant brought the bureau's head into his command headquarters.[18] The systematization of intelligence was (and is) an aspect of change that properly deserves to be described as 'modernized.' Information was not always pursued in such a fashion, but when it was, as by the Blockade Board founded by the Union's Navy Department in 1861, it could be very effective.

The Union and Confederacy faced command tasks that the Prussians did not encounter. The most significant was the creation of new military systems in the context of an unpredictable civil war that put great pressure on the concept and actions of the citizen-soldier. The extent and nature of the terrain was also a problem, and the battlespace was made more difficult by the destruction of bridges and the distances that had to be covered in wet marches.[19] There was plenty of 'fog and friction.'

There were also doctrinal matters that affected campaigning. In particular, there were the issues concerning position warfare and of continuity with base-route systems of advance and retreat. Grant noted the impact of established practice, as represented for instance in the 1854 New York edition of Jomini's *Summary of the Art of War*:

> Up to this time it had been regarded as an axiom in war that large bodies of troops must operate from a base of supplies which they always covered and guarded in all forward movements. There was delay therefore in repairing the road back, and in gathering and forwarding supplies to the front.

Indeed, many American officers, for example McClellan who had been a member of the Delafield Commission of 1855–6 that inspected European methods, have been presented as overly willing to accept the value of a European paradigm of war, rather than developing an American doctrine useful in America.[20] That, however, begs the question of how far the contrast between European and American methods was more than simply a matter of scale, and also what the latter entailed.

There was also the issue of preparing for, and waging, naval and amphibious warfare. The Confederacy, moreover, had to muster up a navy and develop a doctrine and style of naval warfare. This involved a range of environments, from rivers and inshore waters to deep sea operations, as well as responding to the possibilities of new technology, particularly the ironclad warship, but also to mines and submarines; all in all the response touched upon tactical, operational, and strategic realms. The Union was greatly superior in resources for shipbuilding and at sea, and therefore able to mount both a blockade and amphibious operations.[21] Each reflected and contributed to an enhanced capability compared to America's earlier wars, but it is also useful to note the distinctions between capability and execution. In part, this reflected the long-term problem in amphibious warfare of translating the force projection it proposed into a capacity for mobility, and thereby retaining the initiative for troops once they landed.

The contrast between capability and execution was also key in other areas of the war, for example with supply systems. The south to a much greater extent than the Union had to create a manufacturing and distribution base.

To a degree, there was the potential for recent and new technology to overcome constraints, notably with railroads and ironclads. Yet many weapons did not realize their potential, notably submarines, and they were inherently complex systems requiring a number of technologies. Use of the machine gun was likewise limited. The Union Repeating Rifle, or Agar Gun, designed in 1861, demonstrated to Lincoln and deployed that same year, was followed by the Gatling gun, which was invented in 1861 and patented in 1862 and could continue firing as long as the hand-operated crank was turned. However, the Gatling gun was not accepted by the army until 1866 although 12 of the guns were purchased by commanders and used in 1864–5 in the eastern theatre. Machine guns made scant impact in the war. Aside from mechanical problems, high rate of ammunition usage (an operator's dream and a logistician's nightmare), and expense, they suffered from their reputation as eccentric to battlefield and its dispositions and tactics. In part, there were specific causes behind this perception, including many individuals involved. The Union's Chief of Ordnance from 1861 to 1863, Brigadier-General James Ripley, a veteran of the War of 1812, was suspicious of new developments and opposed not only to the adoption of Agar's and Gatling's guns, but also to breech-loading rifles. Reliability and cost factors were important to him, as were the risk surrounding poor fire discipline and the excessive use of ammunitions, but he also reflected the conservatism of his department.

As a comparison, the Prussians were also worried about the fire discipline and ammunition usage elements, while, in the Franco Prussian War of 1870–1, the French had in the *Mitrailleuse* an effective machine gun, but it was used neither extensively nor intelligently. Overall, the failure to develop an appropriate tactical doctrine reduced the impact of new technology, a recurrent issue throughout the war.

In other respects, technological developments brought change but not necessarily revolution. Rail and telegraphs, neither of which changed significantly during the period, did not have the effect of the internal combustion engine and radio. The absence of the latter limited tactical and operational flexibility, affecting the tempo of battles and campaigns, and making the coordination of units difficult. More generally, the introduction of new technology was much more limited than some previous writers have claimed and the degree to which it acted as a "force multiplier" can be challenged. There was also the standard trade-off of industrial production, notably the degree to which potential or real quality was compromised for quantity. Good enough in quantity was what the north and south needed. With that came the subsequent need for effectiveness in use. The latter meant improvement with experience, above all in the response to environmental problems or opportunities—something witnessed in military bridging, in which the army of the Potomac acquired considerable skill.[22]

The Civil War exhibited many of the standard problems of military history, some of which have been accentuated due to the character of collective memory imposed by hindsight, or at least memories, as well as the subsequent presentations of the conflict. It is necessarily the case that the result of the war is known; but it is inevitable that this knowledge is then read backward and affects discussions of the conflict as a whole, as well any consideration of specific episodes. Given the eventual failure of the Confederacy in 1865, it is manifest that everything beforehand is then read in that light. In all these analytical processes, it is always necessary to underline the extent to which all approaches could never exhaust contemporary perceptions nor the contexts within which decisions were made.

Moreover, this degree of uncertainty occurred at all levels of war—tactical, operational, and strategic—and was accentuated by the lack of predictability and clarity in communicating developments at these particular levels. This was further complicated because there was, for example, no set process to allow events at the tactical level to determine outcomes at the operational. Additionally, the flow of consequences was multi-directional, and this greatly added to the uncertainty of conflict.

That lack of knowledge of contemporary factors was crucial; but there is likewise a need for caution before adopting any confident model of determinism in the historical perspective one may choose to take. In one respect, of course the latter benefits from scholarship, not least the ability to scrutinize sources from both sides. Yet, there are also many problems posed by assumptions and by confirmation bias. There was also uncertainty that was particular to land or naval operations, and problems specific to individual theatres, as well as the related determinism.

Discussion at the level of military structures is valuable, but it does not capture the immediacy and range of the experience of service. In this respect, there were similar features to other conflicts of the period, or indeed to warfare taken as a whole; but also contrasting ones. The former included the curious dichotomy of long periods of boredom interspersed by short bursts of fighting, most of it unpredictable and terrifying. The boredom could lead to a range of responses, from the communal experience of music-making, especially when in winter quarters,[23] to the affirmation of individual honor through quarreling, including brawls and dueling, from the search for adventure, such as alligator hunting, to blatant disobedience. Both the search for adventure and disobedience could also be seen in looting, which was a prime motivation in some for participating in war, and other aspects of often cruel conduct to civilians as with the Union troops in Fredericksburg during the battle. The anger and stress built up by many soldiers was apparent through such conduct. Equally, however, a large number of soldiers refrained from such ill behavior. This situation also occurred in the treatment of prisoners: some were mistreated, but others not.

Meanwhile, disease was the major and most consistent killer (not combat), although sniping and skirmishing inflicted a steady toll. The standard problems of disease on campaign, particularly diarrhea and dysentery, were exacerbated by the scale of the war, notably in army size and the length of conflict, both greater than the War of 1812 and the Mexican American War. Moreover, the cities from which many recruits came were already the incubators of disease as well as conduits for international epidemics. This was why 'farm boys' were so much more susceptible to disease than 'city folk.'[24]

Even without epidemics, the health problems posed by the human and animal waste produced by armies challenged water supplies and could make it difficult to stay clean at particular sites where the ground water was quickly contaminated. The crowded nature of encampments was an additional issue. To a degree, armies were moving high-density male slums, the urine and excrement of which destroyed health in particular environments. Wasting away and dying from disease was horrific. Prisoner of war camps could be especially malign, with soldiers crowded together, given inadequate food, and allowed very poor sanitation. Yet there were also features particular to this conflict, notably because this was a civil war and therefore one in which everyone spoke the same language and many of the commanders knew each other.

A major war brought to a relatively rapid close is not the headline many would expect when reflecting on the Civil War. Much of the literature deals with failure of all fronts—strategic, operational, and tactical. Yet that is generally the case with any war. In reality, the Civil War delivered a decisive verdict in four years, and eventually saw its commanders able to handle their forces on campaign and in battle.

Meanwhile, there was a great variety and layers of conflict in the Civil War. This included set- piece battles, smaller clashes, large-scale sieges, naval and riverine warfare, guerrilla and counter- insurgency operations, and raiding and trench warfare. There was also the use of infantry, cavalry, and artillery, but in varying proportions. Mounted raiders represented the overlap of cavalry with mobile infantry.

The fighting inflicted great losses in manpower. Increasingly destructive weapons gave troops little or no time to find shelter. And in a culture of attack—such as it was in the nineteenth century—the cost could be high. The idea that the attack would always win if the attackers had sufficient resolve was based on a poor understanding of changing firepower. As an alternative to the advance of the entire force in regular formations, notably lines and columns, leadership urged forward rushes 'going to ground,' whereas another part of the attacking force rushed forward directly, and the whole process repeated as many times as was necessary to force the enemy back. This was seen as one way to reduce casualties. However, it was difficult given the limits of communications technology and other tools of command and control, which were as significantly debilitating as poor discipline in officers and men, if not more so. Battlefield conduct was also an issue on account of poor training and confusion, notably over the identification of uniforms and of where the enemy was located or concentrated. Moreover, the strain of losses, the impact of morale, and the consequences of inadequate food, all affected discipline and conduct in action.

The high number of military casualties reflects the degree to which the popularly grounded determination of the two sides, each based on a conviction of righteousness, was expressed in military action. In part, this included the use of new firearms. The percussion-lock rifle and the *Minié* bullet fired from rifled (rather than smoothbore) muskets were deadly, and notably so at the expense of frontal assaults that tended to take the form of mass attacks by tightly packed units, whether they streamed forward in lines, columns, or more formless rushes. The halting of advances to engage in close range firefights led to a failure in pressing home (or concluding) attacks and this caused indecisive combat.[25]

Casualty rates are a function of the size of the lethal zone that increased in depth with the greater range and accuracy of rifled firearms. This meant that an attacker was subjected to deadly fire for longer than hitherto had been the case with smoothbore muskets. Even if a bullet missed soldiers at the front of an attacking wave, it could still kill those behind. The lethal zone with rifled muskets, a muzzle-loading firearm with a rifled bore, at the time of the war was about 500 yards deep. A smoothbore had a range of no more than 200 yards and was only accurate for about 50–75 yards. The rifle (a breech-loader) could be accurate to about 600 yards, although this was true of trained marksmen firing in isolation, not massed formations with little or no marksmanship training. The front sights, being the locking lug for the bayonet, were often moved out of alignment due to repeated bumps in the process of fixing and unfixing bayonets, and the smoke from the black powder obscured even the serried ranks, which tended to be somewhat more extended than shoulder to shoulder. Two 700-man regiments facing each other at 150 yards typically each inflicted for each minute of firing seven killed outright and about that number of wounded (requiring treatment) and could average about three rounds a minute. Men generally carried 40 rounds total. This changed when troops were entrenched and firing on attackers. In these circumstances even the smoke tended to be less of a problem, usually rising and allowing clear vision about 1–2 feet off the ground. Cannon at close range, 100–250 yards, inflicted more casualties per discharge, but were also within range of the infantry fire, which was a real conundrum.

Battle ranges, however, were rarely greater than 300 yards, especially if the terrain was difficult (such as in the Battle of the Wilderness on 5–7 May 1864) and often 100 yards or even less. Some exchanges of fire were at no more than 30 yards. Encounter clashes were particularly prone to short-range fire.

The situation was complicated by the vast array of weapons with which the two sides were armed. Although the Enfield 1853 rifled musket was an important weapon, others came from France and Austria (the Lorenz 1854 rifle), and the Union made its own Springfield 1855 and 1861 models. There were also repeating breech-loaders such as the Henry (1860), the Spencer (1860), and the Colt revolving rifle (1855), an early revolving rifle that was the first to be adapted for service by the army, but one that, despite its high rate of fire, had serious design faults. To the extent officers had combat experience, they learned tactics during the Mexican American War, yet before these significant changes to small arms' range, accuracy, and rate of fire. To use the new weapons properly, experienced officers first had to unlearn their own prior experiences.

The issue of rates of fire is complicated by the use of magazine-fed breech-loaders, such as the Henry and the Spencer, which could fire faster than muskets—whether rifled or smoothbore—but were much shorter ranged. The rate of fire of a rifled musket was marginally quicker than a smoothbore because the former needed only seventeen actions to load and fire, compared to the smoothbore that needed eighteen. In practical terms, this was probably insignificant as the rate of fire depended on the calmness (steadiness) when charged or receiving fire, and that calmness (steadiness) came with experience and was also heavily influenced by combat conditions. Aside from these factors, there were relatively few breechloading and magazine-fed rifles.

Although affected by the amount of ammunition they could carry and the problems of resupply, defenders who stood their ground could cut down an attack before it reached them. This undermined infantry tactics as taught at West Point and elsewhere. The accuracy of rifled muskets moved tactics away from the use of volley fire when meeting an attack. Volley fire made up for the inaccuracy of smoothbore muskets. In contrast, although they wasted ammunition if they opened fire too far out, men armed with rifled muskets could take aim at individuals if they chose, which had not been a realistic proposition hitherto. This was aided by the provision of better sights than those that were fitted to smoothbores.

As a consequence, battles could lead to more wounded and to worse wounds, putting pressure on medical care. The worse wounds were a direct result of the greater mass of a conical bullet (at 500 grams) and the increased long range velocity of the round. The lighter round ball (at 400 grams) travelled slower because, though it had a faster initial muzzle velocity, it slowed more quickly. As a result, it often hit bone and rolled around bones or pushed organs aside. In contrast, the conical bullet, travelling faster and heavier, broke bones with compound fractures, and ruptured organs more easily. Already hampered by the state of field hospitals and medicine, the growing pressure on medical care was a serious aspect of the strain of the conflict, one accentuated by it being a civil war fought largely by volunteer armies.

Experience and steadiness were also important with the artillery, the specific location of which was crucial to the course of many battles. For example, on 2 January 1863, in the Battle of Stones River (Murfreesboro), a Confederate advance against retreating Union forces was blocked by concentrated artillery fire from 58 guns that caused 1,800 casualties and obliged the Confederates to retreat. Earlier, on 31 December 1862, the first day of this battle, Union infantry and artillery had eventually beaten off Confederate attacks, ending the Confederate challenge to Nashville and Kentucky. This battle in mid-Tennessee had the highest percentage of casualties on both sides of all the major battles: 3.8 percent killed, 19.8 percent wounded, and 7.9 percent missing or captured.

Aggregate casualty rates could be formidable. The Confederate army of Northern Virginia suffered a casualty rate of 20 percent or more at each of the battles of Seven Days, Second Bull Run, Antietam, and Chancellorsville, leading to 90–100,000 battle casualties in Lee's first year in command (1862–3). More generally, the Confederacy mobilized 80 percent of its military age Whites, but, by the end of the war, a quarter of this manpower-pool was dead and another quarter maimed. These were casualty rates far greater than those in the European wars of the 1860s, in part because the latter were far shorter and were fought over a smaller area, but the length remained the key issue. Single campaign conflicts, such as the Franco-Austrian War of 1859 and the Austro-Prussian War of 1866, could be deadly, but they were also limited wars. Moreover, they were essentially struggles between regulars or trained reservists and did not, as with the Civil War, entail significant guerrilla and counterinsurgency warfare.

In the Civil War, the determination to persist strategically, and the attritional quality of the fighting at the tactical and, sometimes, operational levels, were important, not least due to the limitations of success of maneuvering on the battlefield. Signs of what were later to be seen as total war were also significant. Alongside a willingness, crucially present on both sides, to take heavy casualties, there was an ability to employ large quantities of resources. However, there was an unwillingness on the Confederate side to use the manpower offered by slaves.

The Napoleonic Wars, as then taught notably at West Point in part following the maxims of Antoine-Henri and Baron Jomini (as interpreted by Denis Hart Mahan, Professor at West Point from 1824 to 1871) for a specifically American audience emphasizing the use of earthworks, entrenchments, and keeping casualties low,[26] did not provide a ready guide for fighting the Civil War or, indeed, a helpful one for subsequent analysis of it. Although the Napoleonic Wars had been lengthy overall, individual conflicts between France and either Austria or Prussia were brief in the 1800s and the early 1810s. Moreover, after the Napoleonic Wars finally ended in 1815, Western commentators had become used to short wars, such as those in Europe in 1821, 1823, 1830–1, 1848–9, 1854–6, and 1859–60; and, in North America, the less than long War of 1812 and the Mexican American War of 1846–8. Indeed, the 1815 campaign that ended Napoleon's attempt to regain power (begun on 15 June when Napoleon invaded Belgium and ended at Waterloo on 18 June) can be seen as the first in this trend. It was expected that in future conflicts there would be one major battle that would prove a decisive encounter, and that at any rate, even if this were not the case the conflict would nevertheless be short-lived. This assumption was to be apparently vindicated by the wars waged in Europe between the Polish rising in 1863 and the end of the Second Balkan War in 1913.

A quick war was intended by both sides in 1861 for both political and military reasons. Neither was prepared for a lengthy struggle, and the pattern sought was that of the Mexican American War of 1846–8, the most recent conventional conflict (as opposed to fighting with Native Americans) in which America had been involved, and that in which many American commanders and politicians on both sides had taken part, including Jefferson Davis. As American offensive plans in the War of 1812 for the conquest of Canada demonstrated, America also shared a 'short-war culture': there was no cultural, ideological, political, social, or institutional commitment in America to a long war, one requiring a large-scale mobilization of resource. (The War of 1812 had revealed a lack of mental flexibility in assessing alternatives, and later in 1945 there was palpable frustration with the length of World War II.)

The Civil War could have gone the way of a swift conflict and been the short struggle that World War I was to be for the Americans (1917–18): the Americans came in fresh when other combatants were exhausted. But even so, World War I was a formidable and costly effort for the Americans. As a reminder of the indeterminacy of sides, events, and outcome, political and military factors might have gone in very different directions in 1861. It was not certain which slave states would join the Confederacy. Missouri, Kentucky, Maryland, Delaware, and the parts of Virginia that became West Virginia did not do so; and it was initially unclear that Virginia, North Carolina, and Tennessee would do so (see chapter one). Had these three remained outside the revolutionary secession, events would have been far less threatening. The extent to which British North America had divided in 1775–83, with Canada, Florida, and indeed also the West Indies not following the Thirteen Colonies into revolution, indicated the contingent character of history at that time. (This is more generally the case with civil wars in particular, and also with coalition warfare.)

As another instance of contingency, the Union forces subsequently might have been sufficiently successful in the early stages in persuading or forcing the Confederacy to end the war. On the Union side, pressure for a one-campaign outcome (see chapter two) led to an advance into Virginia and an encounter battle at First Bull Run (Manassas) on 21 July 1861. This battle, in part determined by the arrival of reinforcements, demonstrated that—as was only to be expected given this was the start of a civil war—neither side had an army that matched the seriousness of its task, and Union command proved particularly flawed.[27] Even if the Union won that battle (and it could have), there is no evidence that the Confederacy would have capitulated. It was still a long and by no means easy road to Richmond in 1861, let alone to Charleston.

The Mexican America War of 1846–8 and policing operations against Native Americans provided experience in projecting power, sustaining operations over long distances, experience in operating without a lot of supervision, experience with administration, and experience operating among and dealing with a hostile population. Many officers had cut their teeth in the Mexican War, and although it was different militarily, organizationally, and politically to the Civil War (above all because the latter was a civil war), the experience was still important. Yet, in 1861, the United States army was still only 16,000 strong, and was based in 79 posts that ensured it would have no experience of attacking in significant units; in the thirteen years preceding the Civil War, not one regiment had even ever assembled all its constituent companies in a single place. Neither the Union nor the Confederacy were prepared for a major conflict in 1861: this was especially true of scale, but also of the attitudes of their commanders and of the resources readily available. The ability to make effective use of large numbers of troops had not been developed in peacetime. Among the complexities and organizational problems confronting the (Union) army, there was great confusion wrought by the existence of, functionally, multiple parallel armies and military authorities in the north. The regular army, the volunteer army, and the state militias were all distinct from one another, and officers could simultaneously hold different ranks. Thus, Benjamin Butler held the rank of Brigadier-General of the Massachusetts militia simultancously with the rank of Major General of U.S. volunteers.

George Custer in 1863 simultaneously held the ranks of First-Lieutenant, Brevet Major, and Brigadier General.

Indeed, the year 1861 saw both the creation of a new military structure in the Confederacy (although this basically copied the old structure), and the massive expansion of the military of the American state on the Union side, as well as the greater availability of irregulars. As such, it was a significant expansion in overall Western military capability (yet due to rapid demobilization in 1865 it was only temporary). The Confederacy's remarkable feat of eventually mobilizing most men of military age was strongly facilitated by its slave-based economy. Proportionally, the manpower turnout was probably only ever matched in history by the Romans during the Second Punic War and the Germans in World War Two, both of whom relied heavily on slave labor for their respective economies. Yet, the application of the draft to the Confederacy underlined the cliché—this was a rich man's war and a poor man's fight.

Thanks to the Confederate revival in 1862 (see chapter four), it became clear that this would be a longer war. Pre-war expectations of the nature of conflict had been matched in part in the first phase of the war, but the Seven Days Battle was a significant strategic victory for the Confederacy, ensuring that the war would continue. This realization led, notably on the part of the Union, to the mobilization of resources (with an army of over 600,000 by January 1863) and to changes in strategy, these two processes being linked but also independent. The north had far more resources to mobilize and did so to great effect, aided by the maritime blockade inflicted on the Confederacy, which was an operation on an impressive scale and an important counterpoint to the land war.

Yet, there were also major issues in Union effectiveness: the utilization of resources, the establishment of predictable and regular operating systems, and the creation of battle-winning armies. These points were real challenges at the outset and in the opening campaigns, and onward. Armies fought the in the same way, were equipped in the same way, were organized in the same way, and were led in the same way. As in other wars, an advantage in overall resources (in the Union) while extremely useful, notably when recovering from failure, did not prove easy to turn into capacity and capability, let alone into success. Although far more obvious due to a lack of preparation in 1861, there was a parallel with elements of World War I in that it proved difficult to raise large forces for effective, and even more successful, use in the field, despite the relative ease of raising the mass of armed men. In World War I, as a contrast, by 1917 America benefited from allies who helped provide training in the new technique as well as equipment.

In the Civil War, there were serious problems of supply, training, and command. Training was particularly deficient in infantry-artillery coordination, which was never easy and especially so in encounter battles (as opposed to sieges). An emphasis on the will, morale, and character as the means to victory (an emphasis that drew on the presentation of the French example, notably that of Napoleon I's campaigns) proved a poor substitute for such training and for experience.

As a result, too many assaults lacked coordination, both between units and arms (infantry, artillery, and cavalry). Poor planning and an inability to implement plans, notably the interaction of moves within a planned time sequence, repeatedly strangled vision, as did command flaws at a number of levels. In part, this failure was due to inadequate generals on both sides, although in this manner of evaluation we can overcome the temptations of hindsight.

In addition, and moving beyond individual flaws, important as they were (indeed often crucial), the basis for a systematic process of effective and rapid decision-making was absent, as was one for the implementation of strategic plans in terms of timed operational decisions and interrelated tactical actions. As a consequence, as so often happens in war, strategies frequently lacked implementation, while operations could be poorly judged, and piecemeal tactics led to battles bereft of overall direction. These were, however, simply the limits of the tools provided.

Staff training and doctrine certainly did not match those in Prussia and Germany. Neither side had an effective integrated high command, and many campaigns, despite the theorization of a structure for apt decision-making,[28] were poorly conceived and mismanaged.[29] Furthermore, most generals failed to develop staff that was up to the challenges of moving and controlling large forces and of providing reliable operational planning.

As a result, those commanders, such as Grant, who were able to provide organizational sophistication, operational grasp, and tactical grip under pressure (and just got lucky, which is always a big part of military success) did particularly well. The very lack of effective processes in practice overall directed attention to individual military abilities and styles, and thereby to flaws. Moreover, as dynamic elements, generals needed to be able to adapt their forces to new weaponry and other technology, particularly the railroads, but also to other tactical possibilities, the moves of opponents, and remaining sensitive to political requirements.

Yet, these were not the sole problems. The difficulty in coordinating attacks, at all levels, not least due to the slow nature of communications, was exacerbated by the extent of wooded cover and other terrain issues (for example watercourses on the battlefield of Shiloh[30]), and by dreadful maps. This difficulty was further accentuated when subordinate commanders might not carry out their instructions. This problem was made more frequent by the degree to which many commanders, and for both armies, associated only with the units they commanded and the states from which they came, rather than with the army as a whole.

The legacy of the prevalent interpretation of the Napoleonic Wars encouraged an emulation of what were taught as the methods of Napoleon I, methods that to a large extent were commonsense. As a result, in accordance with the ideas of Antoine-Henri Jomini, although he was not much cited, there was an operational emphasis on moving along interior lines and on defeating opponents in detail—that is, individually. In practice, this was not easy to achieve. There was also tactical stress on turning the opponent's flank.[31] This was sound and commonsense and had been done by Scott in Mexico. An important element at all levels was that of the ability, in both battle and campaign, to create and use an 'open' zone in space and time, with both room for maneuver, which meant gaining the advantage of the flank, and a tempo that maintained the retention of the initiative. Turning the flank could be successful and in pretty much every major battle this was attempted by the attacking party, as at Chancellorsville in 1863. However, the failure to do so in many of the battles was important in producing what (as a consequence of firepower) was either an impasse or a cause of heavy casualties, or both. Trying to defeat opponents in detail can be seen in the Second Manassas (Bull Run) campaign. In the battle, which was fought on 28–30 August 1862, Lee sought to attack the Army of Virginia under John Pope, while the Union forces were divided between that and the army of the Potomac. In turn, Pope tried to destroy Stonewall Jackson's corps while it was separated from troops under Longstreet. Because everyone knew that getting attacked on the flank was dangerous, they tended to pay a lot of attention to flank security, which made attacking this flank a great challenge. Even successful flank attacks tended to do no more than push the enemy back to a stronger position either tactically or operationally—as was the case with Jackson's attack at Chancellorsville and Longstreet's attack at Second Manassas, although they suffered casualties and energy.

Flanking movements by units whose speed was no greater than that of defenders frequently led instead to frontal assaults on the part of defenders who had rapidly altered deployment, although this was dependent on effective situational intelligence. Linked to this, speed and surprise could not be readily achieved or utilized with inexperienced troops and commanders, and in the complex simultaneity of battle. Moreover, this was hard to achieve even with experienced troops, not least in confronting other experienced troops. And as always, the terrain often did not help.

The U.S. Army operated by the bureau system, upon which theoretically the Secretary of War was to draw on in advising the Commander-in-Chief as he directed the war. This was adopted by the Confederacy. However, there are problems with applying more modern notions of strategic clarity and planning because at the time the U.S. Army lacked an equivalent to the navy's Blockade Board. Newly- established in 1861, the latter laid down coherent strategic recommendations that remained valid for the rest of the war.[32] Contemporaries, moreover, were uncertain as to how the geography of the war worked in terms of the relationships between the spheres of operations; and this uncertainty affected discussion of strategy, which in part was a matter of prioritization, but also any political process in terms of goals, means, and methods. These relationships between spheres of operation, in turn, became a matter of scholarly discussion and heightened a concern for the role of geography in the planning and conduct of the war.[33] Yet, this role was less apparent to contemporary foreign commentators than is true now with the benefit of hindsight.

Alongside the many problems at the strategic level, there were serious deficiencies in operations, although the British likewise lacked a developed staff system. The extent to which many officers gained positions through volunteering and political influence[34] and the absence of effective command structures meant that mediocrities were not tested adequately before being entrusted with independent command (nor always removed sufficiently rapidly when proven unfit). Personal staffs frequently clashed with specialized staff drawn from the bureau system. Histories of particular armies and studies of individual generals are frequently simply accounts of squandered opportunities,[35] which is a sign of the inexperience that was a key military reality in the Civil War. Yet, as Britain showed in World War I, there are major problems in rapidly creating large armies and then attempting to sustain their strength in the face of heavy casualties, casualties that included officers as well as soldiers.

Although evidence for every soldier is lacking, there was a tendency for expectations in the war to evolve from a series of heroic contests, in which soldiers could ideally display manliness, to more incessant, machine-like exchanges by 1864–5.[36] This again reflected casualty rates that, when looked at differently, involved major issues surrounding the maintenance of combat quality as well as morale. The latter had many causes to wane, not least of which was unit cohesion and the drive to support colleagues, display resilience, and show courage accordingly, but it was also affected by a sense of necessity from idealistic motivation in terms of mission.

Alongside battle, by land and sea, the railroad was a means and metaphor of mechanization. The railroad, which had expanded greatly in America in the 1840s and 1850s (especially in the north), made a huge difference, tactically, operationally, strategically, and economically in the Civil War. At the tactical level, man-made landscape features created for railroads, such as embankments, played a part in battles. Operationally, the railroad created links along which troops could move. In 1862, General Braxton Bragg, Commander of the (Confederate) army of Mississippi, was able to move his troops 776 miles by rail from Mississippi to Chattanooga, and thus created an opportunity for an invasion of Kentucky. The Confederate concentration at Manassas in 1861 was another impressive use of rail, as was the Union reinforcement of the army of the Cumberland by rail to Chattanooga in September 1863: here 20,000 men from the army of the Potomac moved 1200 miles in 12 days.

Such potential was totally different to the situation during the previous wars in North America, and, if the term revolutionary is helpful, then the capacity to plan for rapid movement was a *significant* development.[37] As a result, rail junctions or river ports where steamship services and railroads were linked—such as Atlanta, Chattanooga, Corinth, Manassas, Memphis, and Nashville—became operationally crucial and the object of campaigning. Corinth, for example, was founded in 1853 as Cross City because it was the junction of the Memphis and Charleston Railroad (*en route* to the Mississippi River) with the Mobile and Ohio Railroad. Control over the junction proved instrumental to the campaigning in northern Alabama. With such junctions, it was necessary to benefit from taking them but also it was key to keep them from enemy occupation.

Union advances aimed at such junctions, which the Confederates struggled to protect or regain. Thus, in 1862, in the campaign that led to the Battle of Second Manassas or Bull Run, Jackson hit the Union supply route along the Orange and Alexandria Railroad, destroying the supply depot at Manassas Junction. Such supply stores were difficult to move, and this provided opportunities for raiders.

Later that year, the Union commander, Ambrose Burnside, planned to move south toward Richmond along the Richmond, Fredericksburg, and Potomac Railroads after he had captured the river crossing point of Fredericksburg, which, in the event, he failed to do thanks to failures in Washington. West of the Appalachians, the Union forces sought both to gain control of the Mississippi River and to advance into the Confederacy along the railroads running southeast through Tennessee and Georgia, here logistics forcefully driving the war.

In 1864, the Union success in cutting rail links led the Confederates to abandon Atlanta on 1 September, which helped ensure Lincoln's reelection that looked less probable earlier in the year. The comparable campaign in the War of American Independence had been the British surrounding Charleston in 1780, but that had been obtained, thanks to amphibious capability, by moving units across rivers, notably the Ashley (on 29 March) and the Cooper (23 April) by boat. The patriots had held on in Charleston, only to surrender rapidly on 12 May once it was bombarded with heated shot.

Technology, employment, and potential combined in the Civil War to ensure organizational precision. The Union created U.S. Military Railroads as a branch of the War Department. This was part of the process of wartime mobilization, the scope of which expanded as a result of the organizational demands stemming from new capacity and needs. The function of U.S. Military Railroads included the building and repair of track and bridges. This function provided a quick-response system to such requirements for transport links as the exigencies of the war required, a system necessary to employ the new technology. The Union benefited from effective direction of the railroad system and the extent to which this railroad expertise was concentrated in the North, and it was further combined with the impressive engineering capability that pushed new construction.

The contrast was clear, for example, in the conflict around Chattanooga, with Confederate movements from Virginia less prompt and effective than comparable Union patterns. Given the significance in battles and campaigns of feeding in fresh troops, this was an important advantage. Very poor Confederate railroad management was a factor, as was the weakness of the local manufacturing base, which made repairs difficult. There was no possibility of using canals as a substitute, whereas in the north these served as a means of moving bulk goods and stores.

At the same time, aside from noting the weaknesses of the Confederacy's railroad system,[38] it is important to put the use of the railroad in context. Armies required railroads or rivers for supplies. Initial railroads were built to supplement pre-existing river systems before the technology was mature enough on its own to be sufficient for logistics. The railroad network did not necessarily determine where the campaigns were fought. Rivers probably had a greater effect on where operations were mounted, although Sherman and Grant's remorseless offensives in 1864–5 moved away from the shackles of a confined geography that rivers and, indeed, railroads imposed on transport systems (even if mountains remained highly significant). There were no railroads in the wilderness, but its proximity to the Orange and Alexandria Railroad was why the armies were there. The problem with drawing an overall conclusion for the war is that, on the one hand, railroads seemed to influence where campaigns and battles were fought, while others were dictated by the presence of navigable rivers. The argument that communications, notably railroads, were a manifestation or cause of the change in the nature of conflict during the Civil War should be qualified by noting a heavy dependence of logistics on such traditional means as wagons and foraging, both on their own and linked to the other aspects of logistics.[39] Thus, the improvement of Union field transport was crucial to William Tecumseh Sherman's successful advance through Georgia and the Carolinas in 1864–5,[40] an advance that destroyed the Confederacy's strategic depth by exposing and using the vulnerability of areas far behind the earlier marked fronts.

Moreover, the technological aspects of railroad warfare were limited. There were no major developments in the specifications of locomotives. Rail design and fabrication methods, as well as railroad construction systems, were crucial to the speed of laying of new track, as well as to the safety of trains on it and the speed they could travel. Changes in these were not driven forward by the Civil War; and economic developments, rather than the war, were responsible for the growth of a large-volume rail system.

As another instance of technological development that both sides employed was the telegraph, which ensured that cavalry raiders made it a point to cut telegraph lines, an important indication of the vulnerability of ground-based communication systems. These lines were more vulnerable than railroads. The use of the telegraph was enhanced by developing 'trains' with insulated wires and poles on wagons designed to extend the fixed telegraph lines to the advancing armies. Lincoln also used the telegraph to keep tabs on the army.

A more abrupt form of capability was provided by artillery. In contrast to the German use of rifled artillery, the emphasis remained on large-caliber muzzle-loaded smoothbore cannons intended to devastate opposing infantry at very close range using direct fire, the so-called "Napoleons." Some rifled guns of different types were available to both sides and provided increased range and accuracy; but they had problems with reliability, as part of the standard trade-offs of capability. It must be remembered that canister shot ruined rifled pieces.

Artillery was responsible for many of the battlefield casualties in the war, and the location of batteries was crucial to the course of many battles. For example, in 1862, cannons were important to the "Last Line" Grant established near Pittsburg Landing that helped his army survive the disaster of a surprise Confederate attack on the first day of the Battle of Shiloh. Edward Porter Alexander, a Confederate artillery general, wrote of the Battle at Fredericksburg in 1863:

> The city, except its steeples, was still veiled in the mist which had settled in the valleys. Above it and in it incessantly showed the round white clouds of bursting shells, and out of its midst there soon rose three or four columns of dense black smoke from houses set on fire by the explosions. The atmosphere was so perfectly calm and still that the smoke rose vertically in great pillars for several hundred feet before spreading outward in black sheets. The opposite bank of the river, for two miles to the right and left, was crowned at frequent intervals with blazing batteries, canopied in clouds of white smoke. Beyond these, the dark blue masses of over 100,000 infantry in compact columns, and numberless parks of white-topped wagons and ambulances massed in orderly ranks, all awaited the completion of the bridges. The earth shook with the thunder of the guns….
>
> Under cover of this storm of shell, the Federal bridge builders again ventured upon their bridges and tried to extend them, but the artillery fire had been at random into the town, and not carefully aimed at the locations of the sharp-shooters. Consequently, these had not been much affected, and presently the faint cracks of their rifles could be heard, between the reports of the guns. The contrast in sound was great, but the rifle fire was so effective that, again, the bridges were deserted. Indeed, the promiscuous fire of bombardments seldom accomplishes any result. Carnot [French Revolutionary commander], in his *Defence of Strong Places*, says that they "are resorted to when effective means are lacking." No citizen was reported injured, though many left the town only

> after firing began in the morning, and some remained during the whole occupation by the Federals.

Alexander was referred to in James Longstreet's recollection of the battle:

> An idea of how well Marye's Hill was protected may be obtained from the following incident: General E. P. Alexander, my engineer and superintendent of artillery, had been placing the guns, and in going over the field with him before the battle, I noticed an idle cannon. I suggested that he place it so as to aid in covering the plain in front of Marye's Hill. He answered: "General, we cover that ground now so well that we will comb it as with a fine-tooth comb. A chicken could not live on that field when we open on it."
>
> A little before noon I sent orders to all my batteries to open fire through the streets or at any points where the troops were seen about the city, as a diversion in favor of Jackson. This fire began at once to develop the work in hand for myself. The Federal troops swarmed out of the city like bees out of a hive, coming in double-quick march and filling the edge of the field in front of Cobb. This was just where we had expected attack, and I was prepared to meet it. As the troops massed before us, they were much annoyed by the fire of our batteries. The field was literally packed with Federals from the vast number of troops that had been massed in the town. From the moment of their appearance began the most fearful carnage, With our artillery from the front, right, and left tearing through their ranks, the Federals pressed forward with almost invincible determination maintaining their steady step and closing up their broken ranks. Thus resolutely they marched upon the stone fence behind which quietly waited the Confederate brigade of General Cobb. As they came within reach of this brigade, a storm of lead was poured into their advancing ranks and they were swept from the field like chaff before the wind. A cloud of smoke shut out the scene

> for a moment, and, rising, revealed the shattered fragments recoiling from their gallant but hopeless charge. The artillery still plowed through their retreating ranks and searched the places of concealment into which the troops had plunged. A vast number went pell-mell into an old railroad cut to escape fire from the right and front. A battery on Lee's Hill saw this and turned its fire into the entire length of the cut, and the shells began to pour down upon the Federals with the most frightful destruction. They found their position of refuge more uncomfortable than the field of the assault.

As in 1914, the use of artillery encouraged the resort to trenches during the eventually successful Union siege of Petersburg in 1864–5. Alexander recorded:

> We soon got our line at most places in such space that we did not fear any assaults, but meanwhile this mortar firing had commenced and that added immensely to the work in the trenches. Every man needed a little bomb proof to sleep in at night, and to dodge into in the day when the mortar shells were coming.[41]

Grant used trenches as economy-of-force measures, to free up forces in 1864–5 for maneuver against Confederate railroad links. Bayonets and rifled muskets were increasingly supplemented by, or even downplayed in favor of, field fortifications and artillery. This was a sign of the future character of war between developed powers. Protection against artillery was to become a major theme in the tactical deployment of military units. To a degree it always had been, but now there was a reconceptualization of fortification in order to respond to stronger artillery as part of a more lethal firepower that the infantry also possessed. The trench warfare of World War I was to be a direct response, but the greater scale and sophistication of the trenches then accentuated the problem of break-in and, subsequently, of moving from break-in to break-out. There was a huge gulf between 1865 and 1914 artillery capabilities, and the use of artillery in the Civil War was more like that of the Napoleonic Wars than of World War I.

Drawing on its superiority in resources, notably iron-production, and also transport capability, the Union enjoyed a major advantage in artillery during the Civil War. This advantage was carefully developed in its main field force, the army of the Potomac, by Henry Hunt, who had played a major part in pre-war changes when he helped to revise field artillery drill and tactics in favor of brigades having batteries for close support alongside an army-level artillery reserve. A graduate of West Point, Hunt served under Scott in the Mexican American War, and was promoted to Brevet Major. He served in Kansas in 1856 and in the conflict with the Mormons in 1857. In 1862, he became a Brigadier General and the Chief of Artillery for the army of the Potomac and was ordered to organize an artillery reserve. This was necessary because at the Battle of Antietam (1862), although the Union had superior artillery, it was unable to ensure a proportional result, a symptom of a more general problem with managing Union resources. Moreover, Confederate guns enfiladed the Union infantry that began the assault. Taking an important role in battle, especially at Fredericksburg and Gettysburg (notably against Pickett's charge and in the siegeworks at Petersburg), Hunt also helped ensure not only that Union artillery had more and better equipment than that of the Confederacy, but also that it was well-trained, for which he emphasized slow and accurate fire.[42]

The Union artillery faced more challenges than its Confederate counterpart: Union forces were far more active in besieging positions, but also engaged in the protection of positions such as Washington against assault, and also participated in very wide-ranging array of offensive operations. In geographical scale, these were more like Napoleon's experience in 1806–13, and even more in 1812, than to the Prussian campaigning in 1866 and 1870.

The extent of the campaign zones in the Civil War, particularly west of the Appalachians, helped ensure that artillery in any one location was not considered plentiful by later standards, while also posing transport problems; these, however, were eased in part by the Union's superiority in rail links and transport. At Gettysburg in July 1863, the Union deployed 372 guns to the Confederacy's 274. In contrast, besieging the major and more distant Confederate fortress of Vicksburg, the Union batteries mounted only 220 cannons over 12 miles of siege line the previous month.[43] In this case, the number of cannons was not the sole issue, for the Union army at Vicksburg benefited from more ammunition and therefore did not have to husband its fire, unlike the Confederate artillery. This was always a particular contrast in sieges: besieged positions could not obtain nor manufacture fresh munitions.

More generally, influenced by inadequate staff work, infantry-artillery coordination in the Civil War tended to be poor on both sides, with many assaults suffering as a result. This issue of poor coordination deserves consideration both from the perspective of infantry and from that of the artillery. Again, and for both the Union and Confederacy, there was a repeated inability to implement plans, especially when it came to the interaction of moves within a planned time sequence.

The use of artillery was affected by the often heavily wooded nature of the terrain. The terrain posed particular problems. Of the wilderness, Grant referred to "the difficulty of making a way through the dense forests."[44] The low density of roads and tracks was also an issue. In some respects, this was similar to the eastern front in World War I and contrasted with the western front at that same time.

Artillery was not yet available in the quantity seen as necessary in World War I, and this enhanced the value of forts that were harder to suppress without plentiful artillery. In the Civil War, there were not the means to sustain such quantities of artillery. The war largely occurred in parts of the country where there were few fortifications other than those, such as Fort Sumter in Charleston harbor, designed to offer protection for coastal positions against British naval attack, a long-term cause of fortification. In Charleston in 1863 and Mobile in 1864, Confederate coastal positions resisted Union naval attacks, as in December 1864 did Fort Fisher, and this protected Wilmington, North Carolina (although it fell to renewed attack the following month). In contrast, there was no system of fortifications in inland Virginia or Maryland prior to the war.

As a result, those forts that were present in and near the field of operations were important. Exposed to Confederate attack, Washington ended up being perhaps the most fortified place in the world, at least in the western hemisphere, with an elaborate system of mostly earthen forts, redans, batteries, and other works that formed a ring thirty miles round the city. In turn, Richmond had lines of defenses around it and there was also the Dimmock Line at Petersburg. The construction of forts, however, was not the sole issue.

There was a process of fort-construction and rapid entrenchment to provide protection. Camps were endowed with defensive facilities. The emphasis was on rapidly built, temporary works intended for use on a short-term basis, and prepared by the troops with the materials at hand. An example was presented by the earthworks at what was called Fort Edward Johnson on the crest of Shenandoah Mountains constructed by the Confederacy on the western periphery of the Shenandoah Valley in April 1862, raised to prevent Union access to the valley and the military depot at Staunton by means of the Staunton and Parkersburg Turnpike. Artillery batteries there were placed on platforms to provide overlapping fields of fire. Access to a constant supply of water was a key element in this location.[45] However, the Confederates gave up the position that month without a fight in order to concentrate their forces near Staunton.

In addition, field fortifications were as important as they had also been in Napoleonic and pre-Napoleonic warfare. Taking forward the European experience during the Revolutions of 1848, railroad lines provided improvised field fortifications, notably the embankments. Breastworks and trenches were designed to protect troops on battlefields, particularly against infantry attacks and against non-plunging cannon shot. Breastworks proved important aids to defenders, although as with trenches it helped against those who focused on frontal advances rather than maneuver.[46] In 1864–5, the trenches dug during the drawn-out Union siege of Petersburg were deeper and the trench systems more complex than ever. Alexander recorded of the Union trenches near Petersburg: "the enemy promptly built a strong line of rifle pits, all along the edge of the dead space with elaborate loop holes and head logs to protect their sharpshooters, and they maintained from it a close and accurate fire on all parts of our line near them."

There was a long tradition of siege warfare and extensive fortifications and trenches. Moreover, recent trench warfare did not originate at Petersburg. For example, the Anglo-French forces that besieged Russian-held Sevastopol in 1854–5, during the Crimean War, had to face a type of trench warfare that was different than earlier sieges in terms of the intensity of artillery fire. Nevertheless, the trenches near Sevastopol can be seen as an aspect of a traditional siege rather than as a development of field entrenchments, the latter being the case in Virginia in 1864–5. The entrenchments there, as at the lengthy battle of Spotsylvania in 1864, looked toward those in World War I, but the more fluid nature of operations in the Civil War ensured that they were less developed. Although a patent was not issued until 1867, barbed wire was in use in the conflict onward from 29 November 1863, when, in the battle of Fort Sanders, an unsuccessful Confederate assault, telegraph wire was attached to tree stumps at knee height to provide some defense for the Union line. This was the key battle in the Knoxville campaign, an unsuccessful Confederate siege by James Longstreet. In Petersburg, however, as in Sevastopol (and also in Rome in 1849), the defenders were not entirely encircled.

There certainly were parallels between trench warfare in 1864–5 and in World War One, for example defensive firepower, the limited value of cavalry, and sappers planning and planting siege batteries, parallels, saps, and wire entanglements; there was also mines, drawing upon methods developed centuries earlier. Those on both sides called their moves "siege operations" and maps were entitled "Siege of Petersburg." The great difference, at least in so far as the western front in 1914–18 was concerned, *was that of scale* in America, and there was no equivalent to the English Channel and neutral Switzerland to anchor the trenches at each end. Furthermore, Lee had to maneuver on a narrow front to defend the key logistical base of Richmond, a situation that has been described as a strategic siege, and the Confederate trenches could be outflanked, as Grant did with Lee in 1865. Lee could not put trenches all the way around Richmond, or he would have been starved out; and to the west, the land went on all the way to the Pacific.

In addition, as far as differences were concerned, it was not necessary to resist lengthy bombardments by heavy guns firing plunging shots, as in World War I, nor was there reinforced concrete with which to protect positions.[47] Petersburg was primarily not a siege but an effort to make the city untenable by cutting off its railroads, with the Union trenches used to counter Confederate trenches and to conserve manpower for maneuver operations against Confederate logistics.

The frequent failure of infantry forces to exploit victory was an instance of the extent to which, although the mass firepower of infantry brought some advantages, it lacked others that the cavalry possessed, especially mobility. However, the war also showed that it was not possible to rapidly mobilize effective mass cavalry forces in the way that infantry can be mobilized. The war also saw a very high 'wastage' of horses. There were many raids to hit opposing supply zones, lines, and communications, as with the Union devastation of the Shenandoah Valley. Cavalry raids also served for morale-boosting propaganda, although on the last day at Gettysburg Lee was thwarted not only in the infantry assault of Pickett's Charge, which lacked sufficient support on its flanks, but also in the simultaneous attempt to send the cavalry (under Jeb Stuart) to outflank the Union right and attack its rear. In the event, a Union cavalry counterattack by a smaller force under George Custer stalled the Confederate cavalry charge. The Confederate cavalry was exhausted because Stuart earlier had led it on a raid toward Washington that had served scant purpose bar denying Lee necessary pre-battle intelligence as well as cavalry support in the early stage of the battle.[48] Stuart's conduct was all-too-typical of the individualism of cavalry commanders, a key element of their mindset, and one that would get Custer into fatal trouble at Sioux and Cheyenne hands at Little Bighorn in 1876.

At the same time, cavalry could be important in battle as it was at Valverde in 1862, a key battle in New Mexico that was a Confederate victory. Yet this involved failure in what turned out to be the only lancer charge of the Civil War, in which a lancer company carrying nine-foot lances was defeated by Union troops who formed a square, a highly traditional form of combat. (The remains of the lancer company then rearmed with firearms.[49])

Cavalry was important in overcoming the great distances of the war, but the use of cavalry ensured the continued problem of providing sufficient fodder, as well as the need for the care of horses. Difficulties in ensuring enough fodder played a role in the Union's failure to prevent Lee's successful retreat after Gettysburg, although the strength of the Confederate cavalry was also significant. The Union's ability to pursue after Gettysburg was affected by the exhaustion of their cavalry, which ensured that, whereas prior to the battle they had provided intelligence and screening, there was now a lack of contact and information, and this owed much to the success of the Confederate cavalry screen.[50]

The assumption at the start of the war was that the Confederacy, with a tradition of Southern gentlemen riders who in many cases provided their own horses, were better natural cavalrymen than the Union forces. This was generally true only for the first two years. At Chancellorsville in 1863, however, Union cavalry was finally able to match its Confederate opponent. Major-General Joseph Hooker's reorganization of the cavalry into a single corps, not least enhancing the command and control, was important to Union success, especially because competent cavalry commanders like Brigadier- General John Buford and Major-General Wesley Merritt also came to prominence. The Gettysburg campaign demonstrated more effectiveness for the Union cavalry than hitherto, part of the process by which the war entailed letting the best commanders rise to the top. The Union cavalry was also helped by better supplies of forage than their Confederate counterparts who had half-starved horses.

The Union cavalry under Major-General Philip Sheridan also clearly benefited in 1864 from not only their experience, but also from a thorough process of training and effective firearms. Brigadier-General James H. Wilson, an engineer hitherto, was appointed Chief of the Cavalry Bureau in February 1864, and both mandated the use of breechloaders and undertook a rapid buildup of an excellent remount service. Promoted to Brevet Major-General, he was assigned to command a division of cavalry under Sheridan and served in the east before being made Sherman's Chief of Cavalry and then taking part in the Battles of Franklin and Nashville. Already in the west at the time of the Vicksburg campaign of 1863, Union cavalry was performing well, as demonstrated by the very disruptive Grierson raid of 17 April through 2 May. This raid diverted Confederate attention from Vicksburg by coming in from southern Tennessee via Mississippi to Baton Rouge—and notably destroying over 50 miles of railroad and attacking Confederate stores along the way. In the east, the strength of the Army of the Potomac's Cavalry Corps helped make it possible to limit Lee options when he retreated in 1865, and thus contributed greatly to his surrender at Appomattox. In the end, Lee lacked the necessary flexibility when his freedom of maneuver was constrained.

The Civil War in large part reflected the American tradition in which mounted infantry in the shape of dragoon 'cavalry' was the mainstay. Reflecting a lack of logistical societal underpinnings in the early years of colonialism, as well as difficult terrain in many areas, this meant that the dichotomy between cavalry and infantry had less meaning in the American context. Indeed, cavalry remained most effective as mounted infantry throughout the nineteenth century. Thus, Philip Sheridan in the Shenandoah and Virginia in 1865, and James H. Wilson in Alabama in 1865, used dismounted cavalry with carbines as infantry to finish off Confederate forces at the end of the Civil War. Yet, this Union cavalry was not just mounted infantry but an extraordinarily flexible force capable of both mounted and dismounted action—employing Spencer repeating carbines, in a powerful example with Sheridan's defeat of the outnumbered Stuart in the Battle of the Yellow Tavern on 11 May 1864. The use by the Union cavalry of breechloading or repeating carbines gave them more firepower compared to infantry that still used muzzle-loaders. This enabled cavalry to act effectively as an operational and tactical tool, as seen with Buford's fight at the first day of Gettysburg, or Wilder's Lightning Brigade in the west (which in fact was mounted infantry). These capabilities contributed to the strategic mounted invasions of the south in the last stages of the war. By 1864–5, the Union cavalry, notably in the army of the Potomac, had developed tactics of 'fire-and-movement' using repeating carbines and mounted charges with swords, tactics two or three decades ahead of any other cavalry. Moreover, the reliance of armies on railroad supply presented the cavalry of both sides with a very vulnerable target.[51]

Naval power was a very different form of the application of power to that of cavalry. It played a key role in the Civil War, even though all the major battles in this war were fought on land. Indeed, this contrast in the use of naval force paralleled the situation during the Cold War and beyond, and thus underlined the extent to which the frequency of naval battles—both prior to 1815 and in the two world wars—did not establish a general model. Moreover, battles at sea were generally rarer than those on land, and decisive ones even rarer. This was a major shift—the blockade had been the major strategic weapon of the (British) Royal Navy in the earlier Age of Sail.

The Civil War began as a consequence of the Union's attempt to maintain Fort Sumter, a position that sat defiantly off the city of Charleston, the leading Atlantic port of the Confederacy. This was an aspect of military synergy in that different arms were given added potency through cooperation, or, alternatively, were lessened by being countered. Confederate coastal batteries prevented relief and compelled the fort to surrender on 14 April after setting fire to the wooden buildings in the fort. This both created a target for Union naval operations and helped set the context for the subsequent naval situation off Charleston by limiting Union options.

Ultimately, the navy of the Union became what was then the second strongest in the world, with over 650 warships, including 49 ironclads. The Royal Navy, in contrast, predominantly invested in blue water—not brown water—units. They were good for command of the sea, but problematic in American waters. During the war, the capability of American ironclads increased, as the Union developed an impressive coastal protection force. Whereas the *Monitor*, a ship that symbolized the power of the machine, had two guns in one steam-powered revolving turret, the Union laid down the *Onondaga*, its first monitor with two turrets, in 1862. The Union also laid down the four dual-turreted river-monitors of the *Milwaukee*-class and the four *Miantonomoh*-class ocean-going monitors armed with four 15-inch guns.[52] These were formidable, to say the least.

Difficulties were encountered when building up naval strength and capability. Superior resources were overwhelmingly at the disposal of the Union navy, although it had to face the uncertainties created by new technology and the pressures of building a great number of ships. The government yards were in the north, but they were not up to the task of building the new navy that was now required. Private contractors therefore played a major role on both sides.

Particular problems emerged when developing the capacity to roll the necessary iron plating, and in building iron ships using the traditional methods of shipbuilding with wood. Nevertheless, the Union's navy was a key strategic asset. This was especially true in economic warfare and in power-projection by means of amphibious capability. The blockade upon the Confederacy was still permeable by small, fast steamships until late in the conflict. However, ably organized by the Blockade Board established in 1861, the Union demonstrated the potency of economic warfare. No less than 295 Confederate steamers and 1,189 sailing ships were destroyed or seized, and the blockade greatly affected the economy of the Confederacy, as well as its morale. Indeed, blockade was the key Union naval policy and means.

In turn, the Confederacy issued letters of marque to a host of privateers in 1861, which posed a major challenge.[53] The Confederate effort failed, however, because of the difficulty, even early on in the war, of bringing a prize home safely through the Union blockade to a Confederate port. As a result, Confederate maritime entrepreneurs turned almost exclusively to blockade-running to make their fortunes, and effective disruption of Union trade came at the hands of raiders who were commissioned in the Confederate navy—such as the *Alabama*, *Florida,* and *Shenandoah*—rather than by privateers. In 1865, the *Shenandoah*, the first composite (iron and wood) hulled cruising warship, wrecked much of the New England whaling fleet in the northern Pacific. It was never defeated.[54] The possibilities of using steam warships to destroy enemy commerce were grasped by Stephen Mallory, the Confederate Secretary of the Navy, and he ordered speedy raiders built in Britain and France. Instead, on account of their seizure, these ships ended up in their navies, as well as in those of Denmark, Prussia, and Japan.

The blockade of the Confederacy drew on American experience against Mexico in the successful war of 1846–8. In turn, the Union blockade was the last major one before, successively, torpedo boats, submarines, and air power transformed the parameters for blockade, especially for close blockade, and indeed for denial of the sea in general. The Union blockade also helped limit Confederate efforts to build up their own fleet. Even before the blockade became effective, the Confederacy had made insufficient efforts to import rolled iron and machinery. This was critical because the Confederacy was so short of iron that it was forced to pull up railroad track. A largely agrarian nation, the Confederacy lacked the capability to create the infrastructure to make many modern products.

Although in February 1865, Henry Halleck, then Chief-of-Staff, writes "his fingers itch to be in everything,"[55] initially the inexperienced

Lincoln played a quite cautious role. The Secretary of the Navy, Gideon Welles, was skillful but there was a serious breakdown in his relations with Rear Admiral Samuel Du Pont, the leading admiral, with respect to the plans for acting against Charleston and, more particularly, over the department's plans for an all-navy operation.[56] However, Lincoln's commitment to the navy led him to become a frequent visitor to Washington's naval yard where he took an interest in the development of naval weapons.[57]

The Union's early strategy included an important amphibious dimension. This led on 1 May 1862 to the capture of New Orleans, which was the largest city and principal port in the Confederacy. In doing so, Commander David Farragut, a Southern Unionist and veteran of the War of 1812 and Mexican American War, and the head of the West Gulf Blockading Squadron in 1862–4, overcame the Confederate warships (the massive *Louisiana* that could not move for want of her engines, whereas the *Manassas* only mounted one 32-pounder) and bypassed at night two substantial forts, but only once the river was freed of obstacles. Off Manila in 1898, at the expense of Spain, Commander George Dewey employed the technique he had observed when taking part in Farragut's attack—namely, passing heavily fortified shore positions at night. Farragut's success had not been matched by the British in 1815. The Union's amphibious capability also tied up large numbers of Confederate troops in coastal defense. The fate of New Orleans furthermore affected Confederate shipbuilding capacity.

Alongside the campaign for the Mississippi, bases on the coastal periphery of the Confederacy were a priority. For example, Port Royal Sound was seized in late 1861 so as to provide a base from which maritime links between Savannah and Charleston might be cut. As a consequence, coastal fortifications were developed on both sides.

The record of '[Union] ships versus [Confederate] forts' was mixed. If troops could be skillfully utilized, as with Grant and Andrew Foot's inland/brown-water operations in early 1862, then forts could be compelled to surrender fairly quickly. Yet this depended on circumstances and it was not so easy at Fort Donelson until the Confederates blundered. Army-navy cooperation was generally, although not invariably, poor for both sides. Without army support, naval attack could prove unsuccessful, as Union warships discovered at Charleston in 1863. Du Pont commanded a powerful force of nine Union ironclads, but they were hampered by mines and exposed to fire from shore batteries. Benefiting from offshore islands, Charleston was protected by a network of defensive positions. One ironclad—the fixed-tower, thinly-armored *Keokuk*—was sunk, while three of the seven monitors were damaged enough to be sent for repairs. Although, (in an important qualification) they were all ready for action within a month and only one man was killed. Charleston withstood all army-navy attacks and was therefore akin to the Russian-held Sevastopol in Crimea in 1854–5, with mines and obstructions playing a crucial defensive role alongside the new and effective land-based rifled artillery.[58]

Furthermore, in what proved a recurrent pattern for amphibious operations, the Union found—as in its failure at Honey Hill on 30 November 1864 when advancing from Boyd's Neck to cut the Charleston and Savannah Railroad—that advancing from coastal positions into the interior was less successful and effective than amphibious attacks on coastal positions. In turn, both were less successful than advancing overland from areas held in considerable depth. Victory indeed was won by the Union on land, and by forces that had advanced overland. Charleston finally surrendered to Sherman in 1865, but not to amphibious assault, thus repeating the fateful trajectory of Vicksburg. Charleston, instead, surrendered after his advance had cut its lines of communications. From another perspective, it was always easier and better to take a position from the rear rather than to attack it directly.

Despite this, the Union's maritime and riverine campaigns were more than incidental to the war's outcome. The early coastal operations greatly contributed to the effectiveness of the blockade by establishing bases for resupply and denying harbors to the south. And so on with successive operations, as when the Union fleet under Farragut successfully fought its way into Mobile Bay on 5 August 1864, despite mines which claimed one ironclad and might have claimed more had they functioned better. The fortifications at the Bay's entrance were the principal Confederate defensive asset in that clash.[59]

The following January, an amphibious operation covered by 58 Union warships—the largest fleet hitherto assembled in the war and one that testified to the size of the Union fleet—captured Fort Fisher, and thus closed the port of Wilmington, North Carolina. However, this assault was carried out with the direct support of an army division of 8,000 troops that had to attack twice before it succeeded in overwhelming the fort.

Such operations faced major logistical problems but maintained the impression and reality of Union pressure. This was particularly so in late 1864 and early 1865, as Sherman maneuvered in the Confederate rear near the coast. By threatening a siege, he forced the surrender of Charleston in 1865: the port was still open, but little traffic came in or out.

In addition, the 'brown-water' (inland) navy repeatedly played a key role in the success of Union operations in the Mississippi basin, notably in the crucial siege of Vicksburg in 1863. These operations severed the Confederacy and secured the midwest and the Mississippi River for the Union. The army was committed to the building of ironclads to aid its operations in the west. The Union army also ably linked river and rail transport to establish an effective logistical system that helped maintain the momentum of the advance.[60]

The Mississippi Marine Brigade illustrated a Union attempt to harness its riverine superiority, as well as shows the complexities of coordinating command. The brigade answered directly to the Secretary of War rather than any army, navy, or marine commander, and received instructions to make amphibious landings throughout the Mississippi basin. It certainly played a role in the Vicksburg campaign in 1862–3. Faced with an industrial backwardness and lack of resources that made competition in shipbuilding implausible, the Confederacy sought to offset Union superiority by using mines and submarines.

Confederate torpedo batteries on rivers and harbors sank 29 Union vessels, more than were sank by Confederate ironclads. This was a variant on the extent to which this was not a war of large naval actions, in part due to the dispersed nature of the Confederate fleet and the southern interest in blockade-running and commerce-raiding. Instead, most of the naval conflict involved clashes between Union warships and Confederate shore defenses—or between individual ships, most famously (and frequently illustrated) the *Monitor* and the *Merrimac* (renamed the

*Virginia* by the Confederates after being salvaged) in Hampton Roads on 9 March 1862. That the first clash between ironclads, an indecisive one, occurred during the Civil War was because the European navies that had already commissioned ironclads had not managed to fight one another—the Anglo-French naval race had been peaceful. In this latter duel, cannon shot could make little impact on the armored sides of the two ships, even though they fired from within 100 yards, which revealed the limited penetration power of the cannon used. This tactical impasse led the Austrians to ram some of their Italian opponents at Lissa in 1866, the larger and more heavily-gunned Italian fleet being less well commanded. The Italians lost two ironclads in this way.[61]

The absence of fleet-sized naval battles left no clear answer as to the full extent to which steam power and iron ships might have changed the nature of naval warfare. This was even more the case because, despite the Union blockade, neither Britain nor France intervened against the Union as had appeared very possible in late 1861 and in 1862 (see chapter three). In preparing for war against the Union, the British and French benefited from their naval race, although it did not make them ready for the conflict they would have faced. The likely consequences of such intervention attracted much discussion and influenced procurement and deployment thereafter during the war. As a result, the Union continued to fortify New York City and San Francisco against possible naval attack.[62]

There were parallels with the War of 1812, but also distinct contrasts. Leaving aside the problems again posed for Britain by the defense of Canada, it was unclear whether Britain's potential for coastal assault could effectively act as a form of strategic deterrent. The prospect frightened Union leaders enough in 1861–2 to lay down a large number of coastal defense monitors, as well as to improve coastal fortifications armed with 15-inch Rodman guns, which were strong cast-iron guns intended to fire shot and shell.[63] This capability was enhanced by the lack of a British standing coastal assault flotilla, a problem for Britain that had also been a factor during the Crimean War (1854–6). A sense of an inability to wage war against increasingly dangerous littorals increased anxiety on the part of the admiralty and compromised the ability of the British government to risk interventionist conflict. The evidence from both Union and Confederate official reports and letters, and from post-war books, was that the prospect of facing naval attack was seen to enhance the significance of coastal defense. After the war, American defense boards emphasized the value of a combination of forts, armed with 15-inch smoothbores and rifled guns, protection minefields and obstructions, and all of this supported by heavily-armed and armored shallow-draft monitors and rams.

After 1862, there was still a fear on the part of the Union and Britain that the Civil War would broaden and 'seep out.' The Union's ironclads were in part designed to resist British warships that had nearby bases, including Bermuda and Halifax. Largely submerged below the waterline, the monitors offered only a concentrated armor protection scheme along the exposed hull and especially the gun turrets. The Union utilized radical new technologies: the *Winnebago* (of the *Milwaukee* class) loaded its guns below deck, as well as rotated the guns and elevated them all by steam. The testing of armor-plate and cannon was an active part of the process of consideration and preparation. The Union's ironclads increased the risk to Britain in intervention, and therefore lessened British political leverage. In order to be any real threat to the Union, the British needed to invest in ironclads that were able to operate effectively in American coastal waters. The Civil War also witnessed an expansion of the American naval presence in the Pacific. The Union sent an ironclad monitor, the *Camanche*, to San Francisco, to protect California from British attack or Confederate raids. The ship was built in 1862–3, then divided into parts and shipped round Cape Horn in a sailing ship—for, as of yet, although it was approved during the war, there was no transcontinental railway. Once it arrived in San Francisco, the *Camanche* was reconstructed.

The likely resilience of the American defense was not the sole factor of non-intervention. In addition, British distrust of France greatly helped hinder the prospect of intervention, as did the significance of trans-Atlantic trade. More generally, longstanding Anglo-American tension over empire and trade were strong in this period, but neither power pressed issues to the point of conflict.[64] They also had a recent history of amicably resolving disputes (see chapter three). This was the most significant instance of the conflicts-that-did-not-occur dimension of the Civil War.

When approached by scholars, the military context of the war is a matter of the enduring impact on the conflict of earlier ideas and practices, and of the conflict upon later ones. Both approaches are important, but there is also the question of the direct impact of, and on, the war at the time. Here the prime context was the immediate background of the learned experience of the war itself, and not only between campaigns but also within them, just as in the Mexican American War the campaigning in 1846 became the lodestar of ideas in 1847, whereas Scott's initial operations established parameters for what followed. This process was made more relevant during the Civil War by the importance of analyzing the capabilities and practices of opponents, as well as factors such as the implications of terrain. There was a pronounced accumulative character to the war, one that set the context for each campaign, but no single element ensured a particular outcome. This is the comprehensive background for our chronological consideration of the conflict.

# 6. 1863: A CHANGING WAR

The third year of the war, like the third year of the War of American Independence, had mixed fortunes for both powers. In 1777, the last full year of campaigning before French entry into the conflict for independence, the British captured Philadelphia, the capital of the Revolution, after defeating the main Patriot field force under the command of George Washington at Brandywine. However, in the later theatre the British army advancing from Canada was forced to surrender at Saratoga. The contrast was important, and emphasized, when at Germantown the Patriots under Washington were able to mount a riposte (albeit an unsuccessful one) that threatened the British position in Philadelphia that encouraged the French to intervene.

The parallel position in 1863 is instructive. If one compares the Confederates to the British, then their renewed offensive is a failure at Gettysburg (which was certainly no Brandywine), and there can be no equivalent to the capture of Philadelphia. If, conversely, the *Union* forces are compared to the British, with both greater wealth and stronger states, there are clearly successes in both theatres for the former—most notably at Vicksburg and Gettysburg—a scenario that the British could not achieve. Yet (and here the strategic situation in each war is enlightening) the victories won did not mean an end to the war, nor a collapse in the resolve of the defeated. The ability of the Patriots to survive the loss of Philadelphia in 1777 throws instructive light on the significance placed on Richmond during the Civil War. To point out that the loss of the latter was rapidly followed by Lee's surrender is only pertinent if it is noted that in 1865 the Confederates were in a far more parlous situation than had been the case for the Patriots in 1777, in part due to the Union overrunning much of the south from 1862 onward.

The British advance on Philadelphia in the year 1777 was that of an amphibious force, rather than what had earlier been considered—that is, an overland advance from New York via New Jersey. As such, the British anticipated the approach taken by McClellan in 1862, although while still benefiting greatly from steamships he moved more slowly once landed, which eroded the advantage of mobility. At the same time, McClellan faced opposing forces from the outset.

The situation was very different for the Confederates as they did not have such an amphibious capability. This also affected their ability to operate inshore or along the coastline. The latter was impossible in the absence of supporting naval power, which helps explain the significance of France's entry into the War of Independence on the Patriot side in 1778. This led to the successful consolidation and use of American and French forces against the British at Yorktown in 1781. There could be no such Confederate use of Chesapeake Bay for army operations, for example in confronting McClellan at Yorktown as Cornwallis had been faced in 1781, let alone for more wide-ranging campaigning or attacking the eastern shore of the bay.

Linked to these parallels is a clear comparison in both wars of both sides showing continued resolve, both governmental and popular. Indeed, the British government easily won the 1780 general election and Lincoln that of 1864. The wars did not end until ultimate responses were given to *military events*—namely, the surrender of a besieged British army at Yorktown in 1781, and that of Lee at Appomattox after the loss of Richmond in 1865. Neither of these, however, on their own forced the respective outcomes, which indeed were very different after the surrender at Saratoga in 1777 and the Confederate loss of New Orleans in 1862, or Vicksburg in 1863, or Atlanta in 1864. The length of political resolve was not determined by military outcomes, though of course linked to it even if in an uncertain fashion. This meant that each year commanders and troops did not know if the campaign would be their last, both in the sense of their own deaths, injury, or collective surrender, and because the war itself might end.

The year 1863 was to be the middle year of the war and, in part, encourages "placing" it on a timeline or giving it a particular interpretation as such. Reaching this point in the timeline, however, was not known by contemporaries. Nor was the significance of particular events always readily apparent. Yet what was clear in 1863 was a change in the tone of the war, and Lincoln had a sense of this when he chose this moment to deliver the Gettysburg Address and issue the Emancipation Proclamation.

Separately, as another instance of this tone, the threat of reprisals came to the fore as the longevity and intractability of the conflict led to increased bitterness. In February 1863, Lyons reported that the Union garrison at Port Royal was holding prisoner a non-combatant, while the Confederacy held a Union officer captured in Florida who was threatened with trial for inciting slaves to rebel. The Union commander had declared that civilian prisoners were hostages for the safety of Union officers and that Confederate officers would be answerable with their lives if the Union officers were killed. This was a breach of the accepted rules of civilized warfare, which the Union commander claimed was a response to the breach by the Confederates, thereby issuing reciprocity of threat. Lyons commented:

> It shows the danger, which seems to be daily increasing, that the present war may degenerate into a contest, in which, under the guise of retaliation on both sides, the usages of civilised warfare will no longer be observed.[1]

The treatment of prisoners, not least black prisoners, caused considerable dispute, with Confederate cruelty attracting criticism. Separately, the practice of bombarding towns and incurring civilian casualties, for example of Fredericksburg in 1862 and Atlanta in 1864 by Union forces, was a matter of considerable controversy.

Lyons was clearly convinced that the north was in difficulty, not only in its military operations but also on the home front. Political opposition at home was matched by problems in recruiting new troops and retaining existing ones in service. Indeed, draft (conscription) agents were getting murdered in Pennsylvania. This view was shared by the French and Russian envoys. On 1 February, in an analysis scrutinizing resources, Lyons suggested that "the war must come practically to an end for want of men and money," adding, a fortnight later, that news from Charleston and Vicksburg was important to the politics of the struggle within the north:

"There is no doubt that the mass of the people are heartily tired of the war and the army not less tired than the rest—but have not yet made up their minds to separation [southern independence], and they see that peace at this moment means separation."[2]

Alongside this sense, there was the idea that operations might influence the prospect of external intervention. This situation was raised in America and abroad, although was far less at the fore than in 1861 or 1862. It therefore becomes one of the many 'might-have-beens' of the war that receive relatively little attention, and, as such, challenge the many other factors that tend to be discussed.

Counterinsurgency, which essentially was the Union cause, involved a process of national mobilization. Claims of necessity were employed to justify the extension of governmental power. This process (overreach) was facilitated by the unprecedented absence of southern representatives in Congress and the relatively weak position of the northern Democrats, who represented the opposition to Lincoln's Republicans. The Democrats were unable to exploit Republican losses in the November 1862 congressional elections, or to make much of the 1863 gubernatorial races, while the idea of a convention of the states gained no traction.[3] Lincoln referred to Ohio as saving the nation when on 13 October 1863 it clearly backed John Brough for governor, a joint nominee of the Republicans and war Democrats who beat Democrat Clement Vallandigham with 288,374 votes to the latter's 187,492. A former member of the House of Representatives who was a supporter of states' rights and a critic of Lincoln, Vallandigham had been convicted in May 1863 by a military court for his criticism of the war. He was then deported to the Confederacy and ran for governor from exile in Canada, being erroneously accused during the campaign of links with the south. The Republicans more narrowly won re-election in Pennsylvania: 51.46 percent to 48.54.

The power of the federal government was enhanced at the expense of the states, and a host of measures, including conscription (signed into law by Lincoln on 3 March 1863 after Congress approved it the previous month) and the establishment of a national banking system, were important in themselves and for what they signified, or at least appeared to signify. On 10 March, Lyons reported:

> The Appropriation Bills have sanctioned military and other expenditure on an immense scale. The Act to provide ways and means for the support of the government has conferred on the Secretary of the Treasury vast powers of borrowing and of issuing paper money and the large discretion left to him in these matters must give him enormous influences and the National Currency Act is intended to cause the government's paper money to be everywhere substituted for the notes of private banks to give the government a control over the banking interests.

Lyons argued that the Conscription Act placed the male population, who were eligible between 20 and 45:

> without restriction at the disposal of the President. The "Act relating to Habeas Corpus" has granted the executive government an indemnity for the arbitrary arrests it has already made, and sanctioned its making arbitrary arrests in future throughout the country. The Act authorising the letters of marque has gone far to transfer the war powers of Congress to the President....
>
> All these measures appear at this moment to find favour with the people at large. Most of the newspapers announce that a dictatorship has been established and make the announcement in a strain of exultation.[4]

The *Habeas Corpus* Suspension Act, which became law on 3 March, was largely passed to ensure that, as the army wished, the underage enlistees on which the Union heavily depended were maintained even in the face of parental opposition.[5] The act permitted the President to suspend the writ of *Habeas Corpus* as long as the Civil War continued.

It proved easier to push through these changes than it had been to mobilize and nationalize resources at the time of the wars of 1775–83 and 1812–14. In part, this contrast reflected the difficulty of maintaining cohesion in a newly-established federal system during 1775–1783 not least given the anti-authoritarian character of the American Revolution.

This situation was altered in the Civil War by the secession of the south as well as by the extent to which practices of government had now been long established in the north.

There was also a different context and content for the assessment of necessity. It was as if the Federalists, who had failed to create more potent and centralized government (being kept in power in 1801 by the Democratic Republicans but who disintegrated by 1816), were now, instead, directing the agenda. Indeed, the critical presidential platform attacking Lincoln, arranged by the Democrats in August 1864, declared that "under the pretense of a military necessity or war power higher than the Constitution, the Constitution itself has been disregarded in every part." This, however, was pushing the matter too hard. Thus, the *Habeas Corpus* suspension had passed the House by 90–45 votes and the Senate by 33–7, and after a joint conference committee, been agreed to by the House by 99–44, and by the Senate on a voice vote. Yet military factors and political circumstances repeatedly encouraged events that would not have been judged appropriate in peacetime. Given the context of the Civil War, treason was an issue, as in the treatment of Vallandigham who in the spring of 1864 took part in talks concerning a northwestern conspiracy that he would help force through peace.

At the same time, the cause of greater power and centralization could take different forms. Major-General Joseph Hooker, an aggressive corps commander and a critic of McClellan, and who succeeded Burnside as commander of the army of the Potomac on 26 January, offered the Napoleonic-style dictum that America might need a dictator in order to overcome the Confederacy, to which Lincoln offered the pertinent rejoinder, "Only those generals who gain successes, can set up dictators. What I now ask of you is military success, and I will risk the dictatorship."[6] Defeated at Chancellorsville on 30 April–6 May, Hooker resigned in June when his request for reinforcements was turned down by Lincoln and Halleck, and was replaced on 28 June by Major General George Meade.

In turn, the Confederate government aroused concern with the expedients it adopted to gain supplies, including conscription, direct taxation, martial law in several areas, and the impressment of supplies in return for paper currency, the latter being very much a necessity during the War of Independence. There were serious pressures on the Confederate home front from the outset. These escalated in 1863 with the so-called "Bread Riots," in which higher prices led to violent opposition—notably looting, mostly by women, especially in Richmond on 2 April, but also in Atlanta, Salisbury, Mobile, High Point, and Petersburg. The militia restored order in Richmond and news of the riots was repressed, while, to alleviate tension, efforts were made to provide supplies for the "worthy poor."[7] There was a general sense of pressure on the home front, one shot through with social tensions.[8]

Conscription, introduced in the Confederacy in 1862, led to additional points of crisis and conflict, not least because the process was violent: the Confederacy used press gangs to enforce conscription. Meanwhile, blacks, both slaves and free, in the south shared growing opposition to the system and displayed increased independence.[9]

Independence of a different type had already emerged in the south. Lee, a keen supporter of conscription (as were many supporters of the war), advocated the subordination of states' rights to the Confederate cause, and believed, as a member of his staff testified, "that since the whole duty of the nation would be war until independence should be secured, the whole nation should for the time be converted into an army, the producers to feed and the soldiers to fight."[10] Davis shared these views, but found state governors, such as Joseph Brown of Georgia, hostile to accepting his arguments from necessity.[11] In the 1863 gubernatorial election in Georgia, Brown won as a states' rights and anti-establishment candidate, who was furthermore hostile to conscription.

These problems repeated those posed by war and the demands of the army in previous conflicts, from the War of Independence to the Mexican American War. Elections on both sides during the war contributed to the need for sensitivity to local views and popular attitudes. On both sides, moreover, there were politicians supporting peace as well as war. At the same time, whatever their views, politicians did not need to heed the opinions of much of the population, certainly as far as elections were concerned. In the south, the majority could not vote, notably women and blacks. This context throws light on the extent to which the 1863 elections revealed strong support for continued bellicosity, as was true in Alabama[12] and North Carolina.

For both sides, discipline became harsher under the pressure of creating large forces willing to fight. This was an aspect of the citizen-armies of Union and Confederate, whether primarily national[13] or state in their identities and loyalties, or even both. Confederate nationalism was a factor, but required more work because the established identity of America was that of the Union.

Conscription led not only to evasion but also to popular resistance that had to be suppressed by troops, notably the New York City draft riots on 13–16 July 1863. In practice, the context and course of conscription did not quite match that of the *levée en masse* introduced by the French revolutionaries in 1793,[14] but it was still very different to earlier practices and this encouraged desertion, which was facilitated by the broken terrain. Sam Watkins, who served in the First Tennessee Volunteer infantry regiment, wrote later of the Confederate Congress's Conscription Act of 1862: "From this time until the end of the war a soldier was simply a machine, a conscript. It was mighty rough on rebels. We cursed the war." He had already noted that soldiers were "deserting by the thousands," which was certainly the case. In 1863, a British military observer wrote of the army of Tennessee, in which Watkins served, that the commander, General Braxton Bragg, had the reputation for "shooting freely for insubordination." Many were also shot for desertion, while in 1864 Joseph Johnston, at that time commander, was regarded as having even more soldiers shot.[15]

There were occupational exemptions in the Confederacy to conscription, including a particular level of slave ownership, which applied to white men aged 17 to 50, but in the end 21 percent of the one million Confederate troops were conscripts. For the Union, where the age range was 20 to 45, it was possible to pay a commutation fee of $300 (a vast sum at the time) or hire a substitute. However, the draft produced only 46,000 conscripts and 228,000 substitutes out of 2.1 million troops. At the same time, these figures possibly minimized its impact, as, on both sides, the draft encouraged volunteering. Conscription increased the problems of discipline and thereby the complexity of managing troops, both in battle and more generally, and notably raised the already serious leadership and managerial pressures on junior officers. The latter faced the harsh problem of implementing 'deadly' instructions.

The need for troops encouraged many Union commanders and politicians to move to support what were termed "U.S. Colored Troops," who came from three sources: free blacks in the north, free blacks, and slaves in the Union border states, and blacks from the Confederacy who had escaped from slavery or were rescued from it by Union advances. They were not paid in an equal amount with other Union troops and were organized not by states, as was the case with most white troops, but essentially at the national level, and officered accordingly. This more centrally controlled force potentially offered greater power to the federal government, not least as a force akin to that of the slave soldiers of earlier Islamic armies for example Ottoman janissaries; but this advantage was not fully tapped. General Orders No. 100, the codification of the laws of war written by Francis Lieber, professor of law at Columbia, hit at slavery in a way that also protected black soldiers in the Union army. Propertied rights over slaves were abolished in favor of the rights of freemen, and any black soldiers that were captured by the Confederates were to have the same rights as other Union soldiers.[16]

The commitment to the emancipation of the slaves in those parts of the south still in rebellion was seen as a way to weaken the southern economy and thus its war effort, as well as a means of providing a clear purpose to help maintain northern morale and assuage the sin that was leading a wrathful God to punish America. Counterinsurgency warfare thus, as so often is the case, extended to include Heaven. A strong sense of religious mission helped empower many of the Union soldiers (although this was also true of the Confederates). Having denied God's support by supporting sectional interests, America was to be made new, an affirmation of faith by the Union that reflected broad chords in American culture and influenced European public opinion. Indeed, for many Americans, emancipation satisfied the longing for a just war, one that would provide a basis for the adoption of "hard war" policies.[17] Yet, by spurring southern anger and Confederate resistance, emancipation also rendered such policies more necessary, which, in turn, stirred more havoc.

Emancipation was a moral cause that, as a result, also lessened the chances of foreign intervention on behalf of the south, while simultaneously working to weaken the south. There emancipation was seen as a race war of northern whites using blacks. From 1862 onward, in what was regarded as applying the "hard hand of war," Union commanders attacked southern private property and inflicted collective punishments as well as deporting Confederate supporters, although, unlike in similar contemporary conflicts, casualties among noncombatants were very few. This shift was encouraged by a larger shift within the Union army away from Democrat commanders hostile to emancipation, notably in the army of the Potomac under McClellan, to commanders and troops who were more radical, especially the army of Virginia under John Pope, and, in particular, and the influence of commanders from the west (Pope coming from Kentucky and Grant and Sherman from Ohio).[18]

At the same time, the move to "hard war" was not consistent or linear, however much there might have been such an intention at the governmental level, given that "hard war" did not have any one definition. Instead, there was a complex interaction of this broader intention with local military exigencies and circumstances, and the latter were generally more prominent. They included the strength of logistical support and consequent availability of supplies, the willingness of the local population to provide supplies, the nature of terrain, cover and weather, the extent of any local resistance, the place of the enemy, the attitude of commanders, the view of soldiers, and so on. This combination was scarcely consistent, geographically or temporally speaking, and this lack of consistency helped undercut any common shaping of change or developments.

Equally, the Confederates were convinced of divine support, a conviction that helped sustain them as the war went badly and in the face of the heavy losses they sustained. Contempt for their opponents also played a major role.[19] There was also fear based upon emancipation as well as foreboding about the future. Keeping slavery alive was central to Confederate strategy as it provided the labor force used during the war (an issue made more serious by the military service of whites), and apparently offered a means toward purpose and prosperity in the future. That meant that slave patrols were not just some ancillary force and or restricted purpose for some southerners, but instead rather crucial. They were an important part of the "small war" within the Civil War. In turn, large black refugee populations readily attached themselves to Union armies.

Although it was not applied to these states, emancipation, and what it might lead to, put a lot of pressure on the Unionist pro-slavery citizens in the border states, leading to an upsurge in neutralism or to Confederate support. Opposition to conscription increased in these states and guerrilla warfare grew in scale. The ambiguities of loyalty that had existed prior to this moment in these states were forced to take sides under the new demands of loyalty produced by the Unionist adoption of radical Republicanism policies and by the use of martial law.[20]

There were more specific pressures for other particular political maneuvers. The November 1862 elections had shown the strength of Democrat support in the midwest, notably Ohio, Illinois, and Indiana, and led to wild talk of a fresh secession. The Democrats won the Indiana General Assembly, only to find it disbanded by the wartime Republican Governor, Oliver Morton, who governed without it.[21] The Confederate invasion of Kentucky in September 1862 underlined longstanding Union concerns about the security of the midwest and made them more immediate. This border state appeared unsteady as well as vulnerable and, to its north, Ohio seemed likewise vulnerable, as it indeed was, which was a factor in the 1863 gubernatorial election. More practically, there was pressure in the Union for the opening of the Mississippi so as to influence opinion in the midwest. Such a political context deserves probing as the source of motivation for other campaigns.

Stones River/Murfreesboro in Tennessee on 2 January gave the Union a necessary victory at the start of 1863, one that offered some compensation for defeat at Fredericksburg the previous month. However, the casualties suffered helped lead the commander, William Rosecrans, to adopt subsequent caution and he did not advance again until late June, capturing Chattanooga on 9 September. His failure to act quickly angered Grant and gave Lincoln much concern. It revealed that removing McClellan had not ended the issue of determination.

Early 1863 also did not begin with decisiveness in the east. In January, Burnside tried to move around Lee's left, only to walk into what became the "Mud March" and be brought to a halt by heavy rain. This hit artillery transport particularly hard as that churned up the soil as well as sinking it.

In contrast, in early May at Chancellorsville, Virginia, Union attempts to outflank Lee were lost to cautious generalship. Joseph Hooker, the Union commander, planned to outflank Lee's left, but initial operational success, based on a brilliant piece of Union deception, was lost on 1 May as Hooker responded in hesitation to engagement with the Confederates. Instead, it was Jackson's Second Corps that made the more successful flank move, turning the Union rightward on 2 May before launching a highly effective attack. However, returning to camp Jackson was shot by sentries who thought he and his staff were a Union cavalry force. He died on 10 May.

Battles always profit from an analysis made in a number of lights. Thus, Chancellorsville was kicked off by a planned Union envelopment but met a Confederate counterplot—namely, that of launching attacks to defeat the Union forces in detail, essentially ensuring that there would be separate battles. A total lack of situational awareness and accurate assessment concerning Confederate moves explains an understandable Union caution that, nevertheless, surrendered the initiative to the Confederate commanders. This produced a successful flank attack on 2 May, followed the next day by the defeat of defending Union units. On 4 May, however, both sides failed to take the initiative successfully, underlining the major problems involved in coordinating units, and on the night of 5–6 May, the Union forces retreated north of the Rappahannock. Hooker had been unable to use his superior numbers to effect, but this is never as easy as it seems. Indeed, famed commanders in iconic battles earlier in the century, for example the Duke of Wellington at Waterloo in 1815, had kept units that were not engaged from entering the battle, in his case in order to protect his flank.

Chancellorsville proved that superiority in men and equipment, and the increased organizational sophistication of the army of the Potomac,[22] could not yet be translated into an effective army capable of defeating the leading Confederate army, the army of northern Virginia. As yet, it was not possible both to bring Union force to bear and to outfight the Confederates. Moreover, on the pattern of 1862, Chancellorsville, by weakening the main Union army and challenging its confidence, represented a shift in opportunity that provided Lee with a chance to advance and attack rather than simply respond. The counterattack at Chancellorsville was to be succeeded by a more ambitious Confederate operational and strategic counterattack.

Chancellorsville not only provided Lee with an opportunity to move north anew, hopefully more successfully than in the Antietam campaign, but also underlined the danger of not doing so. Such a Confederate course presupposed both the need and the ability to deny victory to the numerically larger and better-supplied Union forces in northern Virginia. Completely thwarting Union advances was implausible in the long term, not least due to the strain on supplies and personnel caused in the Confederacy by the war's continuation. Moreover, in so far as Richmond was a key to the war, it need only fall once for the Confederate position in Virginia to collapse, and among other issues its loss would have hit Confederate communications hard and provided opportunities for Union exploitation in a variety of directions.

This was a situation comparable to the Continental Army during a similar stage in the War of Independence. In early summer of 1777 the British were in control of a key central location (New York), had cleared Canada, and were pursuing a plan both to take Philadelphia (which they did on 26 September) and to link their Canadian and New York armies in the Hudson Valley, which they utterly failed to do. In the early summer of 1863, the Confederacy was also under great pressure, notably in the Mississippi Valley and in Tennessee. Both the Patriots in 1777 and the Confederates in 1863 were under enormous economic strains, not least in food supply.

The situation encouraged Lee to attack, especially as his Union opponents did not face any comparable challenge but, instead, maintained morale and an ability to remain in place according to the regular distribution of sufficient supplies. The resulting physical health was one reason for the marches of the army of Potomac that summer.

The Confederates were also encouraged to act by the strong religious revival that affected the army of northern Virginia in winter of 1862–3, not least in the case of Stonewall Jackson. As with other signs of Confederate religious revival, for example in 1864, this Providential Evangelicalism was a response to a need for faith and cannot be explained in crude terms as if it simply were a crisis of a slave-owning society. Religious faith and devotion did not mean that other factors did not play a role. Nor did they characterize all the troops. However, in terms of coherence and morale, these elements were crucial. They were also important for fighting determination and in a situation in which, as for the Union troops, this was not all present in equal amounts.

Morale and food came together for the Confederates in the large number of straggling troops who became a feature of their advances. The search for food was a significant component in this straggling, as was sheer exhaustion that, in part, was due to malnutrition and further compounded by the physicality of the marches that involved distance, heavy loads, poor footwear, dust, and heat.

The strategic situation changed dramatically that summer, for Chancellorsville and its aftermath provided an opportunity for Lee to move north, not least in part to prevent a fresh offensive by Hooker, which would have happened once his army had been revived. Hooker was no Grant or Napoleon as far as continual campaigning was concerned and the army of the Potomac needed reinforcements, supplies, and rest. Nevertheless, there would be another Union attack indeed.

Logistics were fundamental to both sides, not only in overall availability, but in specific access. Supply problems in the Confederacy were far more serious than those for the Union[23] and were becoming worse. These problems encouraged Lee to march into the north in 1862 and 1863: He hoped to gain food, boots, and other supplies, shortages of which were affecting morale and effectiveness. Moreover, safeguarding the Shenandoah Valley offered the possibility of securing Virginia's grain for his army, while operating in Pennsylvania would lessen the burden on Virginia.[24] In addition, the capture of the Pennsylvania coalfield in 1863 would have hit the Union's industry and logistics, given that railways were totally dependent on coal. In turn, the impact of logistical problems, notably the supply of fodder, played a role in the Union's failure to prevent Lee's successful retreat after Gettysburg.[25]

Lee's invasion of the north had major political implications: It helped galvanize support for the war in the Union as the Confederacy now looked like an aggressor, and this also had implications on the global stage. Yet significant Confederate successes would have had positive implications. It would have encouraged both Democrats domestically and interventionists abroad.

Lee advanced on 3 June, moving west of Hooker who, in turn, sought to match him on a northward axis that provided an opportunity to mask Washington. This was a defensive goal, but one that also greatly affected Union requirements and options. Lee was able to cross the Potomac, which was not defended (in contrast to the defense of the Rappahannock earlier by the Confederates against Union advances), and to move north. He invaded—first, Maryland and then Pennsylvania—not only seizing resources but also cutting Union forces off from the west to the extent of reducing risk-free links.

Severing communications would hit not only Union logistics but also its coherence. This would have political, strategic, and operational advantages, whether or not it ever led to a battle. If battle broke out, it was likely to catch the Union forces at a disadvantage, whether it was an encounter battle or the Union attacking the Confederates when the latter was at an advantage. Any such battle would probably result in an engagement with only a portion of the Union forces.

In practice, however, Lee's advance left his forces dispersed, as was only to be anticipated, as occurred for example in Napoleon's 1805 Ulm campaign. Concentration on the battlefield, as Moltke was to do at Austrian expense at Sadowa in 1866 and as played out in a number of Civil War battles, was never easy. However, the nature of transport and logistics, and the scale of the armies, ensured that it was necessary to advance by different routes.

In any event, neither side had adequate intelligence regarding the other in terms of routes and intentions, although the Union Bureau of Military Intelligence had a complete roster of Lee's army by Gettysburg. It was because of this that Sharpe could tell Meade with confidence that any attack on 3 July would be Lee's last throw.

In June, Lyons observed, "A battle, a great slaughter, and no result has hitherto been the end of such a meeting between the armies as seems to be imminent,"[26] but that scarcely described Gettysburg, fought from 1 to 3 July. Lee had moved north, and, in opposition, Major-General George Meade (a long-service veteran who had climbed up in the Civil War through divisional and corps commands) assumed command of the army of the Potomac on 28 June, ordered the previous day by Major-General Henry Halleck, the General-in-Charge, to protect Washington and Baltimore and to give battle to Lee. This would avoid a reliance on the city fortifications and take the initiative away from Lee, who appeared to be advancing via Carlisle on Harrisburg, the state capital of Pennsylvania, which would then provide an opportunity to move eastward threatening all Union communications from Washington. Lee was establishing a series of possible axes for advance, for raiding, or for threatening both. This was a key element in seizing and applying the initiative.

Meade moved north from his base at Frederick, Maryland, to counter Lee's advance while, at the same time, concentrating his forces in order to prepare for the apparently imminent battle. This put his army in a good position for the battle, which developed in an unexpected fashion as fighting began. Gettysburg was a small town that was a major road hub, and such junctions were particularly important for encounter battles. Given the area, as well as the movements and tempo on both sides, it was understandable that a road junction, and not a rail one, was the place of conflict, and that both sides sought to gain position.

In this respect, Meade proved a more effective operational commander, and this restricted Lee's tactical opportunities;[27] although, in part, this reflected the advantage for Meade of being on the defensive in an encounter battle. As later with Grant, operational skill could always trump tactical factors and uncertainties. Lee in effect was reduced at Gettysburg to the tactics of Napoleon at Borodino (successfully in 1812) and Waterloo (unsuccessfully in 1815), in that he sought not to outmaneuver a powerful opposing army, but to defeat it through action in which he actually surrendered his operational maneuvering (even so, the battle revealed the attempts for tactical maneuvers in order to win success). Unsuccessfully so for Lee. He was not helped by the weakness of his cavalry in the battle. It did not serve him much to mount supporting maneuverist blows.

On 1 July, the first day of battle, the Confederates drove the Union forces back off ridges to the northwest of the town, but the latter were not broken, and both sides were able to occupy linear positions. If the Union forces had taken heavier casualties, they could afford them (however brutal that sounds at the individual level) as their forces were more numerous and were consolidating.

On 2 July, the second day of the battle, Meade benefited from the advantage that interior lines along a good defensive position brought to the defense. Lee's attacks on the Union flanks on the second day failed. The movement of Confederate forces to the Union left was observed, and Union commanders were able to switch troops to Little Round Top in order to both block them and to leverage the height of that position. This was a classic instance of the benefit of higher ground. Height gave greater range, aided aim, made it easier to fire on the rear ranks of opponents, and reduced air resistance. This, however, is a tasteless description of the chaos of fighting on the Union left and the extent to which the position based on Cemetery Ridge was only held precariously. Other attacks on the Union center and right failed, in part due to a lack of coordination along the Confederate front. As with other battles, assessment would have been different had Lee succeeded, and the attempt of to gain flanking positions is well-established. However, too many elements of this day for Lee's forces were similar to McClellan's army at Antietam. Lieutenant-General James Longstreet, the Commander of the First Corps, criticized Lee for his emphasis on the attack on prepared Union positions, and instead pressed for a flanking maneuver on the second day. In turn, Longstreet was criticized for a lack of urgency in bringing his troops forward. After the battle, Longstreet was to press successfully to be transferred to the western theatre,[28] although in 1864 he returned to serve under Lee.

On the third day at Gettysburg, the Confederate focus was on the Union center. Pickett's Charge is somewhat misnamed popularly given the participation of the divisions of Pettigrew and Trimble as well as that of Pickett, which was largely shot down as it crossed open ground. Colonel William Aylett writes:

> The brigade moved on across the open field for more than half a mile, receiving, as it came in range, fire of shell, grape, canister and musketry, which rapidly thinned its ranks; still pushed on until the first line of the enemy, strongly posted behind a stone wall, was broken and driven from its position.... By this time the troops on our right and left were broken and driven back, and the brigade exposed to a severe musketry fire from the front and both flanks and an enfilading artillery fire from the rocky hill some distance to the right.

> No supports coming up, the position was untenable, and we were compelled to retire, leaving more than two-thirds of our bravest and best killed or wounded on the field.[29]

The Union artillery proved superior to its Confederate counterpart. There had been a supporting thrust by the Confederate cavalry, which was intended to force a turn in the Union flank and then attack from the rear, but this was stopped by a determined riposte by the Union cavalry under Brigadier General George Custer at the East Cavalry Field.[30]

Having taken heavy casualties without winning success, Lee then rested on the defensive, and Meade in turn did not attack him on 4 July. That night Lee retreated. Although there was some action, Meade's pursuit was cautious, in part due to the heavy casualties of the battle, issues with supplies, and uncertainty about Confederate moves. Nevertheless, and despite criticism, Meade was more active than McClellan after Antietam.[31]

While the Gettysburg campaign developed, both sides sought to pursue opportunities in Virginia. Lee, however, lacked the manpower to develop his notion of another force operating possibly against Washington. The Union, in contrast, had troops to threaten Richmond from the east, but failed adequately to develop this threat, a result owing much to Confederate resistance, poor Union command, and the enervating climate.[32]

Lee's failure at Gettysburg combined with Grant's success in isolating Vicksburg on the Mississippi (driving in its defenders and forcing their surrender on 4 July) suggests that a major shift in the balance of advantage had occurred. The Vicksburg defenders suffered both from supply issues and from the advance of the besiegers, not only in their trenches, but also in undermining the defenses and detonating mines. Lee's army was to escape from Gettysburg and to fight again, but at Vicksburg the Confederacy lost an army, which was a problem when one surrounded position surrendered and helped make a siege more potentially decisive than a battle. Moreover, the western Confederacy in effect shrank, for with the Mississippi lost, the Trans-Mississippi (although still a zone of hostilities) ceased to be an integral part of the war-effort.[33] Any European intervention on behalf of the Confederates now appeared less plausible. This in effect was Germantown (1777) in reverse.

The significance of Vicksburg and the extent to which, in contrast, the war was now far from being an immutable series of Union triumphs, and the question of where to place the emphasis, were all demonstrated by the fate of Port Hudson. The Confederates had established a powerful position there in 1862 on the Mississippi, 25 miles upriver of Baton Rouge, only to meet challenges from Union warships, which were the easiest way to move and protect artillery. Union troops assaulted the position on 27 May and 13–14 June, meeting strong resistance and taking heavy casualties. However, in the face of disease, exhaustion, and depletion of supplies, and following the fall of Vicksburg, the 6,340 strong garrison of Port Hudson surrendered on 9 July. This cemented the Union success on the Mississippi.

In effect, Winfield Scott's 1861 plan for what was called an "Anaconda" strategy (after the snake), that included bisecting the Confederacy on the Mississippi axis, had indeed been achieved, although it had not been a speedy process. By controlling the Mississippi, the Union strangled the essential overseas trade in cotton and forced the Confederacy to fight a two-front war in the western theatre, and created a more wide-ranging sense of Confederate failure.

Grant had shown an impressive flexibility and adaptability at the operational and tactical levels, and inserted himself successfully between the Confederate forces on the Mississippi Valley and Tennessee fronts.[34] At the same time, there was no inevitability to Grant's success, either in the particular steps of the campaign or in the fall of Vicksburg. Indeed, he endured repeated failures, and his eventual plan was criticized by colleagues, including Sherman, whereas Lincoln was skeptical. Crucially, however, Grant remained determined to press on.[35] The Vicksburg campaign exhibited excellent army-navy cooperation, the skillful use of intelligence, effective logistics, and operational art of a high order.

Grant repeatedly provided significant opportunities for exploitation. These reflected his creation of a central position, both within his specific section of the western theatre and more generally in it. He was greatly helped by not facing an army comparable to that of northern Virginia, nor a relative density of opposing troops. In terms of subsequent Union exploitation, the extent to which the Appalachians were hardly the Alps was important. There were potential axes of advance toward and into the eastern theatre.

This was also seen to the west of the Mississippi, notably in 1863 in Arkansas. The interaction of the respective spheres of operation was on full view in the relationship between the Vicksburg campaign and developments there. James Seddon, the Confederate Secretary of War, sought to move troops from Arkansas to divert Grant, and this led to an attack on the Union garrison at Helena north of Vicksburg on 4 July. Badly commanded and poorly-executed, the attack was repelled with heavy losses. Union forces (assisted greatly by success at Vicksburg) responded by moving into Arkansas, taking advantage of river and rail routes and bringing to bear much larger forces that ensured that the Confederates left Little Rock to avoid being destroyed there. It ultimately fell to Union forces on 10 September, which provided control of much of the state, and in particular the Arkansas River.

Water routes were important throughout the Mississippi basin and extended the significance of the control of the main river. The situation led to a crisis for Confederate society, with many fleeing from Arkansas into Texas. Large numbers of slaves, meanwhile, had fled to Union lines, hitting the economy, and several thousand became Union soldiers. The countryside saw Union foraging, Confederate guerrilla activity, and brutal Union reprisals.

Separately, the fall of Fort Smith, Arkansas, on 1 September to an army advancing from Indian territory (Oklahoma), where a Confederate force had been defeated at Honey Springs on 17 July (a battle in which there were many Native Americans on both sides and the more numerous Confederates suffered from poor equipment and leadership) blocked Confederate plans to attack Fort Gibson in that same territory. The Union now had a good route along the Arkansas Valley from the Mississippi to Indian territory, and this helped limit possibilities for the Confederates in the Trans-Mississippi region. Yet the Union presence was not so strong that Confederate forces were unable to advance across the state to attack Missouri in September 1864. Moreover, the failure of the Red River campaign in the spring of 1864 limited the possibility for the Union of exploiting its position in Arkansas.

To the east, the Union forces sustained their strategic advantage in November by defeating the Confederates at the key rail junction of Chattanooga, a basis for offensive campaigning that provided an opportunity for further advance into the south, especially toward Atlanta. The move into the Confederate rear was now possible, and in a very different context to that of amphibious assaults. Indeed, earlier after the Gettysburg campaign this brought about the dispatch under Lieutenant-General James Longstreet of some of Lee's army westward, helping Bragg to secure victory at Chickamauga, Georgia, on 20 September over the army of the Cumberland under Rosencrans who had captured Chattanooga in September. Fighting began on 18 September with the Confederates attacking, which they did in greater numbers on the 19th and even more so on the following day, but on the last day Bragg suffered from his attack starting late. Poor coordination and intelligence problems affected both sides, as did a failure to conform to timing. Crucially, and unlike at Gettysburg, a gap opened up on the Union front and was exploited by a large-scale Confederate attack. The Union units retreated, many in chaos, while others mounted an impressive defense. This helped prevent an effective Confederate pursuit, as did a lack of pontoon bridges and a shortage of artillery horses. The Union forces had 16,170 casualties, the Confederates 18,454, and these amounted to the second highest losses of the war after Gettysburg.[36]

This defeat led the Union forces to retreat to Chattanooga. The army of Tennessee[37] then besieged the Union forces in Chattanooga in October, hoping thereby to compensate for Vicksburg. Jefferson Davis visited the siege, a sign of its significance. However, on 23–5 November, Grant's relief forces, benefiting from bravery, boldness, seizing the initiative, and poor Confederate deployments, defeated the Confederates there, quite similar to Prince Eugene beating the French before Turin in 1706.[38] More generally, the success of the Union in the western theatre helped make the eventually victorious Union campaign of 1864–5 in Virginia possible.

In 1862 and 1863, Union pressure and triumphs there had not prevented Lee from advancing in, and from, Virginia. To a considerable extent, it had been possible for the Confederacy to trade space in the west for time with which to attack in the east. This potentially war-winning formula, however, was unsuccessful. After that, the Union forces were able to exploit their success in the west against Confederate forces (who were facing major problems with resources, logistics, and coherence[39]) in order to attack what might otherwise have been the defense-in-depth the Confederacy enjoyed in the east. That indeed was a key outcome of the 1863 campaign. Yet again, however, it was one that was only apparent in hindsight (and was hardly perceptible after Chickamauga) and also certainly required defense and exploitation in fresh fighting.

The significance of the Confederate defense-in-depth was underlined by the failure of the major Union naval and amphibious assaults on Charleston in 1863, on 7 April and from 18 July to 7 September. On the other hand, it is unclear that the capture of Charleston would have had strategic military consequences, in the same way it would be a very major political blow that would have resonated across the south and also deterred foreign supporters of intervention. Such reflections serve to underline the danger of judging strategic choices too glibly. The significance of the Union failure at Charleston in 1863 might have been apparent only in hindsight, but, even then, it was unclear. The availability of the navy as a strike force encouraged its use accordingly, causing the Confederacy to disperse forces for coastal defense, but that was not the prime value of Union naval strength.

Amphibious power was used more easily on 2 November when, in the face of no resistance, the Union landed 4,500 troops on Brazos Santiago Island at the mouth of the Rio Grande, subsequently advancing up the valley via Brownsville to Roma, while other moves were made along the nearby Gulf coast. This was designed to put pressure on developments in Mexico but did not, as there was no relevance to the campaigning in central Mexico. In July 1864, Grant pulled the force out. The far south of Texas was also marginal to the conflict in Texas as a whole, and the latter was more centrally at stake in the Red River campaign of 1864. The far south of Texas was even more marginal to the Confederacy as a whole.

On 19 November 1863, in front of an audience of about 50,000, the Soldiers' National Cemetery was consecrated at Gettysburg, fulfilling not only a wish for memorialization, but also a practical need to bury the very many dead. A very downtrodden Lincoln, probably suffering from smallpox, gave a dedicatory address that sought to affirm lasting value from the end of what was to be the last major Confederate invasion, closing:

> ...the great task remaining before us—that from these honored dead we take increased devotion to that cause for which they gave the last full measure of devotion—that we here highly resolve that these dead shall not have died in vain—that this nation, under God, shall have a new birth of freedom—and that government of the people, by the people, for the people, shall not perish from the Earth.

Devotion is a key word.

Edward Everett, who had been Professor of Greek Literature at Harvard, President of Harvard (1846–8), Secretary of State (1852–3) and a Massachusetts Senator (1853–4), and Vice-President on the Constitutional Union Party ticket in 1860, who spoke at Gettysburg for much longer than Lincoln, compared the site with that of Marathon in 490 BCE. In doing so, Everett provided an echo of the glorious and successful defense of liberty by the Greeks against the invading Persians, and an account that cast Greek civilization as the progenitor of modern America. This was a comparison that the listeners could be anticipated to understand. It annexed the classical past, and notably Athens that had played the key role at Marathon, for the Union cause and sought to deny it to the Confederacy (whose commentators, in contrast, had made much of the role of slavery in the classical world and highlighted its defense by Aristotle). Everett reinforced prevalent ideas of purpose and conduct, in terms of the eye of history, and the roles of honor, courage, and manhood. With ideas of nationhood and a faith in Providence, these values, however, had to confront the maw of war.

Ironically, Marathon was not similar to Gettysburg in that ten years later a far larger Persian invasion force led by the ruler himself attacked Greece. Moreover, it was initially successful, the Spartans dying bravely at Thermopylae but failing to stop the invasion which was only blocked by Greek naval victory at Salamis and was not to be defeated on land (at Plataea) until the following year. History could be readily used, as Everett showed, but analogies were not necessarily as relevant as they were useful. When he died in January 1865, Everett was to be accused in the South of being 'a superserviceable lackey of Lincoln' who had betrayed his earlier principles.[40]

The pace of the war had increased. This was indicated earlier in 1863 by the number of battles waged by Grant in isolating Vicksburg: Port Gibson on 1 May, Raymond on 12 May, Jackson on 14 May Champion Hill on 16 May, and Big Black River Bridge on 17 May. With an army that had been marching and fighting for over two weeks, Grant fought four battles in six days, against two different armies on two fronts. This level of intensity and remarkable operational tempo, which was reminiscent of Napoleon in northern Italy in 1796–7, and of Scott in Mexico in 1847–8, demonstrated and publicized Grant's ability, and reflected the need for commanders to adapt rapidly to the unexpected moves of opponents. Situational intelligence posed a major problem, forcing the need to in that moment, and more generally, to adapt plans, decide whether or not to persist, and in practice to weave strategy on the move. The classic situational intelligence was provided by encounters with opposing forces, but that offered few indications of their size, intentions, and resolve.

All this continued to play out later in the year in Virginia. This saw advances by Meade in Virginia, first Meade failing in mid-September to advance to defeat the outnumbered Lee, then the Bristoe campaign (13 October–7 November), with Lee, having failed in a counter-offensive, pushing south beyond the Rappahannock River followed, on 7 November, by Meade who forced passage at two locations. This was followed, however, by the Mine Run campaign (27 November–2 December) in which Meade, whose army was larger (81,000 to 48,000), failed to surprise the Confederates south of the Rapidan River. Meade moved too slowly, and a Confederate counterattack, in an encounter battle, saw the advanced Union force pushed back. Meade then decided that the Confederate lines were too strong for a full-scale assault. Although it had faced failures, the army of the Potomac was still a major challenge to the army of Northern Virginia.

The campaigning in 1863 led to serious cumulative damage for the Confederacy, though less than was to follow in 1864. At the same time, alongside numerous desertions, Confederate determination remained high. As of yet, there was no sign that Union successes could be readily transformed into victory of the war. The determination of both sides left pointless the attempt by Alexander Hamilton Stephens, the Confederate Vice-President, to negotiate a peace.

At the same time, the strain on the Confederate home front was greater than that of their opponents, and this was replicated in the respective armies. Lieutenant Robert Hubard of the 3rd Virginia Cavalry, was to write:

> Matters were now very gloomy, the prospects of the Confederacy were very doubtful and many had despaired since the battle of Gettysburg and the fall of Vicksburg and Port Hudson. Our currency was in a hopeless condition of depreciation. Our population had furnished nearly as many soldiers as it could naturally bear and the conscript laws therefore availed but little and the tax and impressment laws had nearly stripped the country of flour, grain, and meat and greatly discouraged production.[41]

## 7. 1864: POLITICS AND COMBAT

The fourth year of the war was totally different from that of the War of Independence in 1778. In large part, this was because of French entry into the War of Independence. It was not so much that this had an immediate military impact in America, but rather because the war thereby became widespread, with Britain having to focus on rivalry with the French in the Caribbean and on the possibility of French fleet attacks in British and American waters. Much later, in 1864, in contrast, there was no foreign intervention, and it no longer appeared to be a prospect as it was in 1861–2. Indeed, the Civil War started to wane with Union forces driving into the heart of the Confederacy. This harkens to an even greater contrast between the "fourth years" of 1779 and 1865, which is discussed in the next chapter.

In 1778, the British also advanced into the south, taking Savannah as the result of an amphibious attack, and thereby preparing the ground for an overland advance on Charleston. This represented a spread of campaigning in the area, a scenario that matched the situation in 1864. This broadening outward was to put great pressure on the Patriots in 1779–81, at least in the south, but the tempo was slower than in the case of Sherman's advance in 1864–5. The British were in a more difficult position, not least in the face of French naval strength and amphibious capacity, as shown by the Franco-American attempt to regain Savannah in 1779. This failed, but nonetheless prefigured the British debacle at Yorktown in 1781 by showing that the French fleet permitted Franco-American cooperation.

In 1864, the difference between Democrats and Republicans led to predictions of change if Lincoln lost the election, predictions made by foreign commentators, such as Lyons, as well as domestic counterparts. In the election, McClellan, the Democratic candidate, was willing to continue the war and wanted reunion as the price of peace, but his running mate, George Pendleton (a Congressman from Ohio), was a Copperhead (or Peace Democrat) and the platform pressed for an armistice. The Democrats were also against an emancipation amendment for the Constitution, which was a policy supported by the Republican Convention. In practice, this policy was one that contradicted the practice of racial segregation and discrimination seen in the Union army and navy,[1] although far less so than in Confederate conduct. More black soldiers were executed, and usually by hanging, whereas whites were shot by firing-squad, which was seen as more dignified.[2] Black soldiers, of whom there were 179,000 in total serving in segregated units, were also paid less and received discarded weapons and were burdened with many manual tasks to a disproportionate extent.[3]

John Frémont, a Georgian opposed to slavery who had served as a major in the Mexican war, playing a major role in the conquest of California, and who had been the unsuccessful Republican presidential candidate in 1856, unsuccessfully sought the nomination again in 1864 before being nominated by the new Radical Democracy Party. They called for the war to be waged without compromise, only for Frémont to withdraw when the campaign failed to gather momentum and upon the danger of a Democrat victory. This was symptomatic of the political tensions on the Union side.

At the same time, the electoral process to a degree helped draw the sting of military disaffection. Despite the significant churn of commanders, there was no equivalent on the Union side to the treason in 1779 of Benedict Arnold, nor to the court-martial in 1778 of Charles Lee, possibly the most talented general in the Continental Army and the second in command. Lee was unfairly accused by some of co-operating with the British. Nor was there an equivalent on the Confederate side, even though civil war more readily provides an opportunity for a shift in loyalty.

Contemporaries were sure that the election would be decided by the campaigning,[4] and it was also seen as important to the success of conscription.[5] Lincoln had found a war-winning general with Grant, but this reality was not apparent at first, and there was the danger he might be the latest in a series of disappointments, a westerner who could not make it back east, and a commander who by failure made the Democrat case.

Appointed Lieutenant-General and General-in-Chief of the Union army on 2 March, Grant's decision to take to the field with the army of the Potomac that remained under the command of Meade until the end of the war, rather than act as military adviser to the government, may be questioned, but, close to Washington, he was more than willing to go there. Grant added strategic purpose and impetus to Union military policy, and helped drive the army of the Potomac, still under Meade's command until it was disbanded on 28 June 1865, to a level of aggression it had not shown hitherto, as McClellan's deliberative caution had been characteristic of his successors, albeit to a varying degree. In doing so, Grant matched Lee's earlier achievement. Grant was also capable of hard and purposed work. He analyzed situations fully but rapidly and issued clear instructions accordingly. He was able to read maps and understand terrain, which was important at every level of war, and an aspect of his ability to gain and use the altitude. Grant was willing to take risks though without disparaging his opponents, but he remained calm and collected while doing so.

To Grant, weakening the opposing society was necessary, and he initially proposed to send 60,000 troops by sea to southern Virginia and then launch a raid into North Carolina to attack the Confederacy's home base, a plan opposed by Halleck. It was possibly as well for Grant's reputation that this plan was not pursued as the mobility of such forces tended to be more hindered than that of defenders. Large-scale amphibious operations might thus be fixed, but re-embarkation was always risky.

Instead, Grant was to show mastery in the established central sphere of operations, albeit as a key element of what was intended to be a series of five coordinated Union attacks that together would overcome Confederate forces, not least by preventing them from moving troops between fronts as had been the case before the battle of Chickamauga. Butler and the army of the James was to follow in the steps of McClellan in 1862 not, however, with the goal of capturing Richmond but in cutting the rail links to Lee's army and in diverting some of his troops. In the event, Grant's and Sherman's attacks were the only two that developed momentum. The maladroit Butler, whose numbers had been cut by Grant, lacked decisiveness, did not cut the rail link, and so an attack on Petersburg on 9 June failed in part due to the determination of the defenders but also because the Union commanders exaggerated their numbers, a defensive habit that had been seen with McClellan and others but one that also reflected intelligence failures.

On 20 April, Grant explained to Lincoln the value of a general advance all along the line, and thus use troops otherwise held on the defense and, in doing so, put pressure on the Confederates.[6] This was an approach that led Grant to criticize those generals who in his view lacked sufficient drive, for example George Thomas, the commander of the army of the Cumberland. With Grant, criticism was not a matter so much of destructive backbiting but rather of a willingness to dismiss such commanders or, as happened with Thomas in early 1865, take units from them.

Grant was also to write, "To get possession of Lee's army was the first great object. With the capture of his army Richmond would necessarily follow."[7] In short, Grant recognized that the center of gravity was Lee's army itself. Grant observed of the Wilderness, "It was my plan then, as it was on all other occasions, to take the initiative whenever the enemy could be drawn from his intrenchments if we were not intrenched ourselves."[8]

In the Overland Campaign of May and June, Grant subordinated the individual battle to the repeated pressure of campaigning against the Confederates. Having fought at the Wilderness, he pressed on to fight anew. This was very different to the earlier experience of the army of the Potomac, and, therefore, of the army of northern Virginia. Attacking the Confederate army became the key (instead of capturing individual positions), although, by driving on Richmond, a powerful psychological blow was struck.

The near-continuous nature of the conflict from his advance that May, which led, initially, on 5 May, to the battle of the Wilderness, was followed by the battle of Spotsylvania from 8 to 21 May, that of North Anna on 23–6 May, and that of Cold Harbor. The assault at Cold Harbor on 3 June saw about 3,500 casualties in a few hours for no gains. Grant was later in his *Memoirs* to express his regret about the losses there, but the attritional warfare compounded the toll taken by supply problems on the morale of the army of Northern Virginia.

There are battles that are more well known, such as that of the Crater on 30 July. Union troops from a mining background had dug a shaft under a major Confederate fort and explosives in the shaft were ignited. The poorly led Union men charged forward into the crater they created, only to be stopped by the crater side, picked off by Confederate defenders and then counterattacked (with the white Union survivors allowed to surrender but the blacks killed when they tried to do so). Combined with the crowded nature of the site and the impact of dehydration and heat stroke, this was a dystopian scene.

There was also a more general pressure of conflict, as with battles at Deep Bottom and Globe Tavern in the stifling humid heat of mid-August. Grant suffered from tensions among his commanders and from Lee's ability to block his moves, which thwarted Grant's wish for a battle in open terrain that would settle the campaign, and thereby the war. Lee blocked this, imposing a delay that was attritional but that was intended to affect the 1864 election. Grant responded by continuing and thus using attrition on the Confederates. This was important to the eventual Union victory.

The campaign finally became to a considerable degree an entrenchment conflict at Petersburg. This spared the troops the burden of constant marching as well as lessening exposure to fire; but entrenchment exacerbated the health hazards posed by one's remaining in a certain, fixed position for a long time. This was not a static campaign, although it had similarities with that at Atlanta in August.

The heavy casualties gave the war in the Virginian theatre an attritional character, which indeed was Grant's intention. Indeed, it was attritional both for the army of northern Virginia and for the Virginian home front. In the long term, although repeated attacks failed to break through the Confederate lines and destroy the smaller Confederate army, Grant's attrition sanded it down, albeit with significantly heavier Union losses (with about 55,000 casualties to about 33,600 for Lee), and a percentage of army strength that was similar. Failure at Cold Harbor meant the end of attempts to defeat Lee north of Richmond and the James River, and this was followed by a new axis south of the James via Petersburg. However, Grant's initial assaults there on 15–18 June failed, in part because the army was tired because of the operational tempo of the campaign, but also due to weak corps commanders.

Grant was also seeking to pin Lee down so that this attritional pressure could be brought to bear while the operational risk of Confederate moves was lessened. These goals, however, were affected not only by the tactical difficulties of bringing force to bear effectively, but also by the logistical problems of supporting significant forces, the sanitary difficulties of coping with large numbers in a small area, and the more general difficulties posed by campaigning in this region.[9] In the short term, the heavy casualties suffered by Grant's army hit civilian morale in the north, as did Sherman's initial failure to capture Atlanta, a failure that led to a five-week Union siege and awakened echoes of McClellan's earlier failure at Richmond in 1862.

Moreover, the Red River Expedition failed, which in part was intended to secure cotton for the textile industry in New England. That is a bald description of a very important operation and serves as a reminder that the war by 1864 was not at all one-sided. Indeed, there is a danger that the process of providing a coherent account of the war risks being misleading. The major Japanese success in China in 1944–5, in Operation Ichigo, similarly tends to be ignored even though it was both significant in and of itself and of wider strategic importance.

The Red River campaign also had wider implications (both strategic and political), the latter contributing to Confederate morale and to a sense that Lincoln might lose the election. He indeed had supported the campaign in part because any economic improvement in New England would help him politically, as would making Texas a Union state and increasing the Union electorate in Louisiana. In turn, the Confederacy would be damaged by the blow to its agricultural infrastructure and to the cotton exported by its blockade runners, as well as by the capture of Shreveport, a center of Confederate economic and military activity. Support from Lincoln and Halleck led to the decision not to use the army of the Gulf in support of Sherman, but instead to employ it for the campaign alongside 10,000 of Sherman's troops, as well as 17 ironclads as part of a major fleet.

Nathaniel Banks, the commander of the expedition as head of the Department of the Gulf, however, delayed operations on the Red River, in part for political reasons. The plan was for his forces to advance on Shreveport, the capital of Confederate Louisiana, joining there with a force sent south-west from Little Rock. In turn, Confederate commanders were divided between the goal of retaking the Mississippi Valley (including New Orleans) or focusing on Arkansas and Missouri. Counterattacking, on 8 April at Mansfield, the Confederates defeated an outnumbered Union force south of Shreveport but, on the next day at Pleasant Hill, a larger Union force repelled a subsequent attack. Banks wanted to press on, but his senior commanders (understandably) lacked confidence, and Banks retreated first to Alexandria and then to the Mississippi Valley. Instead, however, of driving on against Banks, the Confederates sent much of their force to Arkansas where the Union units were pushed back to Little Rock. On both sides, there were recriminations between commanders. The retreating Union forces also inflicted considerable damage including burning Alexandria on 13 May. Civilian anger helped to make subsequent reconstruction highly unpopular.

Sherman was to argue that the Red River campaign delayed the end of the war, maybe by six months. The army of the Gulf had originally been intended for Mobile, and the failure to advance on it enabled Confederate commanders to move about 15,000 troops to take part in the Atlanta campaign, which as a result took longer than it might otherwise have required. All counterfactuals/might-have-beens are problematic, and, indeed, an advance on Mobile, in the sticky Gulf climate, and with many rivers to cross, might have gone badly wrong, just as the Red River campaign had been. Certainly, the Union hopes of success in Louisiana and Texas proved abortive and there were significant opportunity costs, especially prior to a crucial election.

The dismal failure of a far larger force was a salutary warning to anyone who assumed that resources could dictate outcomes. Not only were there much greater troop numbers but also the largest Union fleet deployed on an interior waterway. Furthermore, logistics, although under pressure, were far less problematic than for Confederate forces. The principal Union problem, that the two axes of advance would be defeated sequentially by a united Confederate force, was not at issue, as the Confederate forces were also divided. Instead, the campaign on the Red River was inadequately planned, badly led, and lacked an ability to recover from mistakes.

The Red River failure was matched by others, with Grant thwarted in northern Virginia at the Bermuda Hundred and the Crater, humiliation in the Shenandoah Valley, and the costly fiasco of James Wilson's cavalry raid in south-central Virginia in late June. Faced by a range of bad news, Lincoln feared that he would not be re-elected and, had the elections been held, he may have been correct. Lincoln was under pressure to negotiate and Copperheads pushing for peace were hopeful.[10]

However, Sherman's capture of Atlanta on 2 September turned morale round,[11] not least because it was the product of more wide-ranging pressure in the south, for example the successful raid by Lovell Rousseau from Decatur on the Montgomery and West Point Railroad in July, with much of the rail infrastructure and associated supplies destroyed. The Confederates had sought an active defense of Atlanta, attacking Sherman's forces at Peachtree Creek on 20 July, Bald Hill on the 22 July and Ezra Church on the 28 July; but they lost heavily in these, and this led to a more defensive and reactive stance for what remained of the campaign. The Confederates took heavy losses in these attacks, notably at Ezra Church, and these both hit their morale and helped ensure the success of Sherman's policy of cutting the rail links to Atlanta. During the siege, he mounted a destructive bombardment, and, after the city's capture, there was widespread destruction, notably of buildings, including civilian ones.[12]

Although many hopes had been disappointed, Lincoln also benefited from northern successes elsewhere. The Petersburg campaign proved a disappointment for the Union because although the Petersburg Railroad was reached on 18 August and a counterattack defeated by defensive fire on 21 August, the Confederates stabilized the line in an attack on Reams' Station on 25 August. As so often happens, the potential of defensive fire was destroyed by the attackers finding and using a vulnerable spot. The Shenandoah Valley saw Lee seek to distract Union forces by mounting an advance down the valley and across the Potomac and further by trying to threaten Washington.[13] This proved an impressive advance to and into Maryland, as the Confederates reached Fort Stevens less than four miles from the White House on 11 July, but not in any strength.

These campaigns, however, exacerbated Confederate supply-shortages, increasing the reliance on blockade-runners, which, in turn, the steadily more effective Union blockade thwarted. This blockade was maintained despite technological developments. February saw the first effective attack by a submersible, mounted in Charleston Harbor when the *Hunley* sunk the Union screw sloop *Housatonic*, although she herself sank soon afterward, probably as a consequence of the stresses created by the explosion. Later that year, the first successful torpedo attack occurred in Albemarle Sound, North Carolina, when, with a spar torpedo fitted to a steam launch, the Union sank the Confederate ironclad *Albemarle*.

As a morale boost, the navy delivered success in the battle of Mobile Bay on 5 August, one in which Farragut showed determination and bravery, and won success. To get a better understanding and view of the engagement, Farragut was lashed to the shrouds, and this provided a heroic image of a leader under fire, one taken further by the lines ascribed to him: "Damn the torpedoes! Full speed ahead!" Although Farragut was not subsequently associated with success comparable to Grant or Sherman, he too provided a memorable image of decisiveness and an example of the adroit and determined risk-taking that helped bring the Union victory. In 1866, Grant and Farragut were to become respectively America's first full general and admiral.

The election saw Lincoln draw on Republican Party organization and patronage and confirm political reality since 1861 through the creation of the National Union Party, a coalition of Republicans with War Democrats such as Andrew Johnson and Stanton. Lincoln won by 212 to 21 (Kentucky, New Jersey, Delaware) electoral votes. Nevada being fast-tracked to statehood gave Lincoln three electoral votes. However, the popular vote was far less unfavorable to McClellan than this figure suggests. In addition, in the Border States voting was only allowed after loyalty oaths to the government, which greatly magnified the overall National Union proportion, which was 55.1 percent of the popular vote, their opponents winning 44.9 percent: 2,218,388 votes to 1,812,807. The Republicans also won a substantial majority in Congress, more than countering their losses in 1862. They gained two more Senatorial seats out of the 14 contested, continuing to hold the majority (now by 33 of 50 total seats). In the House of Representatives, 193 seats were contested, and the Republicans had a net increase of 40 seats, winning 150 (of 193) seats. The Democrats suffered from their division between War Democrats and Copperheads.

Lincoln, the first President to win re-election since Andrew Jackson in 1832, and the first northerner to do so, was helped by the backing of the War Democrats and by the army's support: 75.8 percent of the Union soldiers who voted in the presidential election did so for him and the majority in every state where soldiers voted bar Kentucky. This backing reflected the strong sense of religious mission that helped empower many of the Union soldiers and encourage them to prefer war for victory to negotiations. Having denied God's support by supporting sectional interests, America was to be made new, an affirmation of faith that reflected broad chords in American, and indeed British, culture.[14] McClellan, the former general, did not attract this emotional commitment, not least because his stand was depicted by opponents as equivocal, which indeed was the case.

Lincoln's victory on 8 November encourages a benign view of the continuance of the political process during the war, but, again, this view is to some degree an instance of the broad-brush approach of (and to) hindsight; for, at the time, the politics of the war, both at the national and the state levels, and between and within the parties, had proved highly disruptive. Moreover, this divisiveness had absorbed much political and governmental effort, posing problems for the management of the war, as well as greatly affecting the politics of military promotion and command.[15] Diplomats seeking signs of opposition to Lincoln were able to find them in plenty.

This included in the army in 1864, where about a fifth of soldiers did not vote, and court martials and other means were used to silence noisy Democrats. Moreover, the role of the army in the election can be reframed to note that many soldiers who were Democrats left, formally or by desertion, after the Emancipation Proclamation. Furthermore, a large number did not re-enlist after their three-year terms. As a result, the army in November 1864 was not politically what it had been a year earlier.[16]

Lincoln's re-election ended the political options for counterfactual speculation as far as the north was concerned, at least insofar as conventional politics were concerned. Northern morale affirmed Lincoln's position, just as his leadership helped ensure the resilience of this morale. In a sense the way was opened for the option of assassination, which raises the question of what would have happened had Lincoln died or been killed earlier.

The re-election provided the background for the pursuit of a strategy designed to stop southern support for the war by crippling morale and destroying infrastructure, a goal shared by the Union troops.[17] Although Sherman's devastation of an important part of the Confederate hinterland increased the resolve of some southern soldiers and civilians, the ability to spread devastation unhindered across the southern hinterland (a situation that owed something to Confederate military moves), exacerbated the already serious tendency toward desertion that weakened the Confederate forces (as well as the Patriot ones in the War of Independence). This helped destroy civilian faith in the war, and made the penalty for and limitation of guerrilla warfare apparent.[18] However, the amount of damage that Sherman inflicted has been reduced by historians, such that aside from the absence of any political comparison at all, any analogy with the Allied Strategic Air Offensive is doubly problematic. Sherman's method, shared by Sheridan in the Shenandoah that year, was to be described later as "total war," which, however, rests on the mistaken assumption that the latter is readily definable.[19] "Hard war" is likely a more appropriate term.

The slave basis of southern society collapsed as Union forces, 66,000 men strong, advanced from Atlanta, which they left on 15 November, to Savannah, where they arrived on 21 December, after a march characterized by skirmishes and no battle. This was a march whose route was not settled in advance, and one in which logistics and the goal of reaching the support of the navy were key elements. Sherman was concerned about guerrilla attacks, but they were relatively few. Confederate field resistance was nugatory, because John Hood, the commander of the army of Tennessee from 18 July, instead of matching Sherman, moved westward to Gadsden on 20–22 October and Decatur on 27–28 October, finally fighting at Nashville on 15–16 December. This move was intended to attack Sherman's supply lines and thus oblige Sherman to move back to fight a major battle, and after winning Hood was to advance through the Cumberland Gap into Virginia and help Lee. However, Sherman had no intention of following Hood, arguing correctly that this would be to disrupt the necessary strategy.[20] Instead, Hood was heavily defeated at Franklin (30 November) and Nashville (15–16 December) by the Union army of Ohio and army of the Cumberland, respectively.

Thousands of slaves used the opportunities of Sherman's advance to escape their masters, although clogging Union lines with "contraband" as they were known. Moreover, Sherman himself was very unenthusiastic about abolition. He was a very transactional commander, concerned with the immediate goals and needs of his forces,[21] which was understandable albeit somewhat shortsighted in the context of a civil war.

Slave escapes were an important part of a broader collapse of Confederate norms and control. In the latter case, those who fled conscription, which included the conscription of the three-year enlistees, were part of a wider disaffection in white society that variously also encompassed southern Unionists and brigands, and that was given added manpower by Union prisoners of war who escaped in steadily greater numbers. There were particular problems of control for the Confederacy in the foothills of the Appalachians, but, more generally, there were growing difficulties, and these became acute in late 1864. The breakdown in cohesion and control posed major issues for local militia, and for Confederate civilians not in the militia. This, in turn, made it less likely that they would send men to the Confederate army; instead, these demanded its assistance. The interior of the Confederacy had become unstable and militarized prior to Sherman's advance, and this situation helped Sherman greatly magnify the impact of the march, both psychological and practical.[22] In response to the march, Confederate troops treated any soldiers they might capture very harshly.

By making territory his objective, Sherman moved beyond the unproductive nature that that goal and method frequently entailed. These were raids, and very different from conventional campaigns to seize territory. However, without his earlier ability to mount such campaigns, Sherman would not have been able to conduct his raids. Now, he used the passage or temporary occupation of territory to fulfil his goal of focusing on the psychological mastery of southern society, which helped make the episode a cause of lasting grievance.[23] Moreover, in the religious atmosphere of the time, this led to Sherman being given a satanic character, as in the *Daily Dispatch* [Richmond] of 23 January 1865, an issue that commented on large numbers of Confederate refugees, and reported Sherman as in "blasphemous contempt" about "Divine Providence." At the same time, much of Sherman's psychological mastery was a product of southerners believing their own propaganda and its lasting exaggeration of Sherman's ferocity.

Psychological mastery was a goal that proved more productive than that of seeking what had all-too-often proved the chimera of victory in battle,[24] and one that matched the desire (on both sides) to achieve such mastery through humiliation and vengeance.[25] Herman Melville celebrated in his "The March to the Sea":

> From charred Atlanta marching
> They launched the sword again.
> The columns streamed like rivers
> Which in their course agree.

Rivers were seen as natural and unstoppable. The British *chargé des affaires* reported in December, as Sherman neared Savannah:

> If Sherman's plans are brought to a victorious end it will have if not a material certainty a moral result as a march for upwards of three hundred miles across the enemy's country without serious molestation must argue that beyond the Confederate armies at present on foot but little can be spared in other quarters.[26]

Sherman's successful advance through Georgia and then the Carolinas in 1864–5 not only had purpose, but was also an administrative triumph. It was supported by five wagon trains with a total of 2,500 wagons, and nearly a third of the force was used to protect them, which was particularly necessary because Sherman had abandoned his supply lines. The advance entailed the commonplace problem of trying to keep troops and supplies in harness, a problem exacerbated by the state of the roads.[27] They were not designed for such a capacity, which in turn wrecked the roads (although Sherman's impressive engineers helped with bridge and road repairs).

The destructiveness of the Union advance contributed to the implementation of attitudes about the desirable nature of agrarian society, which to Union soldiers, many from the midwest, did not mean slave-labor plantations, rather independent farmers, as well as the overcoming of a rival economy and a hostile environment, both physical and human. There was also, on the pattern of Grant's advance prior to Vicksburg, the seizure of food to the benefit of the Union army.[28] This was necessary if Sherman was to provide adequate supplies for his men, although he did take cattle with him. Sherman's instructions to leave residents with enough food for survival and to favor the "poor and industrious" were frequently ignored by his troops. At any rate, Sherman's harsh treatment of women and children put pressure on Confederate men, Sherman observing: "We are not only fighting hostile armies, but a hostile people." The systematic destruction, however, was of public not private property. Indeed, the forest fires infuriated Sherman because they slowed his march down.

Sherman certainly contributed to a socio-economic crisis across the south, albeit a crisis that was already serious. The shortage of resources exacerbated the inherently divisive social character of the south. This has been seen in a double sense. First, a shortage of resources, especially food and footwear, hit morale and reduced the operational effectiveness of many soldiers. Secondly, the impact on the home front of shortages and of other economic pressures, particularly high inflation, affected military morale, encouraging high rates of desertion—that is, even higher rates of desertion. In short, it has been suggested that military factors contributed to a loss of Confederate will, but that home front factors were what was ultimately decisive. Had it not been for the latter, the desertion rate would have been lower, with important operational consequences. This has been linked to the "class" character of the south, with the soldiers and the home front seen in terms of "plain folk," whose interests were neglected by a plantocracy that directed the war and were, to a certain extent, insulated from its most savage consequences.[29] There were indeed serious social tensions, although that is characteristic of all conflicts that place heavy demands on the home front. The respective weight to be placed on campaigning and on the home front can also be seen in debates over the reasons for German failure in World War I in 1918.

In the Civil War, the experience of occupied areas captured the more general social strain of the war, although only partly so, for a determination by some in these areas to continue resistance was both inherently divisive and made more so by the resulting harshness of occupation. This harshness focused on control over food supplies, which was control by destruction, confiscation, and allocation. Sherman's advancing troops drove this policy to the fore at a greater pace and in areas hitherto spared raiding, let alone occupation.

The Confederates now lacked a viable strategy, both military and political, and many soldiers primarily now sought to defend their homes, a form of strategic neutralism however much shaped by southern values. Security had been destroyed. Indeed, the war was to end in the campaigning season that followed the presidential election. The latter had essentially foreclosed Confederate strategy, which appeared to have shrunk to the task of Lee preserving the position around Petersburg and Richmond. This was one encouragement for the idea of grasping success by seizing or assassinating Lincoln.

As a major part of the developing politics that complemented Sherman, the Confederate attempt to use the army of Tennessee to mount a powerful riposte and regain the initiative was defeated at Franklin and then, more clearly, at Nashville where the heavily outnumbered Confederates broke under attack on 16 December and then retreated into Mississippi. Nashville had been a pivot of Union operations, but it no longer fulfilled this role at the level of grand strategy, although it was important to Union communications and, therefore, logistics. Its fall would greatly have complicated Union operations across a wide front, but in the south these could also rely on ports, notably New Orleans, and also Savannah once it was captured. This was similar to Wellington's use of northern Spanish ports in 1813–14, thus avoiding the need for a supply route back to the Portuguese frontier.

Again, however, there is a degree of hindsight at play. The fall of Nashville would have created many opportunities for disruption and thus for indirect assistance to the Confederate cause in the border states and across the south. It is far from clear, however, that the forces available to Hood would have permitted much in the way of exploitation. Meanwhile, the benefit to Sherman of Hood's absence during his advance had been considerable.

Confederate aspirations remained bold, but at least Nashville was a less unrealistic target than St. Louis, another key logistical center, and the destination of Major-General Sterling Price's invasion of Missouri that September. Price, a political general of energy only in quarrels and hopes, led a small force of 12,000, one that was particularly badly equipped and clearly inadequate. A former governor of Missouri, where he had been a major slaveholder, Price saw the conquest of that state as a key goal, not least with St. Louis offering a way to hit the Union in the Mississippi basin. He was unlucky in his opponents, Major-General William Rosecrans (the head of the Department of the Missouri) and Samuel Curtis (the commander of the army of the border formed by Rosecrans). Price's advance lacked dynamism and, instead of driving on St. Louis, which was probably far too strong a target but the disruption of which offered something, he focused on secondary positions in south-east Missouri, ultimately losing heavily in an unsuccessful attack on Fort Davidson on 27 September. Jefferson City, the state capital, on 7 October was too well defended, and, likewise, near Kansas City on 22 and 23 October, and Price's force was unable to prevail. At Westport on the 23 October, Price deployed many troops for whom he had no arms, an apt sign of a wider Confederate failure. Retreating southward, the Confederate army of Missouri reached shelter at Laynesport on 2 December.

Aside from its failure as a field force, this army had not coordinated well with the numerous Confederate guerrillas in Missouri, instead weakening them by drawing some into field action and by destroying the optimism and support networks of others. In context, scale, and causes, this was a very different failure to that of the Union in the Red River Campaign, which showed the range of possible factors at play in failure (a point that can also be made about success).

A sense of desperation was seen on 7 November when Jefferson Davis, in his annual address to Congress, pressed the need to assess arming slaves as soldiers, a theme advanced by some Confederate commanders from earlier on, for example Richard Ewell (a slaveholder) from July 1862. This idea greatly challenged the logic of slaveholder society and the attendant white supremacist ideology, and thus exacerbated tensions between slaveholders and others, the latter of whom were doing much of the fighting. Indeed, there was no dynamic behind the proposal, which, on 10 February 1865, as part of a more general Confederate maneuvering for peace terms, was to be introduced into Congress but was to be reliant on the consent of owners, many of whom were yet unwilling.[30] The slaveowners were well-represented in the Confederate Congress. This issue was a sign that Confederate society was unable to adapt to win the war. Ultimately, it went to war to preserve its way of life, but that way of life, at least in this instance, lessened the options for success. (The British proved more willing to arm slaves during the War of Independence.)

The year 1778 had seen the arrival in America of the Carlisle Peace Commission, the British government's attempt to negotiate a peace, part of a program that included the repeal of pre-war British legislation unwelcome to the Americans, such as the Massachusetts Government Act. The Peace Commission was authorized to offer self-rule, but, in response, the Continental Congress demanded a recognition of independence or the withdrawal of all troops. The Commission was not authorized to offer these terms, and the negotiations lapsed. The Clinton-Arbuthnot Peace Declaration of December 1780, a British offer of fresh negotiations, was also ignored. In contrast, although Lincoln acquiesced in Horace Greeley being sent in July 1864 as an envoy to Canada (admittedly with little authority) to discuss peace unofficially with Jacob Thompson and Cassius C. Clay, these negotiations were fruitless as the Confederates had no credentials. Indeed, there was no real equivalent in 1864 to the 1778 and 1780 attempts, although Democratic victory in the elections might have led in a different direction, a point also true if the Whig opposition had won the 1780 election in Britain. As the War of 1812 had also shown, political aspects repeatedly set the parameters for military counterparts, and through what did not happen as well as what did.

# 8. WAR CLOSE

On 8 February 1865, Richmond's *Daily Dispatch* was still very optimistic about the war, but this was scarcely realistic. In 1779, the War of Independence had broadened into a world war. Spain joined in on the French side, and the two powers prepared a major invasion of England, albeit without success. In 1865, in contrast, the Civil War came to an end and without evolving into an international conflict as would have happened had the victorious Union declared war on Britain (over Canada) or France (over Mexico). These might not have seemed likely given the pressure to end the war and demobilize, but these were seen as options at the time by many commentators. There was, however, no significant persons within the government calling for such action: the Republicans were not cut from the same cloth as the French Revolutionaries of the 1790s. Indeed, it was the Confederacy that was more interested in such adventurism.

Confederate troops were under pressure across the south. The Confederate armies continued operations but very much in response to their Union rivals. At Waynesboro on 2 March, the Shenandoah campaign was brought to an end when the remains of Jubal Early's force were defeated by cavalry under Brigadier General George Custer, who managed to combine a successful flanking with diversionary pressure on the Confederate center. With their backs to a river across which there were only two bridges, Early's force was broken by defeat and retreat. Union forces were able to raid south into Virginia before joining Grant near Petersburg.

In North Carolina, Johnston pulled together the remains of the army of Tennessee in an attempt to defeat part of Sherman's army and, in thus regaining the initiative, permit the Confederates to bring their two main field armies together. On 19 March at Bentonville, Johnston attacked a wing of Sherman's army, but the Union forces did not break and were eventually supported by reinforcements. During the following two days the outnumbered Johnston held his position, while Sherman chose not to fight a battle he did not need. On the night of the 21–22 March the Confederates withdrew. Nevertheless, Bentonville showed the continued Confederate ability to mount attacks and the willingness to take losses.

On 28 March Lincoln met Grant, Sherman, and David Porter, the commander of the north Atlantic blockading squadron, on the steamer *River Queen* at Grant's headquarters at City Point, Virginia, on the James River. Lincoln said he hoped to avoid another major battle, and wanted the war ended before Congress met in December and might put him under pressure over terms to offer the south. He was concerned about Confederate guerrilla warfare, and Johnston's ability to move south from North Carolina and continue the war. Lincoln emphasized peace and subsequent conciliation.

The *River Queen* had already seen on 3 February the unsuccessful Hampton Roads Conference where Lincoln, Seward, and Confederate representatives had failed to agree because Lincoln rejected an armistice unless the Confederacy first accepted the recognition of the Union. This was unacceptable to the Confederate commissioners. The idea for joint military action against Mexico was also of no interest to Lincoln, who had earlier rejected Jefferson Davis's proposal for a meeting between Grant and Lee.

Grant had initially planned for Sherman's forces to join his by means of transport by sea, a lengthy process but one that would not see losses to enemy action. Sherman, instead, wanted to move north from Savannah by land, thus putting pressure on South Carolina and fulfilling the "hard hand" approach. A concentration near Richmond in accordance with Grant's plan would have helped against Lee, but would have also given the Confederates more room to maneuver into the south, which Lincoln wished to thwart. Sherman's march northward was to be coordinated with an amphibious attack on Fort Fisher, guarding the mouth of the Cape Fear River, which fell on 15 January.

The focus for 1865 is generally on Grant's operations in Virginia, notably the Petersburg campaign from June 1864 to March 1865, but far more was involved. Sherman's advance threatened Lee's rear in Virginia, and was later praised by the military commentator Basil Liddell Hart as an instance of the indirect approach he advocated in the 1920s for British strategy. Columbia, South Carolina, was occupied by Sherman's forces on 17 February and largely ruined by (accidental) fire, while Wilmington fell on 22 February, its garrison pulled back due to the risk of encirclement, and North Carolina was entered the following month.

Once Lee had left Richmond, Sherman advanced not to attack him but rather to drive Johnston to surrender, for Grant saw the "rebel armies" as the remaining "strategic points." Lee's surrender was followed by Johnston and Beauregard at a meeting in Greensboro, North Carolina, on 13 April, a rejection of Davis's wish to continue the war.

Raleigh was occupied the same day. This advance contributed to the situation in which Lee was defeated without his army being destroyed. The Confederate forces lost many men through desertion, in part to protect their homes. This was not only from Union regulars but also from partisans and guerrillas, numbers swelled by blacks, as well as from escaped prisoners-of-war and deserters.

So too was there pressure on the coasts. With Charleston challenged by Sherman's march through South Carolina, its defenders evacuated. Its position challenged by Sherman's arrival at Savannah, Charleston's defenders evacuated the city and its forts on the night of 17 February, blowing up their ironclads and the forts. The mayor surrendered the city on 18 February. On 14 April, the Union flag that had been lowered there in 1861 was formally raised over the ruined Fort Sumter. Meanwhile, Farragut's squadron provided support to forces under Frederick Steele and E.R.S. Camby who in early April captured Spanish Fort and Blakely across the bay from Mobile before entering that city on 18 April, one of the only major cities left in Confederate hands.

In their different ways, Sherman and Grant ensured that the uncertainty of war undermined the Confederacy, for they managed risk and uncertainty as their opponents came to experience its weight in 1864. For example, construction on the South and North Alabama Railroad had begun in 1859 and continued during the war, with slaves used for the purpose. The railroad delivered wood (for charcoal) and coal to the Shelby Iron Works, which had been built in 1844, with a rolling mill following in 1860 that was able to produce finished bar iron. A larger furnace stack was built in 1863. The iron was used for constructing thc

Confederate warships at Selma, including the *Huntsville*, *Tennessee,* and *Tuscaloosa*, as well as for Confederate railroad rolling stock (only for the works to be destroyed in March 1865 by raiding Union troops under James Wilson). This was part of a wider devastation of ironworks in the region, as well as of the University of Alabama. Heavily outnumbered Confederate defenders were defeated at Montevallo, Plantersville, and Selma. Wilson pressed on to take Montgomery on 12 April. The home front was literally collapsing, and this collapse was closely linked to the failure of the Confederate armies, which were diminishing through desertion.[1]

The tempo of Union operations exploited the uncertainty of conflict and directed it against the Confederacy's military as well as its sociopolitical underpinnings, and in so far as was possible pressure was applied simultaneously across the front of operations. Sherman's advance was also the culmination of the long series of Union triumphs in the western theatre. In 1862 and 1863, these had not prevented Lee from advancing in, and from, Virginia and to a considerable extent it had been possible for the Confederacy to trade space in the west for time with which to attack in the east. This potentially war-winning southern formula had failed in the east, not across the Appalachians, but it was only afterward that the Union forces were able to exploit their success in the west in order to attack what could otherwise have been a defense in depth in the east.

This exploitation of northern success was in part a matter of a psychological shift. Grant brought a conviction that victory could be won, a confidence that reflected the repeated Union successes in the west. This conviction replaced the earlier hesitation of many Union commanders in the east, a hesitation born of a caution, if not a lack of confidence, that had been seen with McClellan's deliberative generalship and been encouraged by Lee's attacks.[2] Conversely, Grant's reputation benefited from the usually poor Confederate generalship he had faced in the west.[3]

To John Keegan, Grant was the commander who understood the nature of space in American war-making, whereas Lee, like McClellan, allowed himself to be confined to a European-scale theatre of operations.[4] In practice, there was a diversity of military environments in both Europe and America. Grant was impressive not so much because of his understanding of space as thanks to his dominance of time, a characteristic he shared with Moltke in 1866 and 1870. At the same time, Grant was greatly helped by the possibilities he had and the constraints facing Lee. In particular, the latter was expected to protect Richmond, but this political goal left him exposed to Grant's ability to vary the axis of advance, and notably to advance past Richmond to Petersburg (extending the degree to which Lee was fixed and exposed to attack). In turn, Grant eventually advanced south of Petersburg, avoiding the trenches there and instead, as Sherman had done at Atlanta, turned to cut off Lee's surviving rail links. Meanwhile, the U.S. Military Railroad, a government agency authorized by Congress in January 1862, repaired railroad line and laid new track to help Grant.

Ultimately, Lee ran out of time and space, for, having left Richmond and Petersburg, Lee was pursued and obliged to surrender at Appomattox. Lee's retreat from Richmond was that of a hungry and tired army. Leaving the city on the night of 2 April, Lee sought to join the Confederate army in North Carolina, but this goal was perceived and blocked by Grant who was able to deploy far larger forces. On 6 April, Lee's rearguard was easily defeated at Sayler's Creek. Grant proposed Lee's surrender the following day, but Lee on the 8 April, instead, proposed negotiations. This was unacceptable and meant continued fighting, but at Appomattox Courthouse a Confederate attack on blocking Union forces was defeated. This led Lee to meet Grant on the 9 April and agree to surrender, which was formally observed on 12 April.

This was an event as pregnant for America's future as the British surrender at Yorktown in 1781, and, like Yorktown, brought great prestige, both domestic and international. This was due not only to the act, but also to the manner of the act. The example given in the New World was important to republican and liberal causes elsewhere, notably in neighboring Mexico (but not only).

A very different American geopolitics to that which was created in 1865 was presented by Jefferson Davis who was determined to fight on after Lee's surrender to Grant. The terms, however, were lenient, which was a product of Lincoln's drive for amnesty, as well as the pragmatic need to encourage a wider end to opposition. The surrendering Confederates were paroled not imprisoned, which, again, reflected necessity as well as the goal—namely, the move to reconstruction.[5] The peace, like the war, was to see such attempts to reconcile, or at least align, goals and necessity.

The previous July, Davis had responded to the terms offered in Lincoln's amnesty proclamation of December 1863 by declaring, "We are fighting for Independence—and that, or extermination, we will have …. You may emancipate every Negro in the Confederacy, but we will be free. We will govern ourselves … if we have to see every Southern plantation sacked, and every Southern city in flames."[6] He had lost touch with military and political reality. To that end, although, having been told on 2 May that a new army could not be assembled, he officially dissolved the Confederate government on 5 May. Davis headed for the Trans-Mississippi region. He was captured near Irwinville, Georgia, on 10 May by a detachment of the 4th Michigan cavalry. Because Jefferson had on his wife's overcoat he was inaccurately described as having attempted to flee in her clothes.

In the event, greatly influenced by Lee's surrender, there was to be no further fighting by the other armies. Lee's surrender left three major Confederate armies still active and, more chaotically, a general air across the south of confusion and instability that threatened continued chaos. Managing these armies and bringing them to surrender would clearly be the means to bring clarity and order, not least in stopping the overlap of skirmishing and brigandage. To do so speedily was also necessary in order both to reduce the burden of the war for the Union states and to provide a basis for moving forward politically. This task was highly complicated, at least in the short term, when Lincoln was assassinated on 14 April in Ford's Theatre in Washington by John Wilkes Booth.

The three main Confederate forces were those under Joseph Johnston, newly appointed to command the Department of North Carolina and Southern Virginia, who could offer only a weak shadow to Sherman; that under Richard Taylor in Alabama, Mississippi, and east Louisiana; and that under Edmund Kirby Smith across Mississippi. All were feeling the pressure from Union forces, notably Taylor from the Union cavalry in Alabama, and were affected by a lack of funds for pay or supplies. The *Chicago Tribune* of 17 April commented:

> Jeff. Davis will undoubtedly attempt to revive the courage of the rebels over the assassination of Lincoln, but they are already too badly whipped to make it of any avail. Without a seaport, without artillery, cavalry, arms or clothing, if they are vigorously pressed up by Sherman they cannot long make even a show of resistance. We look for a short, sharp and speedy campaign in North Carolina [against Johnston]….

Aside from the questionable nature of fighting on, there was also the problem of securing mutually acceptable terms, which for the Union meant the template of those granted Lee. The speed with which this was accomplished was surprising given uncertain command lines, poor communications, and Davis' drive to continue the conflict, while there was also the problem of tensions on the Union side over negotiations, particularly between Edwin Stanton, the secretary of war, and Sherman.

That a series of settlements was reached was a testimony not only to Confederate weakness but also by a sense of despair accentuated by the cascading examples of failure following the fall of Richmond and Appomattox.[7] At the same time, the process was scarcely problem-free, and the attempt to negotiate an end to hostilities in Texas failed in mid-March.

Johnston surrendered to Sherman at Durham Station, North Carolina, on 20 April. Johnston had met Sherman on 17 and 18 April, the two men agreeing on an armistice, and that southern state governments would be recognized upon giving an oath of allegiance while southern property and political rights would be guaranteed, and southerners granted legal amnesty. This was a political reach Sherman was not authorized to make, as Grant had been authorized only to discuss military matters. Sherman had promised to do what he did not—namely, offer Appomattox terms. Sherman's agreement was rejected unanimously by President Andrew Johnson and his cabinet.

Under the threat of renewed conflict, and with the Confederate army dissolving through desertion, the two generals met again on 26 April and drafted terms that were approved. This surrender, which was supplemented by an agreement on 27 April providing terms for the paroled troops (including transport home), encompassed the Confederate forces in the Carolinas, Georgia, and Florida, about 89,000 troops. This was the largest surrender of the war.

On 4 May, Taylor, who commanded the last Confederate force east of the Mississippi (a force of nearly 9,000 troops) surrendered at Citronelle, Alabama, to Major-General Canby. This enabled Lincoln's replacement, President Andrew Johnson, on 10 May, to declare armed resistance as virtually at an end. In the Trans-Mississippi, Kirby Smith's army surrendered on 26 May at Galveston.

The last clash, the Battle of Palmito Ranch, occurred near Brownsville, Texas, on 12–13 May. The reasons for the battle, which breached the *de facto* agreement reached earlier in the year in south Texas for no further conflict, are controversial. A search for glory and horses on the part of the Union commander has been alleged, whereas his Confederate counterpart did not wish to surrender to a black force and wanted to stop the confiscation of cotton in the area that was ready for movement into Mexico. Confederate artillery was important to the Union defeat. Yet this was ultimately a minor clash. The Confederacy's currency had collapsed with its government, and the prospects for continued resistance by this army were terrible.[8]

On 23 June, at Doaksville, Oklahoma, Stand Watie (a Cherokee who commanded Native forces on the Confederate side) was the last Confederate general to surrender, while President Johnson declared the blockade ended. This was a rapid close to the war, and certainly so compared to the pace of things in 1864, a year of overall Union success. The last surrender was the CSS *Shenandoah*, on 6 November 1865 at Liverpool. Captain James Waddell surrendered the ship to the British government, and the crew were granted parole.

The prospect of further conventional operations therefore came to an end. There was also to be no guerrilla warfare such as the one anticipated in 1862 by the French envoy after a trip to Richmond, and proposed by Davis in a proclamation after the fall of Richmond (and this very much suggests a new spatial understanding of the south and of the war-zone):

> "Relieved from the necessity of guarding cities and particular points … with an army free to move from point to point …

> ]operating in the interior of our own country, where supplies are more accessible, and where the foe will be far removed from his own base … nothing is now needed to render our triumph certain but the exhibition of our own unquenchable resolve."[9]

This was not an alien concept as guerrilla warfare had already been seen in areas, notably southern Appalachia, where terrain was difficult and the number of regulars limited.[10] In addition, the last stages of the Mexican American War had shown the problems the American occupying forces confronted due to continued opposition,[11] and the same was even more true for the French in Mexico.[12]

Yet, despite the Partisan Ranger Act of 1861, the Confederate political and military leadership had proved largely unwilling to encourage guerrilla warfare that, while particularly widespread and important in Appalachia and in the Missouri-Kansas region, was not so common in the crucial war zones. Furthermore, some of what is now termed guerrilla warfare, with the misleading implication that it was not waged by regulars, can better be described as irregular warfare by regulars, particularly engaged in raiding activities, a form of what was otherwise known as "small war." "Mosby's Rangers" (the 43rd Battalion Virginia Cavalry) that operated in Virginia in 1863–5, was a Confederate force of this type, although the practice of adopting civilian disguise led to the execution of Mosby's men captured out of uniform. The Union forces, indeed, were able to counter these methods, both by defensive means, especially blockhouses and patrols, and by action designed to provide the exemplary threat of retribution and/or to find and engage those directly involved (but Mosby was never captured).[13]

Lee and his fellow generals ignored Davis's call. Such a policy was antipathetical to their understanding of military and social order, unacceptable under both heads, and would jeopardize any peace and reconciliation. Unlike Davis, they put their egos aside. As a result, the most bitter conflict in American history came to a more abrupt end than might have been anticipated. As in the English Civil War of 1642–6, there was an obvious exit strategy through the decision to surrender. As a consequence of this possibility, which rested on a clear command structure, the pursuit of the factors necessary to secure these surrenders were sensible tasks in the English and American Civil Wars. Indeed, Grant in this respect can be compared to Sir Thomas Fairfax, the commander of the New Model Army that brought victory to the Parliamentarians. Established in 1645, the New Model was a product of Parliamentary dissatisfaction with the existing military structure, and the move to greater vigor in the eastern theatre under Grant in 1864 might be seen as a parallel.

In the absence of clear command structures and military discipline, it becomes far harder to secure the end of hostilities; and this poses serious problems for combat in most civil wars. Looked at differently, the Civil War in part subsequently re-erupted in areas like Mississippi during the reconstruction, as with the actions of white militia in the Colfax massacre in 1873 and street fighting in New Orleans. At any rate, with about 145,000 men marching, the Union forces were able to stage the Grand Review of the Armies at Washington on 23–4 May 1865.[14] Maybe five times that number had been killed in the war.

# 9. AFTERMATH

The aftermath was all around them, but not always readily visible. There were the survivors, many using titles or wearing medals reflecting their service, and numerous amputees, with all the issues and thoughts this condition provoked. Others had less visible wounds, especially gunshot wounds that were covered by clothing, intestinal problems (particularly chronic diarrhea), and mental issues, notably what would now be called PTSD. Continuing wartime official conduct, these were handled far less sympathetically, notably in terms of pensions and medical care, as well as postwar social and economic stigma. Disability was widely treated as unmanly and unworthy.[1] Combat trauma was too often masked by victory in the north, but there were long term mental and emotional costs there as well as in the defeated south.[2] At the same time, large numbers of veterans made the transition to civilian life, often finding identity, worth, and pride in their wartime service,[3] and many were helped by the stoical nature of culture and the role of Providentialist assumptions.

The 1864 Presidential election had cemented the political coherence of the north and, as a consequence, created the basis for a political settlement that would entail not only victory over the Confederacy but also a postwar American order able to intimidate other powers in the New World. At the same time, the very decision not to attack the French in Mexico or, even more dangerously, the British in Canada reflected the role of politics. Indeed, the impact of politics on strategy emerged with increasing influence throughout the Civil War, as strategy likewise played a greater role in politics.

These relationships were structural as well as contingent. For example, the very cause of the rebellion helped lessen any chance of success, as the incubus of "state rights" proved a systemic weakness for southern central government. As a very different aspect of the structural character of politics, the frequent removal of Union commanders was a product not only of failures but also of the inherent tensions in the command system, with the divisions over goals and means exacerbating factional and personal differences in the army. At the same time, there was a great number of political elements. These included the multiple tensions between national and state institutions, as well as rivalries between particular armies. To a degree, the political and military divisions of the wartime Union were sustained, although in a different context, from 1865 onward, a period when conflict rather than combat was the social and political reality. Indeed, while military occupation during reconstruction lasted longer than the war, this presence was another aspect of the occupation of Confederate lands during the war itself. The task was made easier by the surrender of the Confederate armies in 1865 but also more difficult because most of the Union army left the service that year. The latter situation made it hard to lend strength to implement those policies that were to be followed, and this encouraged significant adaptation to local circumstances, including with respect to the participation and role of the conquered opponent.

Attitudes among the generals in command of the army in the south during reconstruction were very divided in their views notably toward blacks and Confederates. There were also contrasts in skill in managing circumstances and in political acumen (that is, in being the politicians that most generals did not wish to be).

In racial terms, Union victory in 1865 led initially to the overthrow of the previous system of exclusion, subordination, and oppression. On 31 January, the Thirteenth Amendment was passed, outlawing slavery. In 1866, over the veto of President Andrew Johnson who sought a rapid return to normality through the conciliation of the south, Congress passed the Civil Rights Act giving full citizenship to all born or naturalized in America, and voting rights to all male citizens. Blacks thus gained legal equality. The provisions of this legislation became the Fourteenth Amendment, which was ratified in 1868. The radicalizing nature of the war made it possible to envisage improvements on the provisions decreed by the Founding Fathers. Moreover, the Reconstruction Acts of 1867 dissolved the southern state governments, which had passed racist "Black Codes" designed to limit the effect of slave emancipation; and, instead, reintroduced federal control that gave the army the task of preserving this control against local opposition. Emancipation also affected the slaves owned by Native American tribes, such as the slave-owning Choctaw, who signed treaties with the Confederacy and fought alongside them.

The antipathy of southerners, many of whom were suffused with grievances due to the war and its hardships, was made clear by the joyous response by many to Lincoln's assassination, a response that shocked northerners. In the south, the American army's war powers remained in operation, including the ability to enact martial law and suspend civil courts. This was the background for reconstruction, one further stirred by the final representatives from the Confederacy not regaining their Congressional seats until 1871.[4] The various Confederate states had their representatives admitted to Congress beginning in 1866. By 1870, only Georgia still had no Congressional representation. With control over policy seized by radical Republicans who impeached Johnson, reconstruction was primarily about reunion rather than reconciliation. This was understandably so, as the southern will to fight had translated into a will to resist. The war created a southern nationalism in defeat.

The army was confronted, in the chaos, poverty, and devastation of the close and aftermath of the war, by the strength of white southern belief in their own superiority, and the foundation of the Ku Klux Klan, a Confederate veterans' movement, in 1866, was followed by several thousand lynchings (although not all were by the Klan because there were multiple white supremacist groups).[5]

However, the potential challenge to northern control was lessened by a kind of Confederate diaspora, including to Brazil, Cuba, British Honduras, and especially Mexico, where some fought for Maximilian, although most of these men came back to America after he failed. In another important aspect of the diaspora, many southerners migrated westward.

In the south, due to demobilization and the challenges of conflict in the west with Native Americans, the federal military presence was modest, and the small army was not in a position to support the one-party rule of reconstruction once it was challenged by widespread violence against blacks. Furthermore, the generals were divided, and Democratic leaders typically lacked the zeal of Republican counterparts.[6] Reconciliation at the national level was seen with the good obituaries Lee received in the northern press in 1870, while in 1898 it became acceptable for surviving Confederate generals to be made American generals.

By 1877, the Republican governments in the south had been overthrown, in part by the threat of mob violence, in every state bar in Florida, Louisiana, and South Carolina. It was only in these states that the troops sent to support reconstruction remained. The situation was resolved as the result of a political compromise following the disputed presidential election of 1876. The withdrawal from the three states were crucial, and the Republican candidate, Rutherford B. Hayes, won the election over Democrat Samuel Tilden, only in return for withdrawing the troops, which, in turn, led to the fall of the three Republican state governments. Like Lincoln, a midwesterner and a former Whig with firm anti-slavery views, Hayes had served bravely, was wounded several times, and was breveted to major-general. He was changed by the war and embraced its impact on slavery and race relations, but disapproved of governments that "rested on bayonets." As president, Hayes was willing to use troops against railroad strikes in 1877.

The blacks were left to celebrate emancipation, not least with "Juneteenth," gatherings first held in 1866 in Texas, marking the day in 1865 (19 June) when Major-General Gordon Granger, commander of the District of Texas, arrived in Galveston to deliver the news of the Emancipation Proclamation, and formally recognized in Texas from 1938. In 2021, it became a federal holiday. Blacks, however, were very much second-class citizens in political, social, and economic terms, a situation that persisted until the 1950s and 1960s, only ending when federal pressure resumed. Blacks suffered from the continuation of racism, and in the north as well as the south, irrespective of the end of slavery.

There was also the decision of many of the remaining southern elite to maintain an agricultural society with oppressive labor relations in which they remained at the top of the socio-economic pyramid,[7] rather than to join the new industrial order whose urbanization and mechanization would threaten their superiority in the south. This decision accentuated regional divisions in America, but these rested on many factors, including the availability of liquidity. The south, for example, was not an area of major rail investment, pre- or post-war, certainly comparable to the northeast and the midwest, but railways were important to the south's postwar economic role of providing raw materials for northern industries. A major item was cotton, and the rail system thus served to maintain the socio-political order in the south, with blacks restricted after the failure of reconstruction by disfranchisement and sharecropping. A much blunter demonstration of white control, in the south and elsewhere, was provided by the disproportionate number of blacks in prison and the widespread use of penal labor, notably for public construction, in the late nineteenth and early twentieth century (but also thereafter). This situation has not disappeared, but it has changed.

The treatment of blacks was also seen in the presentation of the war, with their role in the Union forces seriously underplayed. This was the case in the fifty-year Gettysburg reunion that stressed reconciliation between Confederate and Union troops, but only among white soldiers.[8] The year 1914 also saw the unveiling of the Confederate monument at Arlington National Cemetery, with the speech by Bennett Young, Commander of the United Confederate Veterans, who declared the cause a "just" one. Woodrow Wilson, the Democrat President from 1913 to 1921, who unveiled the monument, was a southerner who imposed segregation in government agencies and in 1913, at the fiftieth anniversary of Gettysburg, declared there that the Union and the Confederacy had "found one another again as brothers and comrades in arms." The monument was removed in December 2023. Memorialization had been eased from 1891 onward (beginning with Chickamauga and Chattanooga) by the designation by Congress of battlefield reservations.

The treatment of black soldiers was an aspect of reconciliation, a worthy and necessary goal, but one that might include a wide variety of definitions. Reconciliation was pursued from the outset with the terms of Appomattox offering a way forward, not least as it included in its scope (and the model it set for other Confederate armies) a wide tranche of southern males. This was immediately significant in terms of the possibilities for continued resistance. There was also the immediate impact of penalties for leading Confederates, in a context that called for pressure for action. In June 1865, a federal judged began proceedings against Lee, who was indeed indicted. Convinced that he was covered by the Appomattox agreement, Lee turned to Grant. The latter interceded with President Johnson and the proceedings were dropped, which helped make the postwar order appear less harsh. Jefferson Davis was imprisoned for two years in Fort Monroe, Virginia, initially in harsh circumstances, but was not tried despite a resolution by the House of Representatives in June 1866 for a treason trial. The government feared that he might be acquitted on the grounds that secession had meant he was not a citizen. On Christmas Day in 1868, President Johnson granted amnesty and pardon to all who had taken part in the rebellion.

It was only in 1998 that the "Spirit of Freedom," the African American Civil War Memorial, was unveiled in Washington. Yet, in the second half of the war, the recruitment of blacks for the Union army was a symbol to, and for, the Confederacy of what amounted to total war. Moreover, the recruitment of all-black regiments for the army, numbering more than 120,000 men, was also a major operational help to the Union. Black troops were frequently employed as labor, notably in logistics. However, they were also given combat jobs, the action at Fort Wagner in July 1863 proving a key watershed, and sometimes made up the bulk of a force. The symbolic power of Black troops was shown in February 1865 when the forces that occupied Charleston, the site of thc outbreak of the war, included black troops recruited from former Carolina slaves and a reply to the murderous treatment of black Union soldiers by the Confederates, as at Fort Pillow in 1864, where many men who had surrendered were slaughtered in a particularly vicious instance of the harsh conflict in Tennessee. This was controversial at the time and also subsequently when southern writers rejected well-justified claims of terrible Confederate behavior. This rejection was given added force because the Confederate commander, Nathan Bedford Forrest, subsequently played a formative role in the Ku Klux Klan.[9]

The huge debt left by the Civil War did much to limit American expansionism other than in North America, as did the very rapid post-war demobilization, and the problems of trying to contain white violence in the southern states. This was notably so of New Orleans, where the army intervened to prevent a pogrom of black citizens in 1866. The Knights of the White Camelia were active from the late 1860s, and the White League, which claimed to fight "armed negro militia and metropolitans," sought to seize control in the 1870s. In 1873, in the Colfax Massacre, in Colfax, Louisiana, about 150 Black people were killed. In 1874, in "the Battle of Liberty Place," the White League, in an attempt to wrest control of the state from Vermont-born William Pitt Kellogg (the Republican Governor from 1873 to 1877) occupied several key city-center sites, only for the revolt to be quashed by federal troops. In an ultimately futile attempt to impose a reconstruction that enabled civil rights for black citizens, federal troops remained in Florida and Louisiana until 1877.

However, there was not sufficient federal or local support for the reconstruction to overcome the challenge of white supremacism. Black people lost their hope of land, and many became sharecroppers or worked on estates where they had formerly been slaves. In 1896, the *Plessy v Ferguson* Supreme Court judgment affirmed segregation legislation. Politics in New Orleans by then was very much a competition between two factions of white Democrats: the Ring, which was based on immigrants and organized labor and led by the corrupt machine boss John Fitzpatrick, versus reforming businessmen.

In 1868, the Fourteenth Amendment to the Constitution had guaranteed citizenship and equality for anyone born in the United States, while the Reconstruction Constitution of Louisiana had decreed black male suffrage and equal rights for all to public education and accommodation. A black man, Oscar Dunn, had become Lieutenant-Governor of Louisiana, an outcome that appeared fantastical by 1896. In 1898, white Democrats took firm control of the legislature and introduced a new constitution that segregated public schools and imposed poll taxes and literary tests as qualifications for voting. In the aftermath, as in 1868–80, many blacks left Louisiana where limited opportunities were accompanied by a marked recalibration of control and oppression. After Kellogg, no Republican was elected governor of Louisiana until 1980. It is understandable that in his "I have a dream" speech, delivered on the steps of the Lincoln Memorial in Washington on 28 August 1963, Martin Luther King Jr. declared that, despite the Emancipation Proclamation of 1863, "One hundred years later, the life of the Negro is still sadly crippled by the manacles of segregation and the chains of discrimination."

The fate of the south was important but less so later than prior to the Civil War because America as a whole had been greatly altered.

Constitutional amendments expanded the authority and power of the United States, which was now a singular and not a plural noun just as the country was presented now as a nation and not a union. The expansion of agencies seen in the north during the Civil War was not automatically extended, notably with no need to support a large military and no conscription. Yet, the Republicans, many ex-army, who would become president over the following decades had a psychological and practical commitment to the country as a whole. The entrepreneurial capitalism that was to characterize America as a whole, and rely on free labor, was a lasting legacy of the war. Mark Twain was to observe that the war had "changed the politics of a people, transformed the social life of half the country, and wrought so profoundly upon the entire national character …."

It had done more. The Civil War had changed America's geography. Furthermore, the American west provided an opportunity for post-war Americans both to shape a mythos of the Civil War as well as to forget the war amidst new distractions. Veterans such as Buffalo Bill and Wild Bill Hickok helped settle, portray, and sell the west to easterners, and there were nationally famous bushwhackers, like Jesse James, Cole Younger, the Mason-Henry Gang, and William McWaters, and cowboys, among whom former black soldiers were significantly over-represented. Former soldiers and officers also frequently sought opportunities abroad. Many Union and Confederate officers ended up in the Khedive's army in Egypt, part of a wider process.[10]

With memorialization being an issue from the outset, for example a national military cemetery established on Robert E. Lee's estate at Arlington in June 1864, the Civil War became a subject of a different form of contention, indeed mythmaking.[11] This has continued to the present, but was already quite apparent as veterans explained their war and sought thereby to justify their goals and experiences.[12] At one level, this was very much a presentation of respective merits of north and south, and one that perpetuated, in a very different context, the serious differences of wartime.[13] White southerners frequently presented the struggle with reference to religious themes. William Bennett, who had served as a chaplain, emphasized religious revival among the Confederate forces. The "Lost Cause" (a term originated in 1866), the account of the Civil

War that presented the southern cause as just, heroic, and not centered on slavery, was not a constant. It changed over time, becoming a broad cultural, intellectual, and indeed social movement.

Yet, there was also a quest for more specific explanations and that led to often bitter quarrels between the memorialists on each side. A variety of factors played a role, notably personal experience, partisanship by, and on behalf of, individual generals, armies, units, and states (for example Virginia advocates), and the pressure to refute claims that were seen as challenging. Alongside these came the theme of honor, which had been so important at the time[14] and became, if anything, more significant subsequently as the pressure of wartime exigencies eased. For several decades after the war, there was also the relationship between wartime fame and postwar careers,[15] notably in politics. Honor and vindictiveness all continued to play a role.

Memorialization of the war was heavily political, with five Union generals (Grant 1869–77, Hayes 1877–81, Garfield 1881, Arthur 1881–5, and Harrison 1889–93) and one Union soldier (McKinley 1897–1901) becoming presidents. All were Republicans. The only Democrat, who was a lawyer in Buffalo at the start of the war, was New Jersey born Grover Cleveland (1885–9, 93–7), had paid for a substitute under the Conscription Act of 1863. (The Polish immigrant he paid, George Benninsky, survived the war.) Republicans used their role in the war to justify their claim to guide the nation, while Democrats held onto their anger. (Harry Truman's mother refused to set foot in Lincoln's bedroom in the White House.) Both sides were accused of "waving the bloody shirt" to rally support.

Union victory was also marked in the erection of monuments. Washington became full of equestrian statues of generals. Victory was also marked in the celebration of anniversaries, especially Memorial Day, when graves were decorated, and speeches delivered.[16]

The Civil War was made more vivid on the screen, notably by *Gone with the Wind* (1939), the Ken Burns' Civil War television series of 1990, and the 1993 film adaptation of Michael Shaara's novel about Gettysburg, *The Killer Angels* (1974). *Gone With the Wind* was originally a lengthy 1936 novel by Margaret Mitchell, the top fiction bestseller in America in 1936 and 1937. In it the destructiveness of Sherman's march is a theme, as is southern survival, and the book's portrayal of blacks has been a matter of contention. In 2020, Donald Trump observed, in attacking the Academy Awards at a campaign rally, "Can we get, like, *Gone with the Wind* back, please?"[17] *Gods and Generals* (2003), the film adaptation of Jeffrey Shaara's novel of 1996, was a prequel to Michael Shaara's work, and provided an account sympathetic to Lee and Jackson. There are pro-Union accounts but many, while good, are less influential.[18]

More recently, contention over the Civil War has played a major role in America's "culture wars," for example in bitter disputes over statues, as in Richmond, over the flying of Confederate flags, and with the naming of military installations. Confederate flags were waved when the Capitol was stormed on 6 January 2020. Divisions over the causes, course, and consequences of the war sit heavy, with dissent clear, for example, in contrasting views of the cause of surrender in 1865.[19] The respective role of slavery and states' rights in causing the war continues to be a point of dispute. In 2000, Congressional discussion of the National Park Service's treatment of Civil War sites saw Representative Jesse Jackson Jr. and others complain that many sites lacked appropriate contextualization and, specifically, there was often "missing vital information about the role that the institution of slavery played in causing the American Civil War." The role of these divisions in America's regional politics has become more insistent since the rise of the Republican party in the south and of the south among the Republicans. There is a continuing pattern of commemorating the southern effort in this conflict without drawing attention to slavery as an issue. George Allen, Republican governor of Virginia from 1994 to 1998, declared a Confederate History Month in that state in 1995, 1996, and 1997. Allen proclaimed the Civil War as "a four-year struggle for independence, sovereign rights and local government control." In turn, Mark Warner, the Democratic governor from 2002–6 was unenthusiastic about backing the idea of a Confederate History Month, only for Bob McDonnell, the next Republican governor (2010–2014), to support it in 2010, the year in which there was a Secession Gala in Charleston to celebrate the 150$^{th}$ anniversary of South Carolina's decision to declare independence. Initially, McDonnell did not mention slavery, but he was finally obliged to accept that slavery "has left a stain on the soul of this state and nation." Similarly, Georgia's State Senate supported April as Confederate History Month, with support for tourism being a key rationale and slavery pushed into the background. In 2022, Alabama, Mississippi, North Carolina, and South Carolina still celebrated Confederate Memorial Day.[20]

Ironically, the Republicans of the Civil War were very different, a point that could have a political resonance, as in Steven Spielberg's film *Lincoln* (2012), which was a critical and commercial success. Focusing on early 1865 and the passage of the Thirteenth Amendment abolishing slavery, this film was an account that was surprising for Americans as it showed the political horse-trading by Lincoln necessary for the legislation to pass through the House of Representatives. This account provides an implicit means to defend Barack Obama, the first Black President (2009–17), and to present him as the culmination of American history, and thus as a pattern for the future. Obama himself praised the film. Furthermore, by depicting Lincoln's opponents critically, a harsh light was cast, by implication, on Obama's opponents. That Lincoln was a Republican, as were Obama's opponents, served to indicate that that party had changed its role, and made it appear unworthy of its heritage.

Spielberg himself faced controversy, and for reasons that would not have excited great concern in 1865. The film has been criticized for marginalizing the role of blacks in their own emancipation, a key issue in the case of agency. For example, Frederick Douglass (c. 1817–95), a former slave and prominent abolitionist who was a confidante of Lincoln, was ignored. Yet, the film works for many Americans as a hymn to the USA: it provides a hero with whom it is possible to engage, and through whom development can be understood and a pattern for the future advanced.

As a reminder that varied, as well as overlapping, accounts of the past are possible, Lincoln was differently treated in another medium in 2012, with Vincent Desiderio's painting *Preservation of the Spirit*, which was commissioned by the Abraham Lincoln Foundation to commemorate the 150th anniversary of The Union League of Philadelphia (a body founded to support the Union war-effort). The painting's main focus is not Lincoln himself, but, somewhat more powerfully, a representation of Lincoln in the form of a white, rider-less horse, boots facing backward, the manner in which Lincoln's horse appeared during his funeral procession in April 1865. With a reach to the modern viewer much different from that of Spielberg's film, the painting shows members of the American military from the Civil War to modern times marching across the landscape. Associating this with the institution in question, rather like a medieval triptych or chronicle, the military are joined by founding members of the League as well as more contemporary, representative members, including an African American and two women.

The aftermath of the Civil War has continued to the present, but not at the same levels of intensity across America. In particular there is far less of an interest and commitment in the north than in the south, a change that has particularly developed over the last sixty years. This has been linked to a differing regional response to Vietnam and its aftermath. There is also the degree to which the "Lost Cause" account of Confederate defeat is one that essentially rests on southern identity, including what was planted in the experience of reconstruction and after, rather than solely on a reading of the war itself. Yet that reading is potent, as in the account of Sherman's advance through Georgia.[21] American "populism," initially a southern and western phenomenon, owes much to the anti-authoritarian legacy of the Civil War in the south.

The very nomenclature of the war continues to reveal differences and pose problems. For example, the U.S. Army University Press includes in its relevant work a "Publisher's Note on the Use of Civil War Terms":

> … the legacy of that war is still at the forefront of our national conversation … the traditional terms to describe the opposing sides, North and South, are only used for grammatical variety, as they ascribe generalities that certainly do not apply…. The Army University Press acknowledges that political alliance, albeit an alliance in rebellion, by allowing the use of the terms "Confederate"….[22]

That there is still no agreement is a suitable postscript to the war and, indeed, an important and instructive feature of its aftermath.

# 10. CONCLUSIONS

The war is far from alone among nineteenth-century conflicts in that not only is it difficult to judge their modernity, but also the competence of the protagonists; although in the case of the Civil War there was, as an explanation of the latter, the unprecedented nature of the struggle. It is then scarcely surprising that there were no adequate preparations. At the same time, the war revealed a lack of appropriate strategic, operational, and tactical doctrine. Yet this was also true of other struggles. In the Franco-Austrian War of 1859, the French suffered from the poor military leadership of Napoleon III, who did not match his famous namesake in strategic or tactical skill.

In the Crimean War (1854–6), where strategy occurred almost by accident, there was a lack of purposeful planning, and the British and French were fortunate that the Russians lacked modern weapons. In addition, in the winter Allied siege of Sevastopol, the troops experienced terrible conditions, especially a lack of adequate food, clean water, shelter, and clothing, that helped to lead to very heavy losses from disease. In the case of both the Crimean War and the Civil War, it is possible to underrate the achievement of deploying, supplying, and controlling large forces, and also the extent to which each war ended with a victory. In both wars, the struggle lasted longer and took more lives than had been anticipated, but these are apt to be characteristics of any war.

It is important not to over-estimate the sophistication of the organization on either side of the Civil War. Neither can be described as war machines, if this is intended to suggest predictable and regular operating systems that could be readily controlled and adapted. Furthermore, organization was not only a matter of raising and moving resources. It also involved their effective use in campaigns and on the battlefield. In this sphere, both sides experienced major limitations, with the Union lacking the advantage it had in overall resources. Training was inadequate. The problem of the effective use of resources was seen, in particular, with infantry-artillery coordination, which was later to be very important in twentieth-century conflict, not least in the success of the British in 1918 on the western Front. By these later standards there was woeful inadequacy in all armies in the mid-nineteenth century, but the achievement displayed in 1918 was not prefigured earlier in World War I.

Within the Civil War, there were serious deficiencies in the operational dimensions of conflict. More specifically, resource strength was applied through the "filter" (i.e., chokepoint) of logistical systems that, in the particular circumstances of campaigns, possessed limited capability and effectiveness. This was true not only of the campaigning in the west, where distances were great and logistical infrastructure limited. It was also the case in the east, where the greater numbers of troops put a heavy burden on supply systems.

As another aspect of operational limitations, it proved difficult to secure adequate tactical concentration and cooperation on the battlefield. More generally, the Civil War was in many respects tactically a Napoleonic War fought with more advanced weaponry and across a larger operational sphere, but in a less complex strategic environment due to the absence of any international intervention.

The Civil War saw the familiar contextual wartime geographical issues, including the impact of resources, climate, weather, topography, and cover, on military potential and moves. There was also the influence of conflict on the environment, both human and physical.[1]

Command responses were an aspect of the contextual impact. Poor planning and an inability to implement plans (especially the coordination of units and the interaction of moves with a planned time sequence) repeatedly emerged. They had a particularly serious impact on offensive operations as it made it difficult for units to provide adequate levels of mutual support, a flaw readily apparent in Union conduct at the battle of Antietam in 1862. The field commanders on both sides were seriously hampered at the outset by a shortage of adequate maps, which contributed to the "loose command arrangements."[2] Commanders sought to use maps for strategic, operational, and tactical reasons, not least for devising overall strategy and because of the scale of operations, the need to coordinate and move forces over considerable distances (within and between individual campaigns), the unfamiliarity of much of the terrain, and the need for detail.

Aside from at the level of campaigns, the scale of battle was such that it was no longer sufficient, tactically, to rely completely on the field of vision of an individual commander and his ability to send instructions during an engagement. Instead, it was necessary to plan far more in advance, especially when preparing artillery positions, in mounting and responding to frontal attack, and in coordinating attacks from a number of directions. It was also important to understand terrain so as to control and use it. Specific factors brought this to the fore, notably the interplay of rail links and field operations, and the best use of water routes. At a more detailed level, the heavily wooded nature of much of the terrain posed a particular problem for the understanding of battles as they developed, most prominently with the Wilderness in northern Virginia in 1864.

At the same time, that situation did not dictate an outcome, rather made it harder to control the flow of a battle or ensure that numbers would have a decisive impact. Skills in combat and command were therefore even more significant,[3] as the Prussians demonstrated.

The Union forces had a particular need for maps as they were advancing south into the Confederacy (with which they were not familiar), and also seeking to make best use of their more numerous reserves. Tasking and needs essentially drove mapping. Commercial cartography, however, could not produce sufficient maps. As a result, the Confederate and Union armies turned to establishing their own map supplies. By 1864, the Coast Survey and the Corps of Engineers were providing about 43,000 printed maps annually for the Union army. The production of standard copies was crucial given the scale of operations, and lithographic presses printed multiple copies of maps rapidly. Surveyors and cartographers were recruited for the military. In 1864, the Union's Coast Survey produced a uniform ten-mile-to-the-inch base map of most of the Confederacy east of the Mississippi. The scale and detail were very different to the mapping of the 1750s when British and French forces had fought in the region.[4]

The geography of the war was changed by rail, but more particularly at the organizational (especially logistical), strategic, and operational levels, than at the tactical,[5] despite the significance of railroad banks as cover. The role of railheads, such as Marietta, Georgia, near Atlanta, indicated the interaction of very different transport capabilities at operational and tactical levels.

At the strategic level, geography set the basic parameters in terms of which states seceded, and notably among what became the borderland states. The defection of the upper south from the Union was crucial: Virginia, Tennessee, and North Carolina were each more important in economic and demographic terms than any state in the Confederacy, while it became easier to think of the Confederacy as a bloc of territory that could be defended in a coherent fashion, and this therefore required a coherent strategy in order to bring it down. The secession of Virginia and North Carolina greatly altered the location of the likely field of operations in the east, pushing it far northward.

However, in turn, the Union was able to retain Delaware, Maryland, Kentucky, Missouri, and what became West Virginia, and this blocked invasion routes into the north, and exposed the south to attack, notably in Virginia and Tennessee. Because Maryland stayed in the Union, the central battleground lay between the two capitals—heavily-fortified Washington and Richmond—which helped give a geographical focus to the conflict, cut across the potential expansiveness derived from the scale of the Confederacy (an area of more than 750,000 square miles), and held out the possibility of a quick end to the war, an outcome thwarted by Union failure at the battle of First Bull Run in 1861.

Because the war continued, it was necessary to reconcile the conflict west and east of the Appalachians and, in turn, to deal with competing priorities. Despite the presence of the capitals, there was no geographical determinism, and indeed the eastern theatre became particularly important in part due to the role of the commanders there, notably the influence of McClellan in 1861–2 as both commander of the Union's largest field army and overall strategic director. The possibility of amphibious attack, however, suggested a greater significance for the eastern theatre that was not brought to fruition due to the failure of the Union's Peninsula Campaign in 1862, a failure both to take Richmond, the vulnerable Confederate capital, and to fix the Confederate forces. Yet this possibility was not pursued in 1864.

Further west, which was a more far-flung area of operations, there was a very different force- space ratio, with its resulting requirements and opportunities, notably for mobility. Rivers, such as the Mississippi and the Tennessee, provided invasion routes but did not ensure success. The latter, however, was clearly shown with the Union's ability to capture New Orleans in 1862 and move northward up the Mississippi, obliging the Confederacy to fight a two-front war in the western theatre. Union success was seen with the capture of coastal positions, but, repeatedly, they did not then find exploitation of these locations easy. More positively, the Union strengthened the blockade by these coastal expeditions, and strangled the essential overseas trade in cotton.

In "Strategy and the American War," an article published in 1929, Liddell Hart argued that the Union campaign of 1861–2, with the focus on an unsuccessful direct advance on the Confederate capital of Richmond, indicated the ineffectiveness of the strategy of direct approach, and that instead decision occurred in the west, with the Union capture of New Orleans and Vicksburg, the latter opening "the Chattanooga gateway into Georgia." Again, Grant's 1864 campaign was presented as indecisive in battle, whereas "the geographical advantage of having worked round close to the rear of Richmond—was gained by the bloodless maneuvers which had punctuated his advance." In contrast to Grant, "Sherman's economy of force by maneuver" was praised: "The indirect approach to the enemy's economic and moral rear had proved as decisive in the ultimate phase as it had been in the successive steps by which that decision as prepared in the West." This was not the sole lesson Liddell Hart thought the American Civil War had offered to those preparing for World War I.[6] In turn, another key British military commentator, J.F.C. Fuller, argued that:

> the most effective way to protect Richmond was to base a powerful army on Chattanooga, and carry out a defensive-offensive campaign in Tennessee, while a less powerful army covered the capital. A vigorous campaign in Tennessee would almost certainly have drawn Federal [Union] forces out of Virginia to meet it, and simultaneously have directly protected the vital railway hub Chattanooga–Atlanta, as well as indirectly … Vicksburg.[7]

Fuller ignored the political factor. As a reminder of the difficulty of evaluating strategic choices and consequences, and thus geographical factors, the lack of an effective integration of expeditionary operations within the larger context of Union grand strategy can be regarded as mistaken and something that helped commit the Union to a lengthy war of attrition in Virginia.[8] This attrition exposed the Union to the risk that war-weariness would lead to a change in leadership and policy in the 1864 presidential election. Lincoln was in fact concerned about this possibility.

As in the American War of Independence and the War of 1812, there was a fundamental asymmetry, with the Confederacy unable to cut Union trans-Atlantic supply routes or to mount amphibious attacks on the north. In contrast, the Confederacy, like the earlier Americans, had no control over whether Union (earlier British) pressure would escalate into large-scale amphibious attacks. Steam increased amphibious capability. However, whereas in 1775–83 the British could hope to build up loyalism and neutralism, and in 1812–15 to encourage backing for the neutralist Federalists, in 1861–5 there was no official movement in the Confederacy comparable to the Democrats on the Union side.

In some respects, there was a parallel with the Mexican War of 1846–8, in that the Mexican unwillingness to negotiate forced the Americans both to defeat, repeatedly, Mexican armies and to overrun a large part of Mexico. However, the Confederacy was more united than Mexico, mounted a more sustained effort, and was actually in a position to inflict blows on core Union areas. In contrast, there were no Mexican invasions of America.

The Civil War took far longer than the individual wars of German and Italian unification, but it was far more decisive. The Confederacy ceased to exist as an independent state, a very different fate to that of Denmark, Austria, and France once defeated in 1864, 1866 and 1870–1, respectively. In the Crimean War, the Allies had not sought territorial gains from Russia, while in the Franco-Austrian War of 1859 the French did not press on to attack the powerful Austrian fortresses of the Quadrilateral and conquer the Venetia, which was left to Austria (and only acquired by Italy in 1866).

Although the situation had initially looked different, the Union forces had no such limited option or moderate political goals. Aside from leading to the total fall of the Confederacy, the Civil War eventually transformed the relationship between the federal government and the individual states. Even more, there was a major social change with the ending of slavery and the liberation of four million slaves; again, here there are no comparisons in the European wars.

The relative length of conflicts greatly impressed contemporaries. Although the Napoleonic Wars had been lengthy, later western commentators had become used to short wars and to decisive campaigning. Indeed, Scott's advance on Mexico City in 1847 fit into this analysis. As a result, it was easy to overlook the magnitude of the task facing the north and to regard the war as overly lengthy.

To a certain extent, as already suggested, this was reasonable. Due, in large part, to mismanagement, the opportunity to seize Richmond in 1862 had been lost, while at Antietam McClellan failed to commit his reserve, which might have broken the Confederate center, and subsequently failed to disrupt Lee's retreat both immediately after the battle (or later while the Confederates were retreating across the Potomac). As for the British with George Washington after the battle of Long Island in 1776, there was an opportunity to wreak havoc on an army forced to undertake a difficult retreat from a vulnerable position; and it was not taken in either case. There was no battle—of the type of Napoleon's victories at Austerlitz (1805) and Jena (1806)—that could destroy an opponent's army and bring on a successful peace settlement. Again, there were other serious Union failures, for example not exploiting Gettysburg in 1863, not advancing south of the James River earlier in 1864, and the Red River campaign in 1864.

The north's task was made more difficult because the command capability gap was less clear cut than the situation facing the Piedmontese in 1860 and the Prussians in 1866 and 1870. In those cases, the clearly poorly commanded army was the one on the defensive: Naples, Austria, and France, respectively. These had far more serious command flaws than the Confederacy.

Excepting the unexpected success of Lee, the pattern of the Civil War in early 1862 appeared likely to be that of a short conflict that might match that of the Prussians, or of the French against Austria in 1859: Union victory in a war of the frontiers, that, in the case of thc Civil War, would lead the Confederacy to abandon its struggle to maintain independence. Even then, due to the area in conflict in the first year and, even more, year and a half of the war, a war of the frontiers was a more formidable challenge in America. Union success in early 1862 was so far-flung and extensive that the "frontiers" must be understood in different terms to those of, say, the Metz and Sedan campaign of 1870. For example, the advance of Halleck's army as far as Corinth, Mississippi, was a dramatic demonstration of the extent to which initial successes had provided the basis for long-distance advances. The latter were seen in 1863 and 1864, and these gave the Union both the Mississippi axis and that from Tennessee via Atlanta to the Atlantic. There were long advances in Europe, for example those of Garibaldi fighting his way through Sicily and southern Italy, or Russian forces suppressing nationalist revolutions in Hungary in 1848 and Poland in 1863. Neither, however, matched the logistical challenge and opposition faced by the Union forces, nor brought the reiterated pressure that they did to the Confederacy. More generally, there was a contrast in operating circumstances with the wars of German unification that calls for credit to be given both sides in the Civil War.

Deficiencies in command, and by both Austria and France, enabled the Prussians to out-maneuver them. The Americans should not be thought inadequate in comparison, although, unlike the British, continental European general staffs and commentators were apt to underrate the lessons that could be learned from the Civil War, misleadingly treating it as a war waged by amateur militia,[9] an approach that gravely underrates the tasks, skills, and learning curves involved. Moltke himself was increasingly skeptical about the potential of the strategic offensive for Germany because of increases in defensive firepower and the size of armies. This was to be amply displayed in the German nemesis in World War I; and the Civil War offered important lessons that looked to the future. There was also an important contrast. In World War I, the Germans suffered from their failure to keep or create an open campaign zone with room for maneuver and a tempo permitting the retention of the initiative. The resulting degree of operational immobility, notably on the western front, did not characterize the Civil War. In 1914, however, as with the Union advance on Richmond in 1861, the Germans suffered from having no Plan B once their initial plan to defeat the French had been derailed.[10]

It is valuable to look for parallels and comparisons between the Civil War and conflict in Europe, if only, in part, to focus on the contrasts that emerge. To that end, it is important to note that it is too limited to hold that the wars of German unification defined European warfare and thus provide a ready frame of contrast with the Civil War. Instead, this paradigm model should be rejected, and it is necessary to stress the variety of mid-nineteenth century European warfare. For Britain, there was a particular interest in the Civil War as it appeared to show how a society without the background of conscription could rapidly create an effective military. Army staff candidates being taught at Camberley were expected to study *Stonewall Jackson and the American Civil War* (1898; 3rd ed. 1902) by the Professor of Military History, Colonel George Henderson (1843–1903), and to know the minutiae of Stonewall Jackson's Shenandoah Valley campaign of 1862, in which a mobile Confederate force had outmaneuvered and defeated larger Union forces (a lesson that was believed to be relevant to the British military).

Furthermore, Henderson was one of the first to try to revive interest in the benefits of speed and surprise in an age of fascination with Napoleonic masses and frontal assaults. What would now be termed "lessons of operational theory" underlie the book. The work of Henderson, who also produced a study of the Fredericksburg campaign, looked toward later British interest in the Civil War, including Frederick Barton Maurice's *Robert E. Lee, the Soldier* (1925) and, more particularly, J.F.C. Fuller's *Grant and Lee: A Study in Personality and Generalship* (1932), which was widely cited and also reprinted in America. While military correspondent of *The Daily Telegraph*, Basil Liddel Hart published *Sherman: Soldier, Realist, American* in 1929. This was in the wake of his critique of the World War I focus on the frontal assault and his own argument for the indirect approach.

Variety was also the case with twentieth and twenty-first century warfare, not least that of the last fifty years. As a result, it is clear that the term "modernity" needs to be employed with far greater care than when it was seen to describe the total warfare of the two world wars. "Modernity" today can be seen as encompassing cutting-edge high technology preparations for conflict between "super-powers," as well as the "limited" warfare waged by those powers, and the diversity of conflicts involving lesser states.

From the perspective of modern America, with relatively small forces of regulars prepared for conflict with other major powers, principally China, and for expeditionary-style limited conflicts, it is possible to look back to American military history in the period 1775–1865 and see precursors of modernity in the earlier regular army with its conflicts with Native Americans and with the challenge of British power. In contrast, the Civil War also saw a size of armies very different to the norm today. The comparisons cannot be pushed too far, but they serve to underline the danger of assuming a clear path toward modern war onward from the Civil War.

The Civil War can be differently compared to the Taiping Rebellion in China in 1850–64, a struggle that was longer and involved far more troops than the Civil War, with possibly 10 million combatants and over 20 million casualties, in part due to large-scale massacres. The Taiping were more seriously affected by divisions than the Confederacy, with the killing at the behest of the leader, Hong Xiuquan, in 1856 of a major Taiping figure, Yang Xiuqing, followed by that of Shi Dakai. The Taiping also suffered greatly from foreign intervention on behalf of the imperial forces in the early 1860s, with no comparison for the Confederacy. The war was a total one, as was the subsequent repression, whereas the Civil War was a 'hard' war, but not a total war. The Taiping Rebellion was accompanied by regional insurrections—notably the Panthay Rebellion in southwest Yunnan from 1856 to 1873, and the Dungan Revolt in Xinjiang from 1862 to 1877. Both largely Muslim, these were suppressed with very high casualties. There was no comparable challenge to American control by Native Americans, or indeed blacks. The contexts, however, were very different, not least in the limited numbers of Native Americans. All this underlines the problematic nature of comparisons.

The Civil War has more commonly been compared with the European conflicts, and for obvious reasons of national identity and notions of military modernization. Moreover, unlike the Taiping, the Confederacy built on an existing structure (that of individual states) and sought simply to change one into two federal states. There was no attempt to create a heavenly kingdom for a new dynasty, or a new religion, culture, and social model. The fanaticism and extraordinary views of the Taiping were not matched by the Confederates. However, both they and the Taiping were rebels that sought to overthrow existing government practices. That each failed is notable, although it is not possible to read automatically from one to the other while searching for explanations.

A multiplicity of factors, each operating in particular contexts, and interacting in uncertain fashions, played a role in success and failure.[11] It would be mistaken to establish priorities between and within them. Moreover, it would be foolish to imagine that economic, political, and diplomatic factors were structural, and military ones somehow contingent in a way that, depending on the analysis, could be either conclusive for the structural factors or, somehow, epiphenomena for the contingent ones. There is no such simplicity to war.

Comparison with the standard accounts of the two world wars is instructive. The Germans, like the Confederates, argued that they had been defeated by superior resources and had only been able to hold out for so long due to better fighting quality. This became a version of the "Glorious Cause," albeit one that was very differently phrased due to the postwar reconceptualization of Germany and the absence of anything similar in the case of the Confederacy.

However, scholarship leads in a different direction, for here the emphasis, instead, is on a more complex approach. This provides an opportunity in each case to argue that there were advantages in fighting quality, notably at the tactical level, in the case of the Confederates and the Germans, from the beginning, only for that capability gap to be narrowed by training and experience. Moreover, the tactical skill of Confederates and Germans was not matched in strategic perception and operational acuity. Far more was involved than resources.[12]

The war settled the map of Continental America and, in doing so, ensured the geopolitics of North America and the west. The contingencies and possibilities that had been so apparent prior to the war, notably in the southwest,[13] had been ended. Or, rather, they had been transformed into the differing possibilities provided by reconstruction (see chapter 10) and by the resumption of expansion at the expense of Native Americans.

The Powder River Expedition was launched into Wyoming in the summer of 1865 against the Sioux, Cheyenne, and Arapaho,[14] but much of the preparatory work had been done during the Civil War, and, indeed, there was continuity in the case of that expedition that was a reprisal for raids earlier that year. The notion that it was Civil War veterans, notably Sherman (Commander of the Division of the Missouri from 1865) and Philip Sheridan (Commander of the Department of the Missouri from 1867), who inaugurated a harsher, exterminatory, approach to plains warfare requires qualification as, aside from assuming a misleading consensus in frontier warfare, General William Harney before the war and Brigadier-General James Carleton during the war both advocated wiping out their native enemies and practiced it to the best of their ability.[15] Moreover, during the Civil War, the useful tactic of winter campaigning got its start.

Nevertheless, there were serious problems for the army in the late 1860s. Many commanders from the 1850s were dead or had lost their commissions by serving the Confederacy; and their replacements, trained in and from the Civil War with its emphasis on commanding and fighting large numbers of regulars, were not adept at dealing with the very mobile natives. Moreover, the sharp reduction of the army in the aftermath of the Civil War ensured that there were few troops available for frontier warfare. When, in 1867, Sheridan took command of the Department of the Missouri, which covered much of the frontier, he had only 6,000 troops.

The show of force helped provoke further resistance, as Major-General Winfield Scott Hancock's expedition of 1867 demonstrated with the response of the Cheyenne.[16] Hancock had played an important role as a key corps commander at Gettysburg. Moreover, in operational and tactical terms, it proved difficult to force the mobile natives to battle not least because they knew the terrain and were adept at surprise. The Sioux showed this in 1866–8 in their successful campaigning against the army in Montana and Wyoming in the Bozeman Trail War, also known as Red Cloud's War. The Sioux surrounded and besieged American forts, forcing their abandonment.

As a consequence, the army developed techniques that focused on winter campaigning, which were used in late 1868 in attacks in north

Texas; winter campaigning had been common in the Civil War. Native settlements were particularly vulnerable in the winter as those who escaped risked starvation and death by exposure. This method was employed on 26 November 1868 at the battle of the Washita when Custer annihilated a southern Cheyenne village led by Black Kettle, killing women and children as well. The destruction of crops and villages and the confiscation of pony herds, none of which were new tactics, also brought misery,[17] and the British envoy deplored such methods as "unnecessary" and "wholesale slaughter."[18] The coordination of independently operating columns advancing from different directions was also important to American success.

There was an important shift in government policy after Grant became President in 1869. Believing in "conquest by kindness" in which natives moved to reservations where Christian education and agriculture were to make them good neighbors, where they were civilized and Christianized, Grant followed what has been seen as a peace policy from 1869 to 1874. As a result of the shift in policy, the pace of hostilities declined at the close of the 1860s, although the situation deteriorated in the early 1870s with the peace policy discredited in 1871. That autumn, Sherman sent troops against the Comanche who were seen as putting Texas under excessive pressure. The inexorable nature of this adversary placed the Comanche in unprecedented difficulties.[19] Moreover, Colonel George Crook forced Cochise, the head of the Arizona Apache, to surrender in 1871, although he soon resumed hostilities.[20]

Whatever the pace of conflict, Native American resistance had been largely broken, and a successful military methodology to that end had evolved. Its focus on wrecking civil society (or rather on the notion that there was no civil sphere separate to the military), had been seen in the conflict between north and south in the latter stages of the Civil War. There was no direct linkage between the "hard war" of the Civil War and the campaigns against the Native Americans, not least due to different military and political circumstances. In the west, this system was made especially effective against Native Americans thanks to the mobility of the regulars and their ability through a good logistical system to stage winter campaigns. This success indicated the army's potential to adapt its military style and methods, and its mobility was an important legacy to subsequent American military culture and doctrine.[21] The image of the cavalryman was and remains a key piece of the west. Industrial capacity underlay this mobility as railroads were used to move troops against opponents.

Yet, other factors also continued to play a role. The Americans were still able to obtain local support because of Native American rivalries. In the Sioux Wars (1854–77), most of the other plains tribes joined the Americans against the Sioux, as they saw the latter as a far more immediate threat to their safety than the more distant Americans. The American army used Pawnee and Crow scouts in the major battles of the 1860s and 1870s, as well as Shoshone warriors as auxiliaries.[22] The Sioux, in turn, viewed the Americans as merely one more tribal enemy for much of the time, and alternated attacks on American units and forts with raids against Crow and Shoshone.[23] The same was true of the Comanche. There was no parallel with the Civil War.

The Sioux suffered from the army's adoption of breech-loaders in 1867, which provided a crucial firepower advantage. On 21 December 1866, Captain William J. Fetterman, a Civil War veteran of the Army of the Cumberland, and eighty troops armed with muzzle-loaders were taken unawares and killed outside Fort Philip Kearny, Wyoming, in a matter of minutes by about 2,000 northern Cheyenne, northern Arapaho, and Lakota Sioux, a force far larger than they had anticipated. By the following August, the army had new single-shot breechloaders with copper cartridges able to fire twelve shots a minute compared to the muzzle-loader's three. On two different occasions, on 1–2 August, the Wagon Box fight and the Hayfield fight, three dozen soldiers held off several thousand warriors.[24] The Native American attempt to counter this by acquiring the same technology, not least from defeated opponents, could be deadly, as at Custer's defeat at Little Big Horn in 1876, but suffered from their lack of access to ammunition supplies. Moreover, there were major limits to the changes in native war-making, notably as they moved away from the style of individual fighting that stressed bravery and also the avoidance of casualties. In particular, the Sioux did not attempt to institute anything like military discipline or coercive leadership, and the seasonal nature of their warfare could not be altered.

Red Cloud and his warriors came to the bargaining table for peace shortly after his fighting power had been greatly reduced by the American use of breechloaders. This weapon usage also had an impact in episodes of European expansion in the period, as well as with the case of expansion elsewhere in the New World (although, as in America, a range of factors played a role).[25] By 1867 on the southern plains (Treaty of Medicine Lodge) and 1868 on the northern plains (Treaty of Fort Laramie), most tribes had been sent to a reservation. Those who left without permission were deemed hostile. Although the Fort Laramie treaty created a large Lakota Sioux reservation centered in the Black Hills and without military supervision, this was a new geography of power and control.

It was also a geography in which the army positioned the west into America not solely by enforcing the reservation policy and maintaining security but also by playing a major role in supporting economic integration—notably by building roads and encouraging the building of railroads. Sherman was particularly involved in this process.[26] These policies were part of a wider program by which the railroads fostered public policies that encouraged the stabilization of civil society, including public relief and law enforcement, while the reservations were intended to clear threatening natives from the rail routes—notably from those along the Platte and Kansas valleys, the routes for the Union Pacific and Kansas Pacific lines.[27]

The situation would have been very different had the Confederacy truly succeeded, as there would have been a rivalry for Native American support rather than coordinated action by the army. The anchoring of the west in America was a key conclusion to the Civil War. There was no equivalent for the Native Americans to the successful hostile reaction to the reconstruction seen in the south. In large part, this reflected the maintenance of the constitutional system, with the state structure preserved in the south, as well as the prevalent white racism toward Native Americans and blacks, albeit with racism having very different meanings in particular contexts.

America ended up as a *de facto* white federation of states. Southern separatism had been defeated, but a southern identity remained strong and was able to express itself through state mechanisms and politics. In the west, identity was offered essentially to white settlers who dominated a plural society of Native Americans, Hispanics, and Whites. As with the south, there was no truck for separatism.

This had already been clear in the case of Utah, which also retained a military presence that to opponents seemed like occupation. Founded in 1862, three miles east of Salt Lake City, Camp Douglas, initially occupied by Union volunteers from California and Nevada, became a regular army post after the Civil War. It was renamed Fort Douglas in 1878. Utah was admitted into the Union in 1896, and then only after polygamy had been abandoned as an essential doctrine in 1890. Lincoln had attacked the notion of state sovereignty as an answer to the slavery question by asking whether Utah was to be admitted into the Union if its constitution tolerated polygamy, an issue that very much engaged those who embraced Christian morality.

In contrast, Nevada, which had been separated from the Utah Territory on 2 March 1861, had been admitted as the 36$^{th}$ state on 31 October 1864, providing Lincoln with three electoral votes to support his re-election. Nevada was the location of the Comstock Lode, the first major discovery of silver ore in America, which had been made public in 1859, and in 1861 separated from Utah. Nebraska followed as a state in 1867 and then Colorado, once in large part inside of Utah, in 1876. Nevada, Nebraska, and Colorado represented the Union ideal much more than Utah where the Mormons did not change their teaching regarding blacks until 1978. Nebraska fitted perfectly with the idea of small freeholding farmers, whereas Nevada's economy, which was built almost entirely on the mining industry, exemplified the entrepreneurial spirit and technological progress that characterized Gilded Age America.

The west may appear a strange place to end an account of a war that began off in Charleston. Yet this captures the breadth of the causes and significance of the war (see also chapter 1). In 1912, with New Mexico and Arizona admitted, the whole of the contiguous United States became states as opposed to remaining as territories. Moreover, this was done without the contention seen in the antebellum period—notably from the admission of Missouri in 1821 to that of Kansas in 1861. The divisiveness between the north and south that had politicized the issue of the west had been settled at the federal level, and the era of Republican ascendancy from the Civil War to 1933 saw a pro-business governance that took the west into the Union on terms suitable to liberal capitalism. This was crucial to America's character as a developing major power, indeed *the* major power by the mid-twentieth century. This result would have been impossible if not for Union victory in the Civil War. A struggle that was far from inevitable in both its course and outcome set in motion fundamental consequences for the history and nature of the entire modern world.

# ENDNOTES

## Preface

1 Sumner to Charles Vaughan, former British envoy in America, 15 May 1848, All Souls College, Oxford, Vaughan papers, C 116 no. 3.
2 M. Thistlewaite, "Washington Crossing the Delaware. Navigating the Image(s) of the Hero," in KL. Cope (ed.), *George Washington in and as Culture* (New York, 2001), 53.
3 J. Nagler, "Achilles' Heel. Slavery and War in the American Revolution," in R. Chickering and S. Förster (eds.), *War in an Age of Revolution, 1775–1815* (Cambridge, 2010), 285–97.
4 C.A. Bayly, *The Birth of the Modern World, 1780–1914* (Oxford, 2004), 161–4.
5 A. Brettle, "1864: The Genesis of a New Conservative World?" in J. Black (ed.), *The Tory World: Deep History and the Tory Theme in British Foreign Policy, 1679–2014* (Farnham, 2015), 187–202.
6 P. Wiart and C. Oppenheimer, "Largest known historical eruption in Africa: Dubbi volcano, Eritrea, 1861," in *Geology* 28 (2000): 291–4.
7 T. Nanzig (ed.), *The Civil War Memoirs of a Virginia Cavalryman* (Tuscaloosa, AL, 2007).
8 B.B. Tomblin, *Life in Jefferson Davis' Navy* (Annapolis, MD, 2019).
9 M. Smith, *The Smell of Battle, the Taste of Siege: A Sensory History of the Civil War* (New York, 2015).
10 J. David Hacker, "A Census-Based Count of the Civil War Dead," in *Civil War History* 57 (4) 2011: 30–48. For a critical account of Hacker's assumptions, see M. Flotow, "J. David Hacker's 'A Census-Based Count of the Civil War Dead,'" in *The Journal of the Abraham Lincoln Association* 42(2) 2022: https://doi.org/10.3998/jala.2299.
11 *Daily Dispatch* [Richmond], 25 January 1865.
12 J. Marszalek (ed.), *The Personal Memoirs of Ulysses S. Grant* (Cambridge, MA, 2017), 248.
13 See the effective account of T.B. Smith, *Shiloh: Conquer or Perish* (Lawrence, KS, 2014).
14 D.S. Frazier, Foreword to D.E. Alberts, *The Battle of Glorietta. Union Victory in the West* (College Station, TX, 1998), xii.

## Chapter 1

1 L. Brophy, *University, Court, and Slave: Pro-Slavery Thought in Southern Colleges and Courts and the Coming of the Civil War* (New York, 2016); E. Herschthal, *The Science of Abolition: How Slaveholders Became the Enemies of Progress* (New Haven, CT, 2021).
2 M.A. Morrison, "The Westward Curse of Empire: Texas Annexation and the American Whig Party," in *Journal of the Early Republic*, 10 (1990): 221–49.
3 G. Rable, *God's Almost Chosen People: A Religious History of the American Civil War* (Chapel Hill, NC, 2010).
4 J.G. Dawson, "Jefferson Davis and the Confederacy's 'Offensive-Defensive Strategy' in the U.S. Civil War," *JMH*, 73 (2009): 595.
5 Clarendon to Sir John Crampton, British envoy in Washington, 4 January 1856, Bod. MS. Clar. Dep C. 135 p. 37.
6 D. Gibler and W. Bagley, *The Mormon Rebellion: America's First Civil War, 1857–1858* (Norman, OK, 2011).
7 E.R. Varon, *Disunion! The Coming of the American Civil War, 1789–1859* (Chapel Hill, NC, 2008).
8 R.E. McGlone, *John Brown's War against Slavery* (New York, 2009).
9 See B. Jenkins, *Lord Lyons: A Diplomat in an Age of Nationalism and War* (Montreal, 2014).
10 Lyons to Lord John Russell, from 1861 Earl Russell, Foreign Secretary, 12 Dec. 1859, NA. PRO. 30/22/34, f. 61.
11 Lyons to Russell, 22 Nov. 1859, NA. PRO. 30/22/34, f. 54; D.E. Reynolds, *Texas Terror: The Slave Insurrection Panic of 1860 and the Secession of the Lower South* (Baton Rouge, LA, 2007).
12 W.W. Freehling, *Prelude to Civil War. The Nullification Controversy in South Carolina, 1816–1836* (New York, 1965), 359–60.
13 M.A. Noll, *The Civil War as a Theological Crisis* (Chapel Hill, NC, 2006); H. Horn, *Leonidas Polk: Warrior Bishop of the Confederacy* (Lawrence, KS, 2019).
14 P. Knupfer, "Aging Statesmen and the Statesmanship of an Earlier Age: The Generational Roots of the Constitutional Union Party," in D.W. Blight and B.D. Simpson (eds), *Union and Emancipation: Essays on Politics and Race in the Civil War Era* (Kent, OH, 1997), 57–78.
15 J.D. Sarris, *A Separate Civil War: Communities in Conflict in the Mountain South* (Charlottesville, VA, 2006).
16 E.S. Rafuse, "Former Whigs in Conflict: Winfield Scott, Abraham Lincoln, and the Secession Crisis Revisited," in *Lincoln Herald*, 103 (2001): 18.
17 S.D. Bowman, *At the Precipice: Americans North and South during the Secession Crisis* (Chapel Hill, NC, 2010).

18 M.J. Birkner (ed.), *James Buchanan and the Political Crisis of the 1850s* (Susquehanna, PN, 1996).
19 W.J. Cooper, *We Have the War Upon Us: The Onset of the Civil War, November 1860–April 1861* (New York, 2012); E. Larson, *The Demon of Unrest: A Saga of Hubris, Heartbreak and Heroism at the Dawn of the Civil War* (London, 2024).
20 J. Remak, *A Very Civil War. The Swiss Sonderbund War of 1847* (Boulder, CO, 1993); R. Weaver, *Three Weeks in November: A Military History of the Swiss Civil War of 1847* (Warwick, 2012).

## Chapter 2

1 B.H. Reid, *The Origins of the American Civil War* (Harlow, 1996); R. McClintock, *Lincoln and the Decision for War: The Northern Response to Secession* (Chapel Hill, NC, 2008).
2 D.E. Reynolds, *Texas Terror: The Slave Insurrection Panic of 1860 and the Secession of the Lower South* (Baton Rouge, LA, 2007).
3 R.N. Current, *Lincoln's Loyalists: Union Soldiers from the Confederacy* (Boston, MA, 1992); C.J. Einolf, *George Thomas: Virginian for the Union* (Norman, OK, 2007).
4 W.W. Freehling, *The Road to Disunion II: Secessionists Triumphant* (Oxford, 2007).
5 B.A. Myers, *Rebels against the Confederacy: North Carolina's Unionists* (New York, 2014).
6 W. Davis, *The Battle at Bull Run* (Baton Rouge, LA, 1981).
7 M. Trninic, "A Call to Humanity: Hawthorne's 'Chiefly about War-Matters,'" in *Nathaniel Hawthorne Review* 37:1 (2011): 109–32.
8 Gary Ohls, "Fort Fisher: Amphibious Victory in the American Civil War," in *Naval War College Review* 59:4 (Autumn 2006): 81–99.
9 N.A.M. Rodger, *The Price of Victory. A Naval History of Britain: 1814–1945* (London, 2024).
10 B. McKnight, *Contested Borderland: The Civil War in Appalachian Kentucky and Virginia* (Lexington, KY, 2006).
11 J.M. McPherson, *Drawn with the Sword. Reflections on the American Civil War* (New York, 1996).
12 Graham to Raglan, January 10, 1854, BL. Add. 29696 fol. 87.
13 D. Canfield, "Opportunity Lost: Combined Operations and the Development of Union Military Strategy, April 1861–April 1862," in *JMH*, 79 (2015): 687–9.
14 D. Stoker, *The Grand Design: Strategy and the US Civil War* (New York, 2010).

15 C. Symonds, *The Civil War at Sea* (Oxford, 2009).
16 B.H. Reid, *America's Civil War. The Operational Battlefield, 1861–1863* (Amherst, NY, 2008).
17 *The Personal Memoirs*...op.cit., 205.
18 D. Bosse, *Civil War Newspaper Maps of the Northern Daily Press: A Cartobibliography* (Westport, CT, 1993) and *Civil War Newspaper Maps* (Baltimore, 1993).
19 B.H. Reid, "Historians and the Joint Committee on the Conduct of the War, 1861–65," in *Civil War History* 38 (1992): 341.

## Chapter 3

1 D. Doyle, *The Cause of All Nations: An International History of the American Civil War* (New York, 2015).
2 D.G. Surdam, "The Union Navy's blockade reconsidered," and "The Confederate naval buildup: Could more have been accomplished?", in *Naval War College Review*, 51 (1998): 104, 54; (2001): 121, respectively.
3 Robert Bunch, Consul in Charleston, to Lyons, 9 Jan. 1863, NA. FO. 5/875 fol. 184.
4 Lyons to Milne, 12 May 1861, NMM. MLN/116/1a; R.A. Courtemache, *No Need of Glory: The British Navy in American Waters, 1860–1864* (Annapolis, Md., 1977).
5 Palmerston to Russell, 18 Feb. 1861, NA. PRO. 30/22/21 fol. 432.
6 Russell to Palmerston, 29 Dec. 1860, Russell to Duke of Somerset, First Lord of the Admiralty, 4 May 1861, NA. PRO. 30/22/30 fols 62, 119.
7 Russell to Henry, Earl Cowley, envoy in Paris, 20 July 1861, NA. FO. 27/1378.
8 Lyons to Milne, 27 May 1861, NMM. MLN/116/1a.
9 For example, Lyons to Russell, 25 Ap. 1864, NA. FO. 5/948 fol. 119.
10 Lyons to Milne, 10 June 1861, NMM. MLN/116/1a.
11 Lyons to Milne, 22 July 1861, NMM. MLN/116/1a.
12 Russell to Cowley, 9 Sept. 1861, Gooch (ed.), *Russell*, II, 320.
13 Lyons to Russell, 13 Ap. 1863, NA. FO. 5/881 fol. 167.
14 C.M. Hubbard, *The Burden of Southern Diplomacy* (Knoxville, TN, 1998).
15 Russell to Francis, 10th Lord Napier, envoy at St Petersburg, 11 Dec. 1861, NA. PRO. 30/22/1/4 fol. 65.
16 Russell to Cobden, 2 Ap. 1861, NA. PRO. 30/22/32 fols. 118–20.
17 Somerset to Milne, 1, 15 Dec. 1861, Milne to Somerset, 24 Jan. 1862, NMM. MLN/116/1c.
18 Russell to Napier, 27 Dec., Palmerston to Russell, 9 July and 25 Aug. 1861, NA. PRO. 30/22/48 fol. 69, /21 fols. 503–4, 538–9.

19 K. Bourne, "British Preparations for War with the North, 1861–62," in *English Historical Review*, 76 (1961): 600–32.

20 Palmerston to Russell, 29 Nov. and 6 Dec. 1861, NA. PRO. 30/22/21 fols. 609, 622.

21 Russell to George, 4th Earl of Clarendon, 6 Dec., Russell to Cowley, 16 Dec. 1861, G.P. Gooch (ed.), *The Later Correspondence of Lord John Russell*, II, 321–2; Lyons to Milne, 28 Dec. 1861, NMM. MLN/116/1a. For a view of war as unlikely, see D. Stoker, *The Grand Design. Strategy and the U.S. Civil War* (Oxford, 2010), p. 31.

22 Lyons to Russell, 23 Dec 1861, NA. PRO. 30/22/35 fols. 360–1; Russell to Clarendon, 14 Jan. 1862, Gooch (ed.), *Russell*, II, 324.

23 Lyons to Russell, 30 Jan.1862, NA. FO. 5/824 fol. 62.

24 Russell to Cowley, 9 Dec. 1861, Gooch (ed.), *Russell*, II, 322.

25 Palmerston to Russell, Victoria to Palmerston, both 1 Dec. 1861, NA. PRO. 30/22/21 fols. 612–14.

26 F. Prochaska, *The Eagle and the Crown. Americans and the British Monarchy* (New Haven, CT, 2008), pp. 62–86; E. Tamarkin, *Anglophilia: Deference, Devotion, and Antebellum America* (Chicago, IL, 2008).

27 A.D. Lambert, "Winning Without Fighting: British Grand Strategy and its Application to the United States, 1815–65," in B.A. Lee and K.F. Walling (eds.), *Strategic Logic and Political Rationality* (London, 2003), pp. 178–87; N.B. Ferris, *The Trent Affair: A Diplomatic Crisis* (Knoxville, TN, 1977).

28 D. Brown, *Palmerston and the Politics of Foreign Policy, 1846–55* (Manchester, 2002).

29 A. Hawkins, *The Forgotten Prime Minister: The 14th Earl of Derby* (2 vols, Oxford, 2007), II, 263–4, 279.

30 Lyons to Milne, 19 and 28 Dec. 1861, NMM. MLN/116/1a, Lyons to Russell, 3 and 31 Jan. 1862, NA. PRO. 30/22/36 fols. 2, 24.

31 Lyons to Milne, 23 Dec. 1861, NMM. MLN/116/1a.

32 Lyons to Milne, 21 and 30 Jan. 1862, NMM. MLN/116/1a. For a discussion of the crisis from an instructive perspective, see D.P. Nickles, *Under the Wire: How the Telegraph Changed Diplomacy* (Cambridge, MA, 2003).

33 Russell to Sir George Grey, 28 Oct. 1862, Gooch (ed.), *Russell*, II, 332.

34 William Stuart, Chargé des Affaires, in Lyons' absence, to Russell, 17 and 24 Oct. 1862, NA. FO. 5/838 fols. 23– 4, 84–5.

35 Stuart to Russell, 17 and 27 Oct. 1862, NA. FO. 5/838 fols. 37, 152.

36 A. Roberts, *Salisbury. Victorian Titan* (London, 1991), 47–50.

37 Lyons to Russell, 17 Nov. 1862, NA. FO. 5/838 fol. 308.

38 D. Beales, *England and Italy, 185–60* (London, 1961).

39 *The Personal Memoirs*… op.cit., 760.

40 B.H. Reid, "Power, Sovereignty and the Great Republic: Anglo-American

Diplomatic Relations in the Era of the Civil War," in *Diplomacy and Statecraft* 14 (2003): 64–5.

41 Palmerston to Russell, 2 Oct. 1862, Gooch (ed.), *Russell*, II, 326.

42 D.G. Surdam, *Northern Naval Superiority and the Economics of the American Civil War* (Columbia, SC, 2001).

43 R.B. Ekelund and M. Thornton, *Tariffs, Blockades, and Inflation: The Economics of the Civil War* (Wilmington, Delaware, 2004).

44 Palmerston to Russell, 1 Jan. 1860, NA. PRO. 30/22/21 fol. 1.

45 Russell to Palmerston, 10, 14, and 19 Sept. 1859; Russell to Gladstone, 16 Jan. 1861, NA. PRO. 30/22/30 fols. 17, 24, 27; 20/22/31 fol. 34.

46 W. Bowen, *Spain and the American Civil War* (Columbia, MS, 2011).

47 D. Brown, "Palmerston and Anglo-French Relations, 1846–1865," in *Diplomacy and Statecraft*, 17 (2006): 688.

48 Palmerston to Russell, 31 Jan. 1861, NA. PRO. 30/22/21 fols. 416–17.

49 Palmerston to Russell, 10 Mar. 1861, NA. PRO. 30/22/21 fol. 449.

50 Palmerston to Russell, 3, 10 June 1861, NA. PRO. 30/22/21 fols. 490–1.

51 Palmerston to Russell, 11 Aug. 1861, NA. PRO. 30/22/21 fol. 527.

52 Lyons to Russell, 8 Dec. 1862, NA. FO. 5/839 fol. 296.

53 Palmerston to Russell, 2 Oct. 1862, Gooch (ed.), *Russell*, II, 326–7.

54 Palmerston to Russell, 22 Oct. 1862, Gooch (ed.), *Russell*, II, 328; C.F. Adams, "A Crisis in Downing Street," in *Proceedings of the Massachusetts Historical Society*, 47, 373–424; F.J. Merli and T.A. Wilson, "The British Cabinet and the Confederacy: Autumn 1862," in *Maryland Historical Magazine*, 65 (1970); P.E. Myers, *Caution and Cooperation: The American Civil War in British–American Relations* (Kent, Ohio, 2008); D.A. Campbell, "Palmerston and the American Civil War," in M. Taylor and D. Brown (eds.), *Palmerston Studies* (2 vols, Southampton, 2007), II, 144–67.

55 Russell to G.C. Lewis, 26 Oct. 1862, Gooch (ed.), *Russell*, II, 328.

56 Lyons to Russell, 14 Nov. 1862, NA. PRO. 30/22/36 fol. 292.

57 Sir George Grey to Russell, 27 Oct. 1862, Gooch (ed.), *Russell*, II, 331.

58 Seward to William Dayton, American envoy in Paris, 30 Nov. 1863, NA. FO. 5/877 fol. 152.

59 R. Quinault, "Gladstone and Slavery," in *Historical Journal,* 52 (2009): 376; H.C.G. Matthew (ed.), *The Gladstone Diaries* VI (Oxford, 1978), pp. 156, 160; draft pages, BL. Add. 44752 fol. 51.

60 Somerset to Milne, 15 Nov. 1862, NMM. MLN/116/1c.

61 Palmerston to Russell, 12 Oct. 1862, NA. PRO. 30/22/22 fol. 111.

62 Gladstone diary, 27 Dec. 1862; C. Matthew (ed.), *The Gladstone Diaries* (14 vols, Oxford, 1968–94), VI, 169.

63 George, 8th Duke of Argyll to Russell, 11 and 15 Oct., Granville Leveson–Gower, 2nd Earl Granville to Russell, 29 Sept.; George Lewis to Russell,

25 Oct.; Duke of Newcastle to Russell, 14 Oct. 1862; NA. PRO. 30/22/25 fols. 55–60, 125–8, 197–204, 317–18, 362.

64 Lyons to Russell, 26 Nov.1862, NA. PRO. 30/22/36 fol. 308.

65 Grey to Milne, 31 Oct. 1862, NMM. MLN/116/1d.

66 Russell to Peter Scarlett, envoy in Greece, 2 Sept. and 12 Nov. 1863, NA. PRO. 30/22/108 fols. 63, 69.

67 *Daily Globe*, 9 Feb. 1863; Lyons to Russell, 2, 6, and 16 Feb. 1863, NA. FO. 5/876 fols. 52–3, 139–40, 5/877 fols. 145–6.

68 Lyons to Russell, 6 Mar. 1863, NA. FO. 5/879; D. Carroll, *Henri Mercier and the American Civil War* (Princeton, NJ, 1971).

69 Hawkins, *Derby*, II, 279.

70 Lyons to Milne, 5 Mar. 1863, NMM. MLN. 116/1a.

71 Lyons to Russell, 24 Feb. 1863, NA. FO. 5/878 fols. 109–10.

72 Lyons to Milne, 5 and 27 Mar. 1863, NMM. MLN/116/1a; Russell to Lewis, 24 Mar. 1863, NA. PRO. 30/22/31.

73 F.J. Merli, *The Alabama, British Neutrality and the American Civil War* (Bloomington, IN, 2004).

74 Lyons to Milne, 27 Mar. 1863, NMM. MLN/116/1a.

75 Lyons to Russell, 14 April 1863, NA. FO. 5/882 fol. 61; Lyons to Milne, 8 and 17 April, 11 May 1863, NMM. MLN/116/1a.

76 Russell to Lewis, Russell to Somerset, both 24 Mar. 1863, NA. PRO. 30/22/30 fols. 89 and 129.

77 Somerset to Milne, 17 April 1863, NMM/MLN/116/1c.

78 Russell to Palmerston, 3 Sept. 1863, NA. PRO. 30/22/30 fol. 69. See also, Russell to Somerset, 14 Sept. fol. 131.

79 Palmerston to Russell, 23 Aug., 4, 11, and 21 Sept., 13 Sept. 1863, NA. PRO. 30/22/22 fols. 239, 243, and 258; Gooch (ed.), *Russell*, II, 334; Russell to Palmerston, 3 Sept. 1863, 30/22/30 fol. 60.

80 Lyons to Milne, 31 July 1863, NMM. MLN/116/1a.

81 Sumner to Bright, 4 Aug., 22 Sept., and 6 Oct. 1863: in E.L. Pierce (ed.), *Memoirs and Letters of Charles Sumner, 1860 to Death* (London, 1893), pp. 143–6; H. Jones, *Union in Peril: The Crisis over British Intervention in the Civil War* (Chapel Hill, NC, 1992); J.J. and P.P. Barnes (eds.), *The American Civil War Through British Eyes; Dispatches from British Diplomats* (3 vols, Kent, OH, 2003–5); P. Myers, *Caution and Co-operation: The American Civil War in British-American Relations* (Kent, OH, 2010).

82 George Elliot to Cobden, 27 Mar. 1863, NA. PRO. 30/22/32 fol. 154.

83 Lyons to Russell, 25 April 1864, NA. FO. 5/948 fols. 118–125, printed version, fols. 145–7.

84 Lyons to Milne, 20 Aug. 1863, NMM. MLN/116/1a.

85 Lyons to Russell, 12 Jan. 1864, NA. FO. 5/943 fols. 33–4.

86 Lyons to Russell, 21 Feb., 25 and 31 Mar., 8, 22, and 25 April 1862, NA. PRO. 30/22/36 fols. 48–9, 56, 58, 63, 70–1, and 83.
87 Thomas to Elizabeth Peace, 19 Sept. 1864, Manchester, John Rylands Library, REAS/2/4/25.
88 E.L. Pierce (ed.), *Memoirs and Letters of Charles Sumner, 1860 to Death* (London, 1893), pp. 68–9.
89 M. Kukiel, "Military aspects of the Polish insurrection of 1863–4," in *Antemurale*, 7–8 (1963): 363–96.
90 Lyons to Russell, 25 Feb. 1862, NA. FO. 5/825 fols. 296–303.
91 R.B. Elrod, "Austria and the Polish insurrection of 1863," in *International History Review*, 8 (1986): 416–31.
92 *Chester Record*, 14 Mar. 1863.
93 A. Brettle, "1864: The Genesis of a New Conservative World?" in J. Black (ed.), *The Tory World* (Farnham, 2015), pp. 191–202.
94 M. Cunningham, *Mexico and the Foreign Policy of Napoleon III* (Basingstoke, 2001).
95 Scarlett to Russell, 27 Feb., 18 Mar., and 10 May 1865, NA. FO. 50/385 fols. 118, 203–6; 5/386 fol. 188.
96 K. Hackemer, "Strategic Dilemma: Civil-Military Friction and the Texas Coastal Campaign of 1863," in *Military History of the West*, 26 (1996): 187–214.
97 Lyons to Russell, 23 Feb. 1864, NA. FO. 5/945 fol. 27.
98 Lyons to Russell, 23 May, 20 June 1864, NA. FO. 5/950 fols. 19–22; 5/952 fols. 93–4.
99 A. Foreman, *A World on Fire: Britain's Crucial Role in the American Civil War* (New York, 2011).

## Chapter 4

1 T.J. McGuire, *Stop the Revolution: America in the Summer of Independence and the Conference for Peace* (Mechanicsburg, PA, 2011).
2 See also, Lyons to Russell, 11, 17, 21 Feb. 1862, NA. FO. 5/825 fols. 33–6, 124–5, 244–6.
3 Lyons to Milne, 27 Feb. 1862, NMM. MLN/116/1a.
4 T.W. Cutrer, *Theater of a Separate War: The Civil War West of the Mississippi River, 1861–1865* (Chapel Hill, NC, 2017).
5 T.B. Smith, *Grant Invades Tennessee: The 1862 Battles for Forts Henry and Donelson* (Lawrence, KS, 2016).
6 T.B. Smith, *The Iron Dice of Battle: Albert Sidney Johnston and the Civil War in the West* (Baton Rouge, LA, 2023).
7 *The Personal Memoirs*… op.cit., 249.

8 E.J. Hess, *Civil War in the West: Victory and Defeat from the Appalachians to the Mississippi* (Chapel Hill, NC, 2012).

9 A. Brettle, *Colossal Ambitions: Confederate Planning for a Post-Civil War World* (Charlottesville, VA, 2020); K. Waite, *West of Slavery: The Southern Dream of a Transcontinental Empire* (Chapel Hill, NC, 2021).

10 S. Hoig, *The Sand Creek Massacre* (Norman, OK, 1961); E. West, *The Contested Plains: Indians, Goldseekers, and the Rush to Colorado* (Lawrence, KS, 1998); C. Whitacre, "The Search for the Site of the Sand Creek Massacre," in *Prologue*, 33 (2001): 96–107.

11 V. Deloria and R.J. DeMallie, *Documents of American Indian Diplomacy. Treaties, Agreements, and Conventions, 1775–1979* in 2 volumes (Norman, OK, 1999), I, 587.

12 Lyons to Russell, 22 Jan. 1864 and enclosures, NA. FO. 5/120 f. 139–53.

13 Lyons to Milne, 12 May 1862, NMM. MLN/116/1a.

14 War Department, *The War of the Rebellion* in 128 volumes (Washington, 1880–1901), V, 44.

15 E.J. Hess, *Civil War Torpedoes and the Global Development of Mine Warfare* (Lanham, MD, 2023).

16 Lyons to Russell, 16 May 1862, NA. PRO. 30/22/36 fol. 93; Lyons to Milne, 9 June 1862, NMM. MLN/116/1a.

17 E. Rafuse, *From the Mountains to the Bay: The War in Virginia, January–May 1862* (Lawrence, KS, 2023).

18 W.N. Still, *Iron Afloat: The Story of the Confederate Armorclads* (Nashville, TN, 1971).

19 S.C. Kinnaman, *A Crisis of Loyalties. The Destruction and Abandonment of the Gosport Navy Yard* (Wilmington, DE, 2024).

20 G. Gallagher, "An Old Fashioned Soldier in a Modern War? Robert E. Lee as Confederate General," in *Civil War History*, 45 (1999): 321; *The Confederate War. How Popular Will, Nationalism, and Military Strategy Could Not Stave off Defeat* (Cambridge, MA, 1997), pp. 58–9, 115, and *Lee and his Army in Confederate History* (Chapel Hill, NC, 2001); J.L. Harsh, *Taken at the Flood: Robert E. Lee and Confederate Strategy in the Maryland Campaign of 1862* (Kent, OH, 1999).

21 D.S. Hartwig, *To Antietam Creek: The Maryland Campaign of September 1862* (Baltimore, MD, 2012).

22 J. Black, *The Geographies of War* (Barnsley, 2022), chapter 1.

23 M.V. Armstrong, *Unfurl Those Colors! McClellan, Sumner, and the Second Army Corps in the Antietam Campaign* (Tuscaloosa, AL, 2008).

24 D.S. Hartwig, *I Dread the Thought of the Place: The Battle of Antietam and the End of the Maryland Campaign* (Baltimore, MD, 2023).

25 D.G. Surdam, *Northern Naval Superiority and the Economics of the American Civil War* (Columbia, SC, 2001).

26 R.B. Ekelund and M. Thornton, *Tariffs, Blockades, and Inflation: The Economics of the Civil War* (Wilmington, DE, 2004).
27 M. Warshauer, *Connecticut in the American Civil War: Slavery, Sacrifice, and Survival* (Middletown, CT, 2011).
28 Stuart to Russell, 10 Nov. 1862, NA. FO. 5/838 fols. 272–3.
29 G. Rable, *Conflict of Command: George McClellan, Abraham Lincoln, and the Politics of War* (Baton Rouge, LA, 2023).
30 Lyons to Russell, 28 Nov. 1862, NA. FO. 5/839 fols. 72–3.
31 George Shepley to Lincoln, 9 Dec. 1862, Library of Congress, Abraham Lincoln papers, Series 1, General correspondence.
32 P.R. Kemmerly, "River, Rails, and Rebels: Logistics and the Struggle to Supply [the] U.S. Army Depot at Nashville, 1862–1865," in *JMH*, 84 (2020): 713–46, esp. 744.
33 J. Solonick, *Engineering Victory: The Union Siege of Vicksburg* (Carbondale, IL, 2015).

## Chapter 5

1 J. Black, *Other Pasts, Different Presents, Alternative Futures* (Bloomington, IN, 2015).
2 J.M. McPherson, "If the Lost Order Hadn't Been Lost: Robert E. Lee Humbles the Union, 1862," in R. Cowley, ed., *What If? America* (London, 2005), 101.
3 For an emphasis on contingency, see J.M. McPherson, *The Battle Cry of Freedom: The Civil War Era* (New York, 1988), 858.
4 R.F. Leslie, *Reform and Insurrection in Russian Poland, 1856–1865* (2nd ed., London, 1970).
5 J.C.D. Clark, *The Language of Liberty, 1660–1832: Political Discourse and Social Dynamics in the Anglo- American World* (Cambridge, 1994).
6 W.W. Bennett, *The Great Revival in the Southern Armies* (Philadelphia, 1877); H. Stout, *Upon the Altar of the Nation* (New York, 2006); M.A. Noll, *The Civil War as a Theological Crisis* (Chapel Hill, NC, 2006); R. Gamble, *A Fiery Gospel: The Battle Hymn of the Republic and the Road to Righteous War* (Ithaca, NY, 2019).
7 M.K. Nelson, *The Three-Cornered War: The Union, the Confederacy, and Native Peoples in the Fight for the West* (New York, 2020).
8 J. Matsui, "War in Earnest: The Army of Virginia and the Radicalization of the Union War Effort, 1862," in *Civil War History* 58 (2012): 180–223.
9 A. Bledsoe, *Citizen-Officers: The Union and Confederate Volunteer Junior Officer Corps in the American Civil War* (Baton Rouge, LA, 2015).
10 C. Beemer, *"My Greatest Quarrel with Fortune": Major General Lew Wallace in the West, 1861–1862* (Kent, OH, 2015).

11 B.H. Reid, "1863: Military Turning Points, Gettysburg, Vicksburg and Tullahoma," in *Organization of American Historians: Magazine of History*, 27:2 (2013): 23–7.
12 G. McWhiney and P. Jamieson, *Attack and Die: Civil War Military Tactics and the Southern Heritage* (Tuscaloosa, AL, 1982), 7.
13 P. Griffith, *Battle Tactics of the Civil War* (New Haven, CT, 1989).
14 For example, see P.L. Patterborze, "Crossroads of Destiny: Lew Wallace, the Battle of Monocacy, and the Outcome of Jubal Early's Drive on Washington, D.C.," in *Army History* (Spring 2005): 13.
15 S.E. Woodworth, ed., *No Band of Brothers: Problems of the Rebel High Command* (Columbia, SC, 1999).
16 N.C. Hughes, *General William J. Hardee* (Baton Rouge, LA, 1965).
17 R.L. DiNardo, "Southern by the Grace of God but Prussian by Common Sense: James Longstreet and the Exercise of Command in the U.S. Civil War," in *JMH*, 66 (2002): 1011–32.
18 W.B. Feis, *Grant's Secret Service: The Intelligence War from Belmont to Appomattox* (Lincoln, NE, 2002).
19 *The Personal Memoirs*...op.cit., 280–1, 292.
20 M. Moten, *The Delafield Commission and the American Military Profession* (College Station, TX, 2000), 86, 209–10.
21 D.G. Surdam, *Northern Naval Superiority and the Economics of the American Civil War* (Columbia, SC, 2001).
22 M.A. Smith, "Rivers, Rails and Wooden Bateaux. Civil War Pontoniering in the Eastern Theater," in *Army History* (Summer 2024): 6–27.
23 J. Davis, *Music along the Rapidan: Civil War Soldiers, Music, and Community during Winter Quarters, Virginia* (Lincoln, NE, 2014).
24 M.C. Adams, *Living Hell: The Dark Side of the Civil War* (Baltimore, MD, 2014).
25 E.J. Hess, *Civil War Infantry Tactics: Training, Combat, and Small-Unit Effectiveness* (Baton Rouge, LA, 2023).
26 D.M. Hart, *A Treatise on Field Fortifications* (New York, 1836, 3rd ed. 1852); I.C. Hope, *A Scientific Way of War: Antebellum Military Science, West Point, and the Origins of American Military Thought* (Lincoln, NE, 2015).
27 E. Longacre, *The Early Morning of War: Bull Run, 1861* (Norman, OK, 2014).
28 C. Tolles, "An Army: Its Organization and Movements, First Paper," in *Continental Monthly* 5 (1864): 715.
29 G. Joiner, *Through the Howling Wilderness: The 1864 Red River Campaign and Union Failure in the West* (Knoxville, TN, 2006).
30 T. Smith, *Rethinking Shiloh: Myth and Memory* (Knoxville, TN, 2013).
31 C. Reardon, *With a Sword in One Hand and Jomini in the Other: The Problem of Military Thought in the Civil War North* (Chapel Hill, NC, 2012).

32 K.J. Weddle, "The Blockade Board of 1861 and Union naval strategy," in *Civil War History* 48 (2002): 142.

33 J.F.C. Fuller, *The Conduct of War, 1789–1961* (London, 1961), 102; J. Keegan, *The Military Geography of the American Civil War* (Gettysburg, PA, 1997); *Fields of Battle: The Wars for North America* (London, 1996); and *The American Civil War* (London, 2009).

34 Lyons to Russell, 24 Feb. 1863, NA. FO. 5/878 fols 73–5.

35 S.E. Woodworth, ed., *No Band of Brothers: Problems of the Rebel High Command* (Columbia, MS, 1999); L. Daniel, *Days of Glory: The Army of the Cumberland, 1861–1865* (Baton Rouge, LA, 2004).

36 D.A. Mindell, *War, Technology and Experience Aboard the USS "Monitor"* (Baltimore, MD, 2000), 144.

37 For a valuable cautious note, see A.D. Harvey, "Was the Civil War the First Modern War?" in *History* (2012): 272–80.

38 R.C. Black, *The Railroads of the Confederacy* (Chapel Hill, NC, 1998).

39 E.J. Hess, *Civil War Logistics: A Study of Military Transportation* (Baton Rouge, LA, 2017).

40 E. Hagerman, "Field transportation and strategic mobility in the Union armies," in *Civil War History* 34 (1988): 171.

41 G. Gallagher, ed., *Fighting for the Confederacy: The Personal Recollections of General Edward Porter Alexander* (Chapel Hill, NC, 1989), 435–6.

42 E.G. Longacre, *The Man Behind the Guns: A Military Biography of General Henry J. Hunt* (South Brunswick, NJ, 1977).

43 R. Field, *American Civil War Fortifications, III* (Oxford, 2007), 45.

44 *The Personal Memoirs*…op.cit., 527.

45 C. Geier, "Confederate Fortification and Troop Deployment in a Mountain Landscape: Fort Johnson and Camp Shenandoah, April 1862," in *Historical Archaeology* 37:3 (2003): 31–45.

46 G. Ecelbarger, *Slaughter at the Chapel: The Battle of Ezra Church, 1864* (Norman, OK, 2016).

47 E. Hagerman, "From Jomini to Dennis Hart Mahan: The Evolution of Trench Warfare and the American Civil War," in *Civil War History* 13 (1967): 197–220; R.J. Sommers, *Richmond Redeemed: The Siege at Petersburg* (New York, 1981); E.J. Hess, *Field Armies and Fortifications in the Civil War: The Eastern Campaigns 1861–1864* (Chapel Hill, NC, 2005); *Trench Warfare with Grant and Lee: Field Fortifications in the Overland Campaign* (Chapel Hill, NC, 2007); and *In the Trenches at Petersburg: Field Fortifications and Confederate Defeat* (Chapel Hill, NC, 2009).

48 W.C. Robinson, *Jeb Stuart and the Confederate Defeat at Gettysburg* (Lincoln, NB, 2007).

49 A. Masich, *Civil War in the Southwest Borderlands, 1861–1867* (Norman, OK, 2017).

50 K.M. Brown, *Retreat from Gettysburg: Lee, Logistics, and the Pennsylvania Campaign* (Chapel Hill, NC, 2005).

51 C.W. Ramsdell, "General Robert E. Lee's Horse Supply, 1862–1865," in *American Historical Review* 35 (1930): 758–77; S.Z. Starr, *The Union Cavalry in the Civil War: The War in the West, 1861–1865* (Baton Rouge, LA, 1979); E.G. Longacre, *Grant's Cavalryman: The Life and Wars of General James H. Wilson* (Lanham, MD, 1972); and *Lincoln's Cavalrymen: A History of the Mounted Forces of the Army of the Potomac* (Mechanicsburg, PA, 2000); J. Keenan, *Wilson's Cavalry Corps: Union Campaigns in the Western Theatre, October 1864 through Spring 1865* (Jefferson, NC, 1998); G. Phillips, "Writing Horses into American Civil War History," in *War in History* 20 (2013): 160–81.

52 A. Gibson, *"Our Little Monitor": The Greatest Invention of the Civil War* (Kent, OH, 2018).

53 J. Lemnitzer, *Power, Law and the End of Privateering* (Basingstoke, 2014).

54 D. Hughes, *A Confederate Biography: The Cruise of the CSS Shenandoah* (Annapolis, MD, 2015).

55 Halleck to Francis Lieber, 5 Feb. 1865; S.E. Ambrose, *Halleck: Lincoln's Chief of Staff* (Baton Rouge, 1962), 110.

56 K. Weddle, "'The Fall of Satan's Kingdom': Civil-Military Relations and the Union Navy's Attack on Charleston, April 1863," in *JMH* 75 (2011): 411–40.

57 C. Symonds, *Lincoln and His Admirals: Abraham Lincoln, the U.S. Navy, and the Civil War* (Oxford, 2008).

58 A.S.R. Wise, *Gate of Hell: Campaign for Charleston Harbor, 1863* (Columbia, SC, 1994); M. Laramie, *Gunboats, Muskets, and Torpedoes: Coastal South Carolina, 1861–1865* (Yardley, PA, 2022).

59 R. Browning, *Lincoln's Trident: The West Gulf Blockading Squadron during the Civil War* (Tuscaloosa, AL, 2015).

60 E.J. Hess, *Civil War in the West: Victory and Defeat from the Appalachians to the Mississippi* (Chapel Hill, NC, 2012).

61 G. Scotti, *Lissa 1866* (Trieste, 2004).

62 H. Fuller, *Clad in Iron: The American Civil War and the Challenge of British Naval Power* (Westport, CT, 2008).

63 E. Olmstead, W. Stark, and S. Tucker, *The Big Guns: Civil War Siege, Seacoast, and Naval Cannon* (Alexandria Bay, NY, 1997).

64 N. Eichhorn, "North Atlantic Trade in the Mid-Nineteenth Century: A Case for Peace during the American Civil War," in *Civil War History* 61 (2015): 138–72; Marc-William Palen, *The "Conspiracy" of Free Trade. The Anglo-American Struggle over Empire and Economic Globalisation, 1846 1896* (Cambridgc, 2016).

## Chapter 6

1 NA. FO. 5/877 f. 139–41.
2 Lyons to Milne, 14 Jan., 1, 15 Feb. 1863, NMM. MLN/116/1a; Lyons to Russell, 13, 27 Jan., 2 Feb., 9 Jan. 1863, NA. FO. 5/874 fols 144, 149, 5/875 fols 132–6, 5/876 fol. 63, PRO. 30/22/37 fol. 7.
3 M.E. Neely, *Lincoln and the Democrats: The Politics of Opposition in the Civil War* (Cambridge, 2017).
4 NA. FO. 5/879 f. 162–3.
5 F. Clarke and R. Plant, *Of Age: Boy Soldiers and Military Power in the Civil War Era* (New York, 2023).
6 S.W. Sears, *Chancellorsville* (Boston, Mass., 1996), pp. 57–8.
7 K.R. Titus, "The Richmond Bread Riot of 1863: Class, Race and Gender in the Urban Confederacy," *Gettysburg College Journal of the Civil War Era*, 2: 6 (2011): pp. 86–146; A. Smith, *Starving the South: How the North Won the Civil War* (New York, 2011).
8 T.C. Williams and D. Williams, "'The Women Rising': Cotton, Class, and Confederate Georgia's Rioting Women," in *Georgia Historical Quarterly*, 86 (2002): 49–83.
9 W. Venet, *A Changing Wind: Commerce and Conflict in Civil War Atlanta* (New Haven, CT, 2014); S. Ash, *Rebel Richmond: Life and Death in the Confederate Capital* (Chapel Hill, NC, 2019).
10 G.W. Gallager, "Another look at the generalship of R.E. Lee," in Gallagher, ed., *Lee. The Soldier* (Lincoln, NB, 1996), 285.
11 J. McPherson, *Embattled Rebel: Jefferson Davis as Commander in Chief* (New York, 2014).
12 B. Severance, *A War State All Over: Alabama Politics and the Confederate Cause* (Tuscaloosa, AL, 2020).
13 A. Fleche, *the Revolution of 1861: The American Civil War in an Age of Nationalist Conflict* (Chapel Hill, NC, 2012).
14 H.G. Brown, *War, Revolution and the Bureaucratic State* (Oxford, 1995). Regarding Columbia County, Pennsylvania, in 1864, see R. Sauers and P. Tomasak, *The Fishing Creek Confederacy: A Story of Civil War Draft Resistance* (Columbia, MS, 2013).
15 S.R. Watkins, "*Co. Aytch": A Side Show of the Big Show* (1882; reprinted Wilmington, 1994), 69, 62, 133; A.J.L. Freemantle, *Three Months in the Southern States* (1864; reprinted Lincoln, NE, 1991), p. 145.
16 J.F. Witt, *Lincoln's Code: The Laws of War in American History* (New York, 2012).
17 D.H. Dilbeck, *A More Civil War: How the Union Waged a Just War* (Chapel Hill, NC, 2016).

18 J.H. Matsui, *The First Republican Army: The Army of Virginia and the Radicalization of the Civil War* (Charlottesville, VA, 2016).

19 J. Phillips, *Diehard Rebels: The Confederate Culture of Invincibility* (Athens, GA, 2007).

20 C. Phillips, *The Rivers Ran Backward: The Civil War and the Remaking of the American Middle Border* (Oxford, 2016).

21 J.A. Fuller, *Oliver P. Morton and the Politics of the Civil War and Reconstruction* (Kent, OH, 2017).

22 L. Kreiser, *Defeating Lee: A History of the Second Corps, Army of the Potomac* (Bloomington, IN, 2012).

23 R.D. Goff, *Confederate Supply* (Durham, NC, 1969); W. Blair, *Virginia's Private War. Feeding Body and Soul in the Confederacy, 1861–1865* (New York, 2000).

24 D.G. Smith, "'Clear the Valley': The Shenandoah Valley and the Genesis of the Gettysburg Campaign," in *JMH*, 74 (2010): 1087–95.

25 K.M. Brown, *Retreat from Gettysburg: Lee, Logistics, and the Pennsylvania Campaign* (Chapel Hill, NC, 2005).

26 Lyons to Milne, 22 June 1863, NMM. MLN/116/1a.

27 T. Bruscino and M. Klingenberg, "'Making War Upon the Map': The U.S. Army's Forgotten Map Problem, Meade's Gettysburg Campaign, and Depicting Operational Art," in *Army History*, 131 (2024): 57.

28 W.G. Piston, *Lee's Tarnished Lieutenant: James Longstreet and His Place in Southern History* (Athens, GA, 1987).

29 Quoted in T. Ballard, "Army After-Action Reports, Circa 1860s," in *Army History*, no. 30 (1994): 37.

30 C. Reardon and T. Vossler, *A Field Guide to Gettysburg: Experiencing the Battle through Its History, Places, and People* (Chapel Hill, NC, 2013). 31 B. and L. Gottfried, *Race to the Potomac: Lee and Meade After Gettysburg, July 4–14, 1863* (El Dorado Hills, CA, 2024).

32 H. Newsome, *Gettysburg's Southern Front: Opportunity and Failure at Richmond* (Manhattan, KS, 2022).

33 M.B. Ballard, *Vicksburg* (Chapel Hill, NC, 2004), 430.

34 T. Smith, *Bayou Battles for Vicksburg: The Swamp and River Expeditions, January 1–April 30, 1863* (Lawrence, KS, 2023).

35 T.B. Smith, *The Decision Was Always My Own: Ulysses S. Grant and the Vicksburg Campaign* (Carbondale, IL, 2018).

36 S.W. Woodworth,ed., *The Chickamauga Campaign* (Carbondale, IL, 2010).

37 The Confederate Army of Tennessee was different to the Union Army of Tennessee.

38 D.A. Powell, *Battle Above the Clouds* (El Dorado Hills, CA, 2017).

39 L. Daniel, *Conquered: Why the Army of Tennessee Failed* (Chapel Hill, NC, 2019).

40 *Daily Dispatch* [Richmond], 24 Jan. 1865.
41 T. Nanzig, ed., *The Civil War Memoir of a Virginia Cavalryman* (Tuscaloosa, AL, 2007).

## Chapter 7

1 M.J. Bennett, "'Frictions': Shipboard Relations between White and Contraband Sailors," in *Civil War History*, 47 (2001): 128.
2 F. Nudelman, *John Brown's Body: Slavery, Violence, and the Culture of War* (Chapel Hill, NC, 2004).
3 B. Luke and J. Smith, *Soldiering for Freedom: How the Union Army Recruited, Trained, and Deployed the U.S. Colored Troops* (Baltimore, MD, 2014).
4 Lyons to Russell, 4, 22 March, 19 April, 18, 26 July, 15 August 1864, NA. PRO. 30/22/38 fols. 19, 26, 37, 72, 79, 92.
5 Lyons to Russell, 26 July 1864, NA. PRO. 30/22/38 fol. 79.
6 *The Personal Memoirs*…op.cit., 490.
7 Ibid., 487.
8 Ibid., 523.
9 A.W. Green, *A Campaign of Giants: The Battle for Petersburg* (Chapel Hill, NC, 2018).
10 J. Weber, *Copperheads: The Rise and Fall of Lincoln's Opponents in the North* (New York, 2006).
11 Lyons to Russell, 15 August 1864, NA. PRO. 30/22/38 fol. 92; J.M. McPherson, *The Mighty Scourge. Perspectives on the Civil War* (Oxford, 2007), 178; E.J. Hess, *July 22: The Civil War Battle of Atlanta* (Lawrence, KS, 2023).
12 S. Davis, *What the Yankees Did to Us: Sherman's Bombardment and Wreckage of Atlanta* (Mercer, GA, 2012).
13 M.J. Forsyth, "The Military Provides Lincoln a Mandate," in *Army History*, 53 (2001): 11–17.
14 O.V. Burton, *The Age of Lincoln* (New York, 2007).
15 M.E. Neely, *The Union Divided: Party Conflict in the Civil War North* (Cambridge, MA, 2002).
16 J. White, *Emancipation, the Union Army, and the Reelection of Abraham Lincoln* (Baton Rouge, LA, 2014).
17 J.T. Glatthaar, *The March to the Sea and Beyond: Sherman's Troops in the Savannah and Carolinas Campaigns* (Baton Rouge, LA, 1995).
18 P.S. Carmichael, *The Last Generation: Young Virginians in Peace, War and Reunion* (Chapel Hill, NC, 2005); M.A. Weitz, *More Damning than Slaughter: Desertion in the Confederate Army* (Lincoln, NE, 2005).
19 J. Black, *The Age of Total War, 1860-1945* (Santa Barbara, CA, 2006).

20 N. Trudeau, *Southern Storm: Sherman's March to the Sea* (New York, 2008).
21 K. Teters, *Practical Liberators: Union Officers in the Western Theater during the Civil War* (Chapel Hill, NC, 2018).
22 L. Foote, *The Yankee Plague: Escaped Union Prisoners and the Collapse of the Confederacy* (Chapel Hill, NC, 2016).
23 A.S. Rubin, *Through the Heart of Dixie: Sherman's March and American Memory* (Chapel Hill, NC, 2014).
24 A. Jones, "Jomini and the strategy of the American Civil War, a reinterpretation," in *Military Affairs*, 34 (1970): 130–1.
25 C. Royster, *The Destructive War: William Tecumseh, Sherman, Stonewall Jackson, and the Americans* (New York, 1991).
26 NA. FO. 5/964 f. 210–11.
27 N.A. Frudeau, *Southern Storm: Sherman's March to the Sea* (New York, 2008).
28 L. Brady, *War Upon the Land: Military Strategy and the Transformation of Southern Landscapes during the American Civil War* (Athens, GA, 2012).
29 D. Williams, *Johnny Reb's War. Battlefield and Homefront* (Abilene, 2000).
30 P . Dillard, *Jefferson Davis's Final Campaign: Confederate Nationalism and the Fight to Arm Slaves* (Macon, GA, 2017).

## Chapter 8

1 J.T. Glatthaar, *General Lee's Army: From Victory to Collapse* (New York,2008).
2 M.C.C. Adams, *Our Masters the Rebels: Speculation on Union Military Failure in the East, 1861–1865* (Cambridge, MA, 1978).
3 T.L. Connelly, *Autumn of Glory: Army of Tennessee, 1862–1865* (Baton Rouge, LA, 1971).
4 J. Keegan, *The Military Geography of the American Civil War* (Gettysburg, PA, 1997), 23–7. See also his *Fields for Battle: The Wars for North America* (London, 1996).
5 E. Varon, *Appomattox: Victory, Defeat, and Freedom at the End of the Civil War* (New York, 2015).
6 J.M. McPherson, "No Peace without Victory, 1861–1865," in *American Historical Review* (2004): 10.
7 S. Ramold, *Obstinate Heroism: The Confederate Surrenders after Appomattox* (Denton, TX, 2020).
8 Frederick Bruce, British envoy, to Russell, 19 May 1865, NA. FO. 5/1018 fols. 159–62.

9 Lyons to Russell, 25 April 1862, NA. PRO. 30/22/36 fols. 74–5; N.A. Trudeau, *Out of the Storm: The End of the Civil War, April –June 1865* (Boston, MA, 1994).

10 M. Fellman, *Inside War: The Guerrilla Conflict in Missouri During the American Civil War* (Oxford, 1989); S.M. O'Brien, *Mountain Partisans: Guerrilla Warfare in the Southern Appalachians, 1861–1865* (Westport, CT, 1999); M. Crawford, *Ashe County's Civil War: Community and Society in the Appalachian South* (Charlottesville, VA, 2001); D.E. Sutherland, *A Savage Conflict: The Decisive Role of Guerrillas in America's Civil War* (Chapel Hill, NC, 2009).

11 Percy Doyle, British envoy in Mexico, to Palmerston, 13 January 1848, NA. FO. 50/219 fol. 7.

12 Scarlett to Russell, 28 April, 9 June 1865, NA. FO. 50/386 fols. 146–7, 210.

13 R.R. Mackey, *The Uncivil War: Irregular Warfare in the Upper South, 1861–1865* (Norman, OK, 2004); C. Mountcastle, *Punitive War: Confederate Guerrillas and Union Reprisals* (Lawrence, KS, 2009).

14 Bruce to Russell, 26 May 1865, NA. FO. 5/1018 fols. 199–202.

## Chapter 9

1 S. Handley-Cousins, *Bodies in Blue: Disability in the Civil War North* (Athens, GA, 2019).

2 S.M. Grant, "Reconstructing the National Body: Masculinity, Disability and Race in the American Civil War," in *Proceedings of the British Academy* 154 (2008): 273–317; "Feeling Right about the Civil War: The Union's battle for Emotional Health," in *American Nineteenth Century History* 24 (2023): 1–28.

3 P. Cimbala, *Veterans North and South: The Transition from Soldier to Civilian after the American Civil War* (Denver, CO, 2015).

4 G.P. Downs, *After Appomattox: Military Occupation and the Ends of War* (Cambridge, MA, 2015).

5 A.W. Trelease, *White Terror: The Ku Klux Klan Conspiracy and Southern Reconstruction* (New York, 1971); K. Allerfeldt, *The Ku Klux Klan: An American History* (Stroud, 2024).

6 G. Downs, *After Appomattox: Military Occupation and the Ends of the War* (Cambridge, MA, 2015).

7 R. Ransom and R. Sutch, *One Kind of Freedom?: The Economic Consequences of Emancipation* (Cambridge, 1977); S. Decarrio, "Productivity and Income Distribution in the Postbellum South," *Journal of Economic History*, 34 (1974): 422–46.

8 J. Hopkins, *The World Will Never See the Like: The Gettysburg Reunion of 1913* (El Dorado Hills, CA, 2023).
9 B.S. Wills, *The River Was Dyed with Blood: Nathan Bedford Forrest and Fort Pillow* (Norman, OK, 2014).
10 D.B. Ralston, *Importing the European Army. The Introduction of European Military Techniques and Institutions in the Extra-European World, 1600–1914* (Chicago, IL, 1996).
11 W. Moody (ed.), *Seven Myths of the Civil War* (Indianapolis, IN, 2017).
12 E.J. Hess, *The Union Soldier in Battle* (Lawrence, KS, 1997), 168.
13 C.E. Janney, *Remembering the Civil War: Reunion and the Limits of Reconciliation* (Chapel Hill, NC, 2013).
14 C. Keller, *Chancellorsville and the Germans: Nativism, Ethnicity, and Civil War Memory* (New York, 2007).
15 B. Miller, *John Bell Hood and the Fight for Civil War Memory* (Knoxville, TN, 2010).
16 S. McConnell, *Glorious Contentment: The Grand Army of the Republic, 1865–1900* (Chapel Hill, NC, 1992).
17 R.Slotkin, *A Great Disorder: National Myth and the Battle for America* (Cambridge, MA, 2024).
18 For a particularly impressive short story, see S. Costa, "The Knife Sharpener," in *Alfred Hitchcock Mystery Magazine* (July/August 2003).
19 E.R. Varon, *Appomattox: Victory, Defeat, and Freedom at the End of the Civil War* (New York, 2013).
20 M. Tyler-McGraw, "Southern Comfort Levels: Race, Heritage Tourism, and the Civil War in Richmond [Virginia]," in J.O. and L.E. Horton (eds.), *Slavery and Public History. The Tough Stuff of American Memory* (New York, 2006),167; K. Walker, "United, Regardless, and a Bit Regretful: Confederate History Month, the Slavery Apology, and the Failure of Commemoration," in *American Nineteenth Century History* 9 (2008): 315–38.
21 E. Caudill and P. Ashdown, *Sherman's March in Myth and Memory* (Lanham, MD, 2008).
22 T Heck and W. Mills (eds.), *Armies in Retreat: Chaos, Cohesion, and Consequences* (Fort Leavenworth, KS, 2023), iii–iv.

## Chapter 10

1 For an emphasis on logistics, see W.E. Grabau, *Ninety-Eight Days. A Geographer's View of the Vicksburg Campaign* (Knoxville, TN, 2000); R.K. Krick, *Civil War Weather in Virginia* (Tuscaloosa, AL, 2007). See, more generally, L.M. Brady, *War Upon the Land: Military Strategy and the Transformation of Southern Landscapes during the American Civil War*

(Athens, GA, 2012); J. Browning and T. Silver, *An Environmental History of the Civil War* (Chapel Hill, NC, 2020).

2 B.H. Reid, *The American Civil War and the Wars of the Industrial Revolution* (1999), 41.

3 J. Ehlen and R.J. Abrahart, "Effective Use of Terrain in the American Civil War: The Battle of Fredericksburg, December 1862," in Doyle and Bennett (eds.), *Fields of Battle*, 63–97; A.H. Petty, *The Battle of the Wilderness in Myth and Memory* (Baton Rouge, LA, 2019).

4 C. Nelson, *Mapping the Civil War* (Washington, D.C., 1992).

5 E.J. Hess, *Civil War Logistics: A Study of Military Transportation* (Baton Rouge, LA, 2017).

6 London, King's College, Liddell Hart Archive, Liddell Hart papers 10/5/1929/1. Article published in *Quarterly Review* (July 1929).

7 Fuller, *The Conduct of War 1789–1961* (London, 1961), 102.

8 D. Canfield, "Opportunity Lost: Combined Operations and the Development of Union Military Strategy, April 1861–April 1862," in *JMH* 79 (2015): 687–9.

9 J. Luvaas, *The Military Legacy of the Civil War* (Lawrence, KS, 1999).

10 A. Mombauer, *Helmuth von Moltke and the Origins of the First World War* (Cambridge, 2001).

11 C. Keller (ed.), *Southern Strategies: Why the Confederacy Failed* (Lawrence, KS, 2021).

12 J. Black, *Strategy and the Second World War: How the War Was Won and Lost* (London, 2021).

13 K. Waite, "The Brittle West: Secession and Separatism in the Southwest Borderlands during the Civil War Era," in *Southwestern History Quarterly* 127 (2023): 28.

14 D.E. Wagner, *Patrick Connor's War: The 1865 Powder River Indian Expedition* (Norman, OK, 2010).

15 R. Wooster, *The Military and United States Indian Policy, 1865–1903* (New Haven, CT, 1988).

16 W.Y. Chalfant, *Hancock's War: Conflict on the Southern Plains* (Norman, OK, 2010).

17 L. Janda, "Shutting the Gates of Mercy: The American Origins of Total War, 1860–1880," in *Journal of Military History* 59 (1995): 26; J.A. Greene, *Washita: The U.S. Army and the Southern Cheyennes, 1867–1869* (Norman, OK, 2004); G.C. Anderson, *The Conquest of Texas: Ethnic Cleansing in the Promised Land, 1820–1875* (Norman, OK, 2005).

18 Thornton to Clarendon, 12 April 1870, Bod. MS. Clar. Dept. C. 481 fol. 75.

19 P. Hämäläinen, *The Comanche Empire* (New Haven, CT, 2008), 333–4.

20 C.M. Robinson, *General Crook and the Western Frontier* (Norman, OK, 2001).

21 R. Weigley, "The Long Death of the Indian-Fighting Army," in G.P. Ryan and T.K. Nenninger (eds.), *Soldiers and Civilians: The U.S. Army and the American People* (Washington, 1987), 27–39.

22 T.W. Dunlay, *Wolves for the Blue Soldiers: Indian Scouts and Auxiliaries with the United States Army, 1860– 1890* (Lincoln, NE, 1982).

23 A. McGinnis, *Counting Coup and Cutting Horses: Intertribal Warfare on the Northern Plains, 1738–1889* (Evergreen, CO, 1990).

24 J.H. Monnett, *Where a Hundred Soldiers Were Killed: The Struggle for the Powder River Country in 1866 and the Making of the Fetterman Myth* (Albuquerque, NM, 2008).

25 J.O. Gump, *The Dust Rose Like Smoke: The Subjugation of the Zulu and the Sioux* (Lincoln, NE, 1994); B. Vandervort, *Indian Wars of Mexico, Canada, and the United States, 1812–1900* (London, 2006).

26 R.G. Athearn, *William Tecumseh Sherman and the Settlement of the West* (Norman, OK, 1956); R.G. Angevine, *The Railroad and the State: War, Politics and Technology in Nineteenth Century America* (Palo Alto, California, 2004).

27 M.L. Tate, *The Frontier Army in the Settlement of the West* (Norman, Oklahoma, 1999); R. Wooster, *The American Military Frontiers: The United States Army in the West, 1783–1900* (Albuquerque, NM, 2009).

# INDEX